EDITED BY **DONALD M. LEWIS**
AND **RICHARD V. PIERARD**

GLOBAL
EVANGELICALISM

Theology, History and
Culture in Regional
Perspective

IVP Academic

An imprint of InterVarsity Press
Downers Grove, Illinois

InterVarsity Press
P.O. Box 1400, Downers Grove, IL 60515-1426
World Wide Web: www.ivpress.com
Email: email@ivpress.com

InterVarsity Press® is the book-publishing division of InterVarsity Christian Fellowship/USA®, a movement of
students and faculty active on campus at hundreds of universities, colleges and schools of nursing in the United States
of America, and a member movement of the International Fellowship of Evangelical Students. For information about
local and regional activities, write Public Relations Dept., InterVarsity Christian Fellowship/USA, 6400 Schroeder
Rd., P.O. Box 7895, Madison, WI 53707-7895, or visit the IVCF website at www.intervarsity.org.

Scripture quotations marked NIV are taken from the Holy Bible, New International Version®. NIV®. Copyright ©1973,
1978, 1984 by International Bible Society. Used by permission of Zondervan Publishing House. All rights reserved.

Scripture quotations marked NRSV are from the New Revised Standard Version of the Bible, copyright 1989 by the
Division of Christian Education of the National Council of the Churches of Christ in the USA. Used by permission.
All rights reserved.

Cover design: Cindy Kiple
Interior design: Beth Hagenberg
Image: © epic11/iStockphoto

ISBN 978-0-8308-4057-1 (print)
ISBN 978-0-8308-9662-2 (digital)

Printed in the United States of America ∞

Library of Congress Cataloging-in-Publication Data
Global evangelicalism : theology, history & culture in regional
perspective / edited by Donald M. Lewis and Richard V. Pierard.
    pages cm
  Includes bibliographical references and index.
  ISBN 978-0-8308-4057-1 (pbk. : alk. paper)
 1. Evangelicalism. I. Lewis, Donald M., editor. II. Pierard,
Richard V., 1934- , editor.
  BR1640.G56 2014
  270.8'2—dc23
                                                               2014022813

P	20	19	18	17	16	15	14	13	12	11	10	9	8	7	6	5	4	3	2	1
Y	31	30	29	28	27	26	25	24	23	22	21	20	19	18	17	16	15	14

This book is dedicated to

the memory of Ogbu Kalu.

CONTENTS

PREFACE

THIS EDITED VOLUME IS THE PRODUCT of years of collaboration involving an international group of scholars. The origins of the initiative can be traced back to conversations in the late 1980s between some of the leading historians of evangelicalism: Mark Noll (then professor of Christian thought at Wheaton College), Edith Blumhofer (then director of the Institute for the Study of American Evangelicals at Wheaton) and the late George Rawlyk, professor of history at Queen's University in Kingston, Ontario. A conference on "Evangelicals, Voluntary Associations and American Public Life," sponsored by the Institute for the Study of American Evangelicals, was held at Wheaton in June of 1991. Mark Noll drew together an initial core of historians to talk about how to advance the academic study of evangelicalism and to share the results of such research with a much wider audience. They included Mark Hutchinson from Sydney, Australia; J. W. (Hoffie) Hofmeyr from the University of Pretoria; John Wolffe of the Open University in England; Richard V. Pierard (then at Indiana State University); and Donald Lewis of Regent College in Vancouver, Canada. The group soon expanded to include many other experts. An initial conference was held in Sydney, Australia, in 1997, and resulted in the publication of *A Global Faith: Essays on Evangelicalism and Globalization* (Centre for the Study of Australian Christianity, Sydney, 1998), edited by Mark Hutchinson and Ogbu Kalu.

In the late 1990s funding was secured for the Currents in World Christianity Project (CWC) based at Cambridge University and headed by Brian Stanley. The CWC went on to sponsor several key international consultations and conferences in England, New Zealand and South Africa. One of the initiatives of the CWC was aimed at producing a single volume of essays that would acquaint a wide international audience with the latest research on global evangelicalism, and it was hoped that this volume would be translated into a number of languages and help many audiences beyond the confines of Western academia to understand this movement. This is that volume.

Our thanks and gratitude must be expressed to the Pew Charitable Trusts of Philadelphia, Pennsylvania, for the funds that made the Currents in World Christianity Project possible, which in turn underwrote the costs of putting this volume together.

We also wish to express our sincere gratitude to Mark Hutchinson for his work in initially pulling articles together for this volume; in spite of his heroic efforts, after a few years of trying to complete the project he found himself overwhelmed with teaching and administrative duties, and as a result, we volunteered to see the volume to the finish line. There are a host of individuals who need to be thanked for their hard work in reading and critiquing the volume in various stages of its preparation: chiefly Doug Hills, whose administrative gifts were so helpful, but also to Hanna Dutko, Danae Yankowski, David Lewis, Laura Werezak, Tim Proudlove, Matthew Thomas and Paul Gutacker.

Thanks also needs to be expressed to Brian Stanley for his patience with us as we have endeavored to finish the editing process. Daniel Reid of Inter-Varsity Press has outshone Job in terms of patience with us; we are very much in his debt.

Donald M. Lewis and Richard V. Pierard

INTRODUCTION

Donald M. Lewis and Richard V. Pierard

IN THE SECOND HALF OF THE TWENTIETH CENTURY, proponents of the "secularization thesis" asserted that religion was a historical phenomenon associated with premodern societies and that its demise was inevitable in the modern world. This process would, of course, take time, but religion's slow disappearance would become evident once a period of cultural lag had run its course. It is now widely recognized that these theorists were wrong. Instead of receding, religions throughout the world have been growing and often have been rigorous in their engagement with the public sphere. In response to these developments, some social theorists are now seeking to construct "postsecular" theories in order to explain where and how the "secularization thesis" went wrong.

Much scholarly attention is now given to the development of Islamic identities, but there is relatively little understanding of how various forms of evangelical Christianity have emerged as the mainstream Christian expression in many parts of the world, and in particular, in the non-Western world. Evangelicalism and its history have been effectively marginalized in the academy in spite of the fact that a case can be made that alongside popular Islam, evangelical Christianity is the most dynamic and expanding religious expression in the world today. However, many academics remain essentially ignorant of evangelicalism as a movement, unable to differentiate between basic terms such as *evangelist, evangelism, evangelical* and *evangelicalism*. Unfortunately, scholars who work in the field have not been very effective in communicating their findings or in persuading scholars that the global expressions of evangelicalism are important or interesting.

The nature of evangelicalism as a popular movement makes it particularly difficult to track and categorize, and this has contributed to its marginalization in the academy. Like popular Islam, its strength comes from the very diverse grassroots base on which it rests—a base made up of individuals, small groups, small and large churches, all spread across a bewildering variety of distinctly evangelical Protestant denominations—while many evangelicals are to be found within "mainline" denominations that are not self-consciously evangelical. In fact, some of its most influential thinkers and personalities are members of denominations that are not widely identified as "evangelical," which would be true in many ways of evangelicalism within Anglicanism in the West. (Here one thinks immediately of George Carey, the former Archbishop of Canterbury and head of the worldwide Anglican communion; of his successor, Justin Welby, the current Archbishop of Canterbury; the late John Stott, leading evangelical author and pastor; and professor N. T. Wright, formerly Bishop of Durham and currently professor of New Testament at St Andrew's University in Scotland.)

Another difficulty related to the term *evangelicalism* is that in the North American setting the term is often associated with a specific political agenda and closely aligned with laissez-faire capitalism, while in other areas of the world these associations would not be made (especially in Latin America). Thus it is often the case that many North American evangelicals hesitate to use the descriptor of themselves, lest they be linked in the broader culture with aspects of what some have come to associate with the term *evangelicalism*.

A third problem related to the marginalization of evangelicalism is its lack of visibility as a global religious entity. Unlike Roman Catholicism, evangelicalism has no visible focal point of unity. It has no Vatican, no St. Peter's in Rome, no grand and imposing ancient buildings linking the movement and its followers to the past, no trappings of church-state links that still linger in western Europe, no pope claiming to be the visible representative of Christ on earth, no crowds of international media waiting for the election of a new leader, no global pronouncements emanating from a central headquarters. In the past several decades, the nearest thing to a visible global expression of evangelicalism has been the Lausanne Movement, which under the leadership of the World Evangelical Alliance has brought together evangelicals in three global conferences (Lausanne 1974, Manila 1989 and

Cape Town 2010). And yet, although evangelicalism has no geographical center as such, it has succeeded in indigenizing popular forms of Christianity in widely diverse areas of the world where a Rome-centered Catholicism and Eastern Orthodoxy have long been unable to set down roots (one thinks of both Korea and China in this regard).

Such marginalization of evangelicalism in the academy and the media is therefore understandable and yet regrettable because it means that this powerful international movement is not well understood by outsiders or—for that matter—by insiders. Many evangelicals themselves have little understanding of their own historical roots and little appreciation of the movement's diversity across many cultures and nations. This book is an attempt to address these concerns, tracing the movement's roots from the North Atlantic world of the eighteenth century, its spread outward from the West in the nineteenth century, and its development as an indigenous movement in cultures across the globe in the twentieth century. It has been written by a group of scholars broadly sympathetic to the movement and who are recognized experts in the study of evangelicalism, in order (first) to help evangelicals understand their roots and the diversity of the movement and (second) to enable those outside the movement to come to understand some of its internal dynamics.

Its primary intended readership is college, university and seminary students throughout the world, and it is the hope of the organizers and funders of this project that it be translated into the five major languages of the world and made available on every continent. So it is in one sense an "in-house" history, but it is also meant to be rigorously fair-minded and accurate, and it is hoped that it will be read by those outside the movement who seek to gain understanding.

For many evangelicals around the world, questions of identity are uppermost. Embracing an evangelical Christian identity in societies dominated by radical forms of other religions can be a matter of life and death, particularly if the person is a recent convert. An evangelical convert to Christianity in Nepal may find him/herself excluded from family and kinship networks, unwelcome to participate in the annual harvest, isolated from those closest to him or her. For African evangelicals, the legacy of colonialism may cause them to question the compatibility of evangelical

Christianity with their African identity. Latin American evangelicals struggle with the fact that Roman Catholic spokesmen and secular academics oppose them by identifying them with foreign powers and dismissing them as mere "sects," untrustworthy as part of the body politic.

This book's main purpose is then to trace the recent history of evangelical churches and evangelical movements while providing a general introduction to the beliefs, practices and characteristic emphases of evangelical Christianity. A second important purpose is to offer a worldwide survey of where evangelical movements have come to exist and of the greatly varying conditions under which evangelicals now carry on their work.

USING THIS BOOK

This is a textbook for people who wish to approach the study of global evangelicalism. The book is broken up into three major sections. The first section provides historical and theological background and offers a discussion of the vexed question of evangelicalism's relationship to the process termed *globalization*. The second section offers surveys of evangelicalism's history in different geographical areas of the world. The final section includes discussion of important themes in evangelical history.

It is hoped that readers will find the book useful and enlightening, either as a reference book or as a starting point to more in-depth study. Of course, no single book can cover any globally extensive subject exhaustively, let alone a subject with the complexity of world evangelicalism. To assist you, we have included sections on further reading at the end of each chapter, and a glossary at the end of the book.

PART ONE

THEORETICAL ISSUES

(1)

DEFINING EVANGELICALISM

Mark A. Noll

At the start of the twenty-first century, evangelical Christianity constituted the second largest worldwide grouping of Christian believers. Only the Roman Catholic church enjoys more adherents in today's world Christianity than the evangelical churches. By comparison with other world religions, evangelical Christians—taken only by themselves rather than as part of the world's two billion Christians—are more numerous than all but Muslims and Hindus.

So, who are the evangelicals and where are they to be found? The need for a survey volume such as this is great because the twentieth century witnessed a nearly unprecedented globalization of distinctly evangelical movements and of movements that share many evangelical features. Not that long ago, evangelical Christianity was predominately restricted to Western Europe and North America. According to one estimate, in 1900 well over 90 percent of the world's evangelical Christians lived in Europe or North America.[1] For a number of reasons having to do with Western missionary activity, cooperative efforts at translating the Bible into local languages, the dedicated efforts of national Christians in many parts of the world, and developments in worldwide trade and communication, that earlier situation has been dramatically transformed. Today, the number of evangelicals in each of Africa, Latin America and Asia exceeds the total in Europe and North America combined.[2] Increasingly, those people who most effectively

---

[1]David B. Barrett, George T. Kurian and Todd M. Johnson, *World Christian Encyclopedia*, 2 vols., 2nd ed. (New York: Oxford University Press, 2001), 1:13-14.
[2]Ibid.

contribute to the spread of evangelical Christianity are recruited from the southern rather than the Northern Hemisphere.

But, of course, before there can be a history of evangelicals and the evangelical presence as it exists on all the continents of the earth today, we must have a definition of evangelical Christianity. Providing a workable definition for a book with a worldwide perspective, however, is surprisingly complicated. Much of the complexity arises from the necessity to define *evangelical* alongside a number of other terms like *Pentecostal, charismatic, fundamentalist, apostolic* and *indigenous* that are often used in conjunction with the term (see the glossary at the end of the book).

After attempting definitions of these key terms, this chapter then goes on to several other necessary preliminary tasks. It sketches with very broad strokes the historical emergence and spread of evangelical Christianity, outlines where evangelical and evangelical-like Christian groups now exist in the world, and specifies the main Christian denominations and Christian movements that are the principal carriers of evangelical energy in the world today. But definitions are the place to begin.

DEFINITIONS

The word *evangelical* designates a set of beliefs, behaviors and characteristic emphases within the broad Christian tradition. That broad Christian tradition has itself appeared in many forms in many places throughout the nearly two thousand years of Christian history. Missiologists (those who study the transmission of Christianity from place to place and generation to generation) say it is possible to identify several characteristics shared by virtually all of the world's Christian movements.[3] First and foremost, Christians affirm that ultimate meaning is found in the person of Jesus Christ. They also turn to the sacred writings of the Bible for authoritative guidance on who Jesus was and what his person and work continue to mean for all the world. The Bible is important for both its New Testament, which speaks directly of Christ, and its Old Testament, which tells of the people of Israel from whom Jesus was born. Almost all Christians also think of themselves

---

[3]This general definition follows Andrew Walls, "The Gospel as Prisoner and Liberator of Culture," in *The Missionary Movement in Christian History: Studies in the Transmission of Faith* (Maryknoll, NY: Orbis, 1996), pp. 6-7.

as joined with other believers through history back to the time of Christ. Most also practice water baptism as an initiation rite, and celebrate the Lord's Supper (or communion, or the Eucharist) as a way of focusing attention on the death and resurrection of Jesus as key elements in the sacred story. Where Christian bodies have come to intellectual self-consciousness, they regularly affirm God as a Trinity, one supreme deity who exists in three persons (Father, Son and Holy Spirit).

Throughout history, the designation *evangelical* has been applied to many different movements within this broader Christian story. The word itself has several legitimate senses, but all are related to the original sense of "good news." The English word comes from a transliteration of the Greek noun *euangelion*, which was used regularly by the writers of the New Testament to signify the glad tidings—the *good news*—of Jesus' appearance on earth as the Son of God to accomplish God's plan of salvation for needy humans. Translators of the New Testament usually used the word *gospel* (which meant "good news" or "glad tidings" in Old English) for *euangelion,* as in passages such as Romans 1:16:

> I am not ashamed of the gospel (*euangelion*), because it is the power of God for the salvation of everyone who believes. (NIV)

Thus, "evangelical" religion has always been "gospel" religion, or religion focusing on the "good news" of salvation brought to sinners by Jesus Christ. As "news" it implies the need for the message to be spread—indeed, evangelical Christianity takes the "speaking" and "Word" elements of the faith as definitional. An unspoken faith is no faith at all—and thus foundational to evangelicalism is the need to witness to the "good news" of Jesus Christ, to "go into all the world." At its core, it is a faith with a global vision. This emphasis also creates some of the unique tensions in the movement—some expressions of evangelicalism (the Reformed or Calvinistic tradition, for example) emphasize the external and rational in ways that are foreign to evangelicals who place an emphasis on the heart and on the "evidence" of experience. As either "word spoken" or "word lived," however, both forms have demonstrated an extraordinary ability to cross borders, to locate themselves in many places and within a wide variety of organizational forms, and yet, in adapting, to retain their essential character.

During the sixteenth century the word *evangelical* began to take on a more specific meaning associated with the Protestant Reformation. In this usage, "evangelicals" were those who protested against the corruptions of the late medieval Western church and who sought a Christ-centered and Bible-centered reform of the church. Because of these efforts, the word *evangelical* became a rough synonym for *Protestant*. To this day in many places around the world, Lutheran churches reflect this older sense of the term (for example, the Evangelical Lutheran Church of Papua New Guinea, the Evangelical Lutheran Church in America, or [in India] the Tamil Evangelical Lutheran Church).

Since the eighteenth century, however, the word has taken on an even more restricted usage, and it is this usage that refers to the movement this book takes for its subject. This usage refers not to Protestants in general but to those Protestants who, beginning about three hundred years ago, placed a heightened emphasis on experiencing the redeeming work of Christ personally and on spreading the good news of that message, whether to those with only a nominal attachment to Christianity or to those who had never heard the Christian gospel. In one of the most useful definitions, the British historian David Bebbington has identified four key ingredients of this kind of evangelicalism:[4]

- **Conversion:** Evangelicals stress the need for a definite turning away from self and sin in order to find God in Jesus Christ.

- **The Bible or "Biblicism":** Evangelicals may respect church traditions in varying degrees and may use schooling, reason and science to assist in talking about Christianity, but the ultimate authority for all matters of faith and religious practice are the Christian Scriptures;

- **Activism:** Evangelicals have historically been moved to action—to works of charity, sometimes to works of social reform, but above all to the work of spreading the message of salvation in Christ—because of their own experience of God.

- **The Cross or "Crucicentrism" (cross-centeredness):** Evangelicals have also consistently stressed as the heart of Christian faith the death of

---

[4]D. W. Bebbington, *Evangelicalism in Modern Britain: A History from the 1730s to the 1980s* (London: Unwin Hyman, 1989), pp. 2-17.

Christ on the cross and then the resurrection of Christ as a triumphant seal for what was accomplished in that death. Evangelicals have regularly emphasized the substitutionary character of this atonement between God and sinful humans whereby Christ receives the punishment due to human sins and God gives spiritual life to those who stand "in Christ."

While holding to such core essentials, evangelicals are often flexible about nonessentials, which has been a key to their spread around the world. So one sees not only revivalistic fervor (the religion of the heart) in South America, but also Reformed revivals in the Southern Baptist Convention in America, and among Anglicans in Sydney, Australia. In this sense, evangelicalism is compatible with global expansion, particular local emphases and strong denominational identities.

Consequently, though evangelicals are marked out by Bebbington's four commitments, important questions still remain concerning the use of other terms that often arise when considering the worldwide dimensions of evangelicalism:

Fundamentalism is a term that arose in the United States during the early years of the twentieth century to designate conservative evangelicals who protested against what they saw as the undermining of orthodoxy by rationalist and modernist ideas (called "liberalization" or "liberalism").[5] Fundamentalists insisted on holding to traditional Christian teachings concerning the *infallibility* of the Bible, the virgin birth of Christ, the substitutionary nature of the atonement and the return of Christ at the end of history. In general, fundamentalists were strident in defense of the supernatural elements in the Christian Scriptures that were being questioned in some academic and church circles. In more recent decades, some groups have used the term *fundamentalist* with regard to themselves in order to demonstrate their separation from other forms of Christianity (including Roman Catholic, liberal Protestant and other varieties of evangelicalism) and to maintain a strict view of the Bible's errorless character. In North America, fundamentalists have also contributed a moral urgency to politically conservative movements like the New Christian Right.[6] Most evangelicals have

---

[5]See especially, George M. Marsden, *Fundamentalism and American Culture: The Shaping of Twentieth Century Evangelicalism, 1870–1925* (New York: Oxford University Press, 1980).
[6]For expert assessment of political-religious connections involving recent fundamentalist activity,

not been fundamentalists, but many fundamentalists do fit within the traditional bounds of evangelicalism.

Pentecostalism is a term that arose about the same time as *fundamentalism*. It describes evangelical believers who placed fresh stress on the active
work of the Holy Spirit and on the restoration of the direct experience of
God commonly reported in the New Testament. In its classic form, Pentecostals taught that "the baptism of the Holy Spirit" would be marked by
"speaking in tongues" (unlearned speech produced by the Spirit's direct
agency) and also by miracles of healing and prophecy. Around the end of
the nineteenth century, Pentecostal-like expressions began to emerge among
Christians in many parts of the globe, particularly those who had roots in
Methodism or the Keswick "higher Christian life" circles in England. Revivals occurred in Australia, India, Wales and among indigenous peoples
(giving rise, for instance, to the variegated African independent churches)
who were coming to terms with modernization and rapid cultural change.
In 1906, one of these outbreaks intersected with one of the more dynamic
and globally open cultures in Los Angeles, in what is often referred to as the
"Azusa Street Revival," and from that point, Pentecostal beliefs and practices
have spread like wildfire. Today Pentecostal and Pentecostal-like churches
make up the fastest growing segment of world Christianity. Pentecostalism
grew directly from historical evangelical emphases, and most Pentecostals
fit securely into historic channels of evangelical Christianity.[7]

Charismatics are Christians not associated with Pentecostal churches
who nonetheless adopt some Pentecostal practices.[8] During the second

---

see John C. Green, James L. Guth, Corwin E. Smidt and Lyman A. Kellstedt, *Religion and the
Culture Wars: Dispatches from the Front* (Lanham, MD: Rowman & Littlefield, 1996).

[7]For helpful orientation, see Walter J. Hollenweger, *The Pentecostals* (London: SCM Press, 1972);
Edith L. Blumhofer, "Transatlantic Currents in North Atlantic Pentecostalism," in *Evangelicalism:
Comparative Studies of Popular Protestantism in North America, the British Isles, and Beyond,
1700–1990*, ed. Mark A. Noll, David W. Bebbington and George A. Rawlyk (New York: Oxford
University Press, 1994), pp. 351-64; and Grant Wacker, *Heaven Below: Early Pentecostals and
American Culture* (Cambridge, MA: Harvard University Press, 2001).

[8]Helpful descriptions of the many and varied expressions of charismatic religion can be found
in the now standard source on the subject, *The New International Dictionary of Pentecostal and
Charismatic Movements*, ed. S. M. Burgess and E. M. Van der Maas (Grand Rapids: Zondervan,
2002). See also K. Poewe, ed., *Charismatic Christianity as a Global Culture* (Columbia: University of South Carolina Press, 1994), and such local studies as Peter Hocken's *Streams of Renewal:
The Origins and Early Development of the Charismatic Movement in Great Britain* (Exeter, UK:
Paternoster, 1997).

half of the twentieth century, charismatic movements appeared in many of the older, more traditional Protestant denominations, and also in the Roman Catholic Church. Like Pentecostals, charismatics stress the direct presence of God through the activity of the Holy Spirit, but do not necessarily organize entire churches, denominations or agencies defined around this special work of the Holy Spirit. Theologically, charismatics have attempted to maintain the link between their personal experience and traditional Christian theology by deemphasizing the uniqueness of speaking in tongues as a sign of the baptism in the Holy Spirit. Charismatic movements have been important in the shaping of recent evangelicalism, especially for making modified versions of historical Pentecostal practices much more common among evangelical churches in the Western and non-Western worlds alike.

Part of the genius of evangelicalism is its ability to adapt to local cultures, but this adaptability makes clear-cut definitions more difficult to maintain. The most difficult groups to categorize with respect to historic evangelicalism are the "Apostolic," "Zionist" and other indigenous Christian movements that proliferated in the Southern Hemisphere over the course of the twentieth century. In Africa, these groups are sometimes known as "aladura" churches, from a Yoruba word meaning "owners of prayer," or are called African independent (or initiated) churches (AICs). Examples from literally thousands of possibilities include the Zion Christian Church of Southern Africa and the Cherubim and Seraphim Society of West Africa. But churches and movements with many similarities have also proliferated in other parts of the world, such as the Universal Church of the Kingdom of God in Brazil, the house church movements in China, and many other rapidly developing church networks in India, the Philippines, Pacific Islands, Africa and Latin America.[9] Through missions and migration, many of the practices and emphases of these non-Western groups have spread back to First-World churches.

As the names suggest, these indigenous Christian movements usually exercise a high degree of independence in charting their own courses, they

[9]For introductory insights, see Elizabeth Isichei, *A History of Christianity in Africa* (London: SPCK; and Grand Rapids: Eerdmans, 1995), pp. 279-88; and Allan Anderson, *Zion and Pentecost: The Spirituality and Experience of Pentecostal and Zionist/Apostolic Churches in South Africa* (Pretoria: University of South Africa Press, 2000).

are usually well adapted to the religious and social practices of their different regions, and they are as determined to recover the supernatural practices of New Testament Christianity as the Pentecostals. Their variety and global spread has caused some concern among traditional evangelicals regarding the nature of their faith and threats to the traditional ways the term (and so the identity) of *evangelical* has been used. The result has been ongoing, and quite vigorous, debates over the meaning, inspiration and role of the Bible, and repeated reorientations of evangelical groupings. These indigenous groups are sometimes criticized by more traditional evangelicals for exalting the prophetic powers of their leaders or subordinating the work of Christ to the work of the same leaders. Some critics see too much ancestral religion surviving in these groups, as well as a penchant for promoting Christianity as a means to gain health and wealth in this life. But there is no doubt that a history of modern evangelical Christianity must pay considerable attention to such groups. Many of them originated from contact with historic evangelical missionaries and most of them promote beliefs and practices that overlap with traditional evangelical emphases. Case by case analysis is the only way to discern whether such independent movements are best studied as merely another variant of evangelical Christianity or should be classified as something other than evangelical. Some methodological rigor is also required in not simply identifying popular revival movements with previous layers of shamanism or popular religion that exist elsewhere in the community in question.

Efforts to define *evangelicalism* will always remain somewhat imprecise because the phenomenon designated by the word represents a set of beliefs and practices rather than a single organization. A survey conducted in North America, for example, was deliberately constructed to probe the dimensions of evangelicalism in Canada and the United States.[10] It found that not all of those who called themselves "evangelicals" or use a related term

---

[10]The survey was conducted by the Angus Reid Group of Toronto in 1996, with 3,000 respondents each in the United States and Canada. The late George Rawlyk of Queen's University, Ontario, who was the key consultant in shaping the survey, oriented religious questions toward the four characteristics of evangelicalism as defined by David Bebbington. For further examination of its results, see "How Very Different: A Poll Shows How Canadian and U.S. Attitudes Vary on Family, Politics and Religion," *Maclean's*, November 4, 1996, pp. 36-40; and Mark A. Noll, *American Evangelical Christianity: An Introduction* (Oxford: Blackwell, 2001), pp. 30-38.

held to traditional evangelical beliefs (although 74 percent in the US did so, with 51 percent in Canada). It also discovered that many people who did hold traditional evangelical beliefs were to be found among members of the Roman Catholic Church (13 percent of the Americans and 25 percent of the Canadians who called themselves "evangelical"). And it found that only about half of those in the denominations descended from historical evangelical movements used terms like *evangelical* to describe themselves (44 percent in the US, 57 percent in Canada). In other words, there is (as with fundamentalism) an increasing vagueness in the use of terminology about evangelicalism, both by scholars and among evangelicals themselves.

Yet if disciplined rather than ideological distinctions are observed, much of the imprecision fades away. As several historians have recognized, evangelicalism can be described as a series of *three overlapping constituencies* that differ in their self-consciousness but are at least loosely related in their shared history and convictions.[11] What we might call *intentional evangelicals* form relatively small numbers of individuals and agencies—often active in networks of voluntary societies or mission agencies—who deliberately label themselves and their efforts as evangelical. Much larger numbers are associated with formal churches and other institutions embedded securely in *historical evangelical* movements. And still larger numbers from throughout the world, who may have only loose connections with original evangelical movements, nonetheless share the historic beliefs and practices of evangelicalism and so may *functionally* be included in wider considerations of evangelicalism as well.

Later chapters in this book will refine questions of definition, and indeed also the relevance of conceptual boundary marking as applied in the various corners of the globe. Enough has been said here, however, to show why the study of worldwide evangelicalism is both a defensible and necessary task.

BRIEF HISTORY

Protestant Christianity was transformed in the century that followed the close of religious warfare in early modern Europe—that is, from the Peace of Westphalia on the continent in 1648 that brought to an end the Thirty Years

---

[11]In this threefold categorization, I am following George M. Marsden, "Introduction," *Evangelicalism and Modern America* (Grand Rapids: Eerdmans, 1984), p. ix.

War and the Restoration of the English monarchy in 1660 following the Puritan Commonwealth period. That transformation involved many factors. Some were obviously religious, but others (like adjusting to new demands of commercial society or resisting grabs for power by divine-right monarchs) were more subtle in their relationship to faith. The most overt religious factor in the transformation of Protestantism was spiritual renewal expressed as a multifaceted protest against ecclesiastical formalism and an urgent appeal for a living religion of the heart. The form of Christianity that historians describe as "evangelicalism" originated in these movements of pietistic revival.[12]

On the European continent the emergence of such emphases is usually dated from the publication in 1675 of Philipp Jakob Spener's *Pia Desideria* (Pious or Heartfelt Desires). This was an appeal for heartfelt religion and for lay study of Scripture in the Lutheran state churches of Germany. Positive responses to this booklet marked the beginnings of the Pietist movement, which spread from Germany to many other parts of Europe. It influenced later English-speaking evangelicalism in many ways, and also pioneered in missionary proclamation of the gospel beyond European borders. But similar longings after "true religion" were also evident in English-speaking areas, as indicated by the nearly simultaneous appearance in England of John Bunyan's *Pilgrim's Progress* (1678, 1684), an allegorical account of Christian existence that moved from the cross of Christ (and the joyful loss of the burden of sin) through the trials of earthly existence to final entrance into the Celestial City. Such stirrings could also be found in other parts of England, in Scotland, Wales and Ireland, as well as in the American colonies.

During the first half of the eighteenth century, Pietist protests against cold, formal religion gathered increasing strength even as the widening search for a "true religion of the heart" broadened and deepened.[13] In the English-speaking world the result was evangelicalism. From the 1720s and 1730s—in London and English market towns, the Scottish Highlands and Lowlands, Wales, Ireland and the North American colonies—English-speaking Protestantism was significantly renewed through a series of often

---

[12]The two best general accounts of this period and the origins of modern evangelicals are by W. R. Ward, *The Protestant Evangelical Awakening* (New York: Cambridge University Press, 1992); and *Christianity Under the Ancien Régime* (New York: Cambridge University Press, 1999).

[13]For a general picture, see Ted Campbell, *The Religion of the Heart: European Religious Life in the Seventeenth and Eighteenth Centuries* (Columbia: University of South Carolina Press, 1991).

intense religious "awakenings." The most visible human agents of these revivals were larger-than-life figures—the spell-binding preacher George Whitefield (1714–1770), the indefatigable evangelist John Wesley (1703–1791) and the brilliant theologian Jonathan Edwards (1703–1758). But if these and other leaders (like Howell Harris in Wales, John McLaurin in Scotland, or Gilbert Tennent in America) were foremost in the public eye, experiences of ordinary men and women made up the driving force of the evangelical awakening.[14] From the start, news about evangelical experiences in particular places was passed on with great excitement to other interested parties in the North Atlantic region. In Scotland, Wales, Ireland and England, concerned Protestants read about the experiences of Abigail Hutchinson of Northampton, Massachusetts, who on a Monday morning in 1735 was turned from despair and alienation to God. As her minister, Jonathan Edwards, explained the event, when "these words came to her mind, 'The blood of Christ cleanses from all sin' [they were] accompanied with a lively sense of the excellency of Christ, and his sufficiency to satisfy for the sins of the whole world. . . . By these things," Edwards concluded, Abigail "was led into such contemplations and views of Christ, as filled her exceeding full of joy."[15] Not long thereafter Protestants throughout the English-speaking world could read in the published journal of John Wesley what had befallen him at a small group meeting organized by Moravians, a group of German Pietists who had recently come from the continent to England. It was on Wednesday, May 24, 1738, at the Moravian gathering on Aldersgate Street in London, "where one was reading Luther's preface to the *Epistle to the Romans*. About a quarter before nine, while he was describing the change which God works in the heart through faith in Christ, I felt my heart strangely warmed. I felt I did trust in Christ, Christ alone for salvation; and an assurance was given me that He had taken away *my* sins, even *mine*, and saved *me* from the law of sin and death."[16]

---

[14]For expanded treatment of these themes, see the early chapters and the introduction (which is the source for the next few paragraphs) of Mark Noll, David Bebbington and George Rawlyk, eds., *Evangelicalism: Comparative Studies of Popular Protestantism in North America, the British Isles, and Beyond, 1700–1990* (New York: Oxford University Press, 1994).

[15]*The Works of Jonathan Edwards*, vol. 4: *The Great Awakening*, ed. C. C. Goen (New Haven: Yale University Press, 1972), p. 193.

[16]Nehemiah Curnock, ed., *The Journal of John Wesley*, 8 vols. (London: Epworth, 1938), 1:475-76.

Many English-speaking Protestants followed just as closely reports concerning the great crowds that came out to hear George Whitefield as he traveled through Britain and North America and then news of the extraordinary revival at Cambuslang, near Glasgow in Scotland, which began in February 1742 and continued for several months.

Soon congregations and small gatherings of believers through the North Atlantic region were singing new hymns that described these life-changing experiences. As would regularly occur in the history of evangelicalism, fresh outbursts of religious fervor were sustained and encouraged by the writing of creative congregational songs. Most of evangelicalism's early hymn writers wrote of what they had personally experienced. John Newton, a slave trader become Anglican priest, wrote such words in a hymn that became especially popular in the last half of the twentieth century:

> Amazing grace! how sweet the sound
> that saved a wretch like me!
> I once was lost, but now am found,
> was blind, but now I see. . . .
>
> 'Twas grace that taught my heart to fear,
> and grace my fears relieved;
> how precious did that grace appear
> the hour I first believed.[17]

The public preaching of repentance and free grace, new institutions arising to perpetuate that message, hymns expounding its effects, and experiences like those of Abigail Hutchinson and John Wesley constituted the origins of the evangelical movement.

From the mid-eighteenth century, evangelicals expanded their activities first in Britain and North America, but then soon also in other parts of the world. For much of the nineteenth century white evangelical Protestants constituted the largest and most influential body of religious adherents in the United States, as also in Britain and Canada. Methodists, Baptists, Presbyterians, Congregationalists and some Episcopalians shared broadly evangelical convictions, and evangelical elements were prominent

---

[17]See especially, D. Bruce Hindmarsh, *John Newton and the English Evangelical Tradition* (New York: Oxford University Press, 1996), pp. 276-78.

among Lutherans, German and Dutch Reformed, and the Restorationist churches (Churches of Christ, Disciples of Christ) as well.

Although evangelicals often combated each other aggressively on the details of those convictions, in 1846 delegates from many churches in Britain and North America, as well as a substantial representation from the European continent, created the Evangelical Alliance, a voluntary interdenominational organization whose doctrinal basis succinctly illustrated major points of mutual evangelical agreement. The founding convictions of the Alliance remain central to evangelical movements around the world today. Well before 1846, however, evangelicals had also begun to take a growing interest in spreading Christianity to other parts of the world. In such efforts, English-speaking evangelicals lagged considerably behind their Continental Pietist colleagues.

Early in the eighteenth century, Bartholomäus Ziegenbalg and Heinrich Plütschau, German Lutherans who had studied at the University of Halle, traveled to the territory of the Danish king in Tranquebar, South India, where they expended great energy in preaching and educating as well as translating and printing the Scriptures, and, in general, preparing the way for the spread of Christianity. These pioneering ventures in crosscultural missionary service were followed by many other Continental Pietists over the course of the eighteenth century. Apart from a few efforts to reach native American Indians with the gospel, however, significant missionary labors by English speakers did not begin until the end of the century. The ex-American slave David George immigrated to Sierra Leone in 1792 as a dedicated preacher of revival just as that West African colony was being opened for outside settlement under the auspices of Anglican evangelicals. The next year, the English Baptist William Carey set out for India. In 1797 Dutch evangelicals formed the Netherlands Missionary Society. In the English-speaking world, the Baptist Missionary Society (1792) was joined by the London Missionary Society (1795), The (Anglican) Church Missionary Society (1799), the interdenominational American Board of Commissioners for Foreign Missions (1810), the Wesleyan Methodist Missionary Society in the UK (1818), and many other evangelical bodies in what would rapidly grow into great efforts of missionary proclamation. They were quickly followed by German and Dutch missions such as the Basel (1815) and Berlin Missions

(1824), and a flowering of *voluntary missionary societies*. The missionary movement was a very important expression of evangelical zeal in English-speaking countries. It became even more important for planting seeds of Christianity in other parts of the world that would grow vigorously into strong indigenous Christian churches.

In the twentieth century, evangelicals remained important in the broader Christian histories of Britain and North America. But the great story of the recent past has been the flourishing of evangelical churches and movements in other parts of the world.[18] Even as the Pentecostal, Zion/Apostolic and indigenous churches of the non-Western world have proliferated to an incredible degree, however, evangelical movements in Britain and North America have had their ups and downs. Evangelicals from around the world continue to come to Britain, the United States and Canada for training, but so now do missionaries from the Two-Thirds World arrive to spread the gospel among fellow immigrants in the West, and also to evangelize among secular Westerners. To be sure, the newer evangelical churches of the world also face many difficulties of their own: instability, at times lack of wise leadership, shortage of educational materials, ethnic violence, numbing poverty and more. But from these churches insights, practices, songs, and doctrinal emphases have also begun to flow back toward the original evangelical homelands. As one commentator has written with a focus on the Pacific, "New Zealand Maori, like other indigenous peoples, valued evangelical Christianity for its acknowledgment of the supernatural. . . . The results may put *pakeha* [New Zealanders of European descent] back into the beginners class of spiritual things."[19] The histories contained in the chapters that follow reveal some of the dynamics by which these great developments of the twentieth century occurred.

---

[18]For orientation, see David Martin, *Tongues of Fire: The Explosion of Protestantism in Latin America* (Oxford: Blackwell, 1990); Martin, *Pentecostalism: The World Their Parish* (Oxford: Blackwell, 2001); Poewe, *Charismatic Christianity as a Global Culture*; Murray Dempster, Bryon D. Klaus and Douglas Peterson, eds., *The Globalization of Pentecostalism* (Oxford: Regnum, 1999); Allan H. Anderson and Walter J. Hollenweger, eds., *Pentecostals After a Century* (Sheffield: Sheffield Academic Press, 1999); Richard Shaull and Waldo Cesar, *Pentecostalism and the Future of the Christian Churches* (Grand Rapids: Eerdmans, 2000); and Allan Anderson, *An Introduction to Pentecostalism* (Cambridge: Cambridge University Press, 2006).

[19]John Roxborogh, "Mapping the Evangelical Landscape in New Zealand," in *Mapping the Landscape: Essays in Australian and New Zealand Christianity: Festschrift in Honor of Professor Ian Breward* (New York: Peter Lang, 2000), p. 327.

Geographical Spread

Different measures can be applied to suggest the transformation of evangelicalism into a thoroughly global presence. The Angus Reid Group conducted a survey with a significant set of religious questions in 33 different countries. When counting the number of Protestants who reported practicing evangelical-like faith—that is, those who considered religion to be very significant in their lives, who prayed at least once a day, who attended church at least weekly, and who had committed their lives to Christ and considered themselves "converted Christians"—it found that the same percentage of South Africans as Americans (28 percent) answered positively to all four questions. Next in order, the Angus Reid survey ranked three nations where there had been virtually no evangelical presence a century ago: Brazil, the Philippines and South Korea (each 10 percent of the population).[20]

Even broader evidence of the worldwide evangelical presence is contained in the 2001 edition of David Barrett's *World Christian Encyclopedia*, which presents an exhaustive country-by-country enumeration of Christian believers throughout the whole world. Using Barrett's narrowest definition of *evangelical*, the *Encyclopedia* found that more "evangelicals" lived in the United States (40.6 million) than anywhere else in the world, but also that the next most populous "evangelical" countries were two where almost no evangelicals had existed one hundred years ago: Brazil (27.7m) and Nigeria (22.3m).[21] Of the next 4 countries where Barrett found the largest number of evangelicals, 1 was a historical center of evangelical strength (the United Kingdom, 11.6m), but 3 had witnessed the growth of substantial evangelical populations mostly in the past century (India, 9.3m; South Korea, 9.1m; South Africa, 9.1m). Of the remaining 24 countries where Barrett found at least one million evangelicals, only 3 were in Europe (Germany, Romania, Ukraine) and 1 in North America (Canada). Fully 10 of these others were in Africa (Angola, Congo-Zaire, Ethiopia, Ghana, Kenya, Mozambique,

---

[20]*Angus Reid World Monitor,* January 1998. The countries that came next in rank order by Protestants responding positively to all four questions were Canada (8%), Australia (7%), Norway (6%) and the United Kingdom (5%). South Africa was the only nation in the continent of Africa surveyed in this Angus Reid poll.

[21]The *World Christian Encyclopedia* (ed. Barrett, Kurian and Johnson) defines "evangelicals" like this: "A subdivision mainly of Protestants consisting of all affiliated church members calling themselves Evangelicals, or all persons belonging to Evangelical congregations, churches or denominations; characterized by commitment to personal religion."

Rwanda, Tanzania, Uganda, Zambia); 5 were in Asia (China, Myanmar, Indonesia, Philippines, Australia); and 5 were in Latin America (Guatemala,
Haiti, Mexico, Argentina, Peru).

If Barrett's more diffuse categories of "Pentecostal," "Charismatic" and
"Neo-Independent" are employed, the worldwide distribution of evangelical-
like Christian movements is underscored even more dramatically.[22] In the
enumeration of these categories, Brazil leads all the rest (79.9m), followed
then by the United States (75.2m), China (54.3m), India (33.5m), South
Africa (21.2m), the Philippines (20.0m), Congo-Zaire (17.7m), Mexico
(13.0m) and then many other countries from Asia, Latin America and Africa,
as well as Europe. In places like China, it is difficult to count evangelicals, as
the "official" church is in fact only a part of the religious landscape. And, as
recent sociological studies are indicating, the "Chinese" or "Latin American"
evangelical presence is not just a factor in China or Latin America. "In
American society," for instance, "most post-1965 immigrants are from Asia,
South and Central America, and many of the new immigrants have joined
conservative churches, such as Pentecostals among Latin Americans and
evangelicals among Korean and Chinese immigrants and Southeast Asian
refugees."[23] In a global age, one learns to think of such evangelical churches
both in their local sense and in the sense in which the ever-present fact of
mass migration makes them worldwide churches. The consequences are
obvious—attacks on evangelicals in Ghana, Nigeria, China or elsewhere
very quickly become global issues.

Of course all such efforts at counting things must be treated with caution.
Evangelical Christians should be the first ones to agree with the assertion by
Leigh Eric Schmidt: "Most of the things that count most about Christianity
cannot be counted, like the warmth or coldness of prayer, the resonance or
hollowness of scriptural words, the songs or silences of the saints in heaven,

---

[22]There is some overlap in the *Encyclopedia*'s enumeration of these three categories and the "Evangelical" category. The *Encyclopedia*'s definitions are as follows: "Pentecostals" = Adherents of
traditional Pentecostal denominations. "Charismatics" = "Baptized members affiliated to non-
Pentecostal denominations who have entered into the experience of being filled with the Holy
Spirit; the Second Wave of the Pentecostal/Charismatic/Neocharismatic Renewal." "Neocharis-
matics/Independents" = Members of the Third Wave of the Pentecostal/Charismatic Renewal
characterized by the adjectives Independent, Postdenominationist and Neo-Apostolic.
[23]Fenggang Yang, "Chinese Conversion to Evangelical Christianity: The Importance of Social and
Cultural Contexts," *Sociology of Religion* 59 (1998): 237-57.

the presences or absences in the sacrament."[24] Yet with proper cautions in place, research results such as those found by Angus Reid and David Barrett testify to how extensive any worldwide history of evangelical Christianity must be today. They also testify to how essential it is to attempt such a history.

DENOMINATIONS, MOVEMENTS

Evangelicalism is not an organized religious movement like the Roman Catholic Church, and it has no "holy place" such as Mecca. Rather, it represents an ever-diversifying series of local churches, parachurch agencies, national and international ministries, and interlocking networks of publications, preachers and personal contacts. Mission agencies have always contributed substantially to the circulation and ligaments of the worldwide evangelical body. Among evangelical mission agencies that recruit their personnel from a broad range of countries and are active in many locations are the Wycliffe Bible Translators/Summer Institute of Linguistics, World Evangelical Alliance, the formerly named Overseas Missionary Fellowship (now known as OMF International), Operation Mobilisation, the early Student Volunteer Movement, Youth With A Mission and the International Fellowship of Evangelical Students. While not strictly "missions" as such, agencies such as the International Bible Society and Scripture Union have had a dynamic impact on international Christianity.

Worldwide denominational connections among Anglicans, Assemblies of God, Baptists, some Lutherans and some Presbyterians strengthen international networks for evangelicals. The international ministries of leading preachers, Bible expositors and evangelists also function to provide a measure of coherence for worldwide evangelicalism. Of such figures in the second half of the twentieth century, the American evangelist Billy Graham, the Church of England minister John Stott and "Mr. Pentecost" David J. Du Plessis have encouraged the broadest range of international contacts.[25] Before World War II, the overlap between social improvement campaigns

---

[24]Leigh E. Schmidt, "Mixed Blessings: Christianization and Secularization," *Reviews in American History* 26 (1998): 640.

[25]Billy Graham, *Just As I Am: The Autobiography of Billy Graham* (San Francisco: HarperCollins, 1997), with Graham's very extensive international trips outlined on end papers; Timothy Dudley-Smith, *John Stott: A Biography*, 2 vols. (Leicester, UK: Inter-Varsity Press, 1999, 2001), with Stott's incredible range of international travel catalogued in the indices, 1:511-12, 2:533-34.

(against slavery, alcohol abuse, child labor, etc.) and evangelical concerns meant that evangelism and social activism were often closely linked. Here among the great names of those who worked to better the world while spreading the gospel are many leading women as well as men: the Women's Christian Temperance Union, for example; the promoter of holiness teachings Phoebe Palmer; the Keswick and missions speaker Hannah Whitall Smith; the wealthy patron of George Whitefield known as Selina, the Countess of Huntingdon; cofounder of the Salvation Army, Catherine Booth; Pentecostal evangelist Aimee Semple McPherson; the Indian social reformer Pandita Ramabai; the missionaries Gladys Aylward and Amy Carmichael and authors Carrie Judd Montgomery and Jessie Penn Lewis. The men included Anthony Ashley Cooper (the seventh Earl of Shaftesbury), Hudson Taylor, the founder of the China Inland Mission, and the early John Mott. After 1945, there are some whose names are perhaps more important outside the West than inside it: Oral Roberts, Reinhard Bonnke, T. L. Osborn, the healing evangelist Katherine Kuhlmann, and the international head of the Salvation Army, Eva Burrows, are just some of the names that could be mentioned.

The important thing to note about this list is that not only does it feature many women, who (in the First World at least) were much more restricted in terms of the roles available to them, but many of these were not "ordained," professional clergy. Missionaries lived between the worlds of clergy and laity, moving to and fro also between the First and Two-Thirds World—they could act both as "men of God" and "humble mechanicks." So in China, a missionary such as Mary Andrews found herself performing all the tasks that the church back in Sydney, or New York, or London, refused to allow her to do. A shoemaker such as William Carey could rise from a position of social insignificance to become a figure of real historical significance. Likewise, we can think of the great merchants whose piety and finance drove many evangelical concerns—Lyman and Milton Stewart of the Union Oil Company, funders of the *Fundamentals* series of books, and cofounders of Biola University; or J. Howard Pew of the Sun Oil company, whose support assisted the global campaigns of Billy Graham and founded one of America's largest charitable trusts; the Young family, wealthy cane growers in Australia who founded the South Seas Evangelical Mission; or the Griffiths Bros Tea and Coffee Company, who sent out generation after generation of their young men and women to work in the Pacific. The preferred organizational form for evangelicals—the voluntary society—made this close relationship between clergy and laity an essential part of the evangelical story. It also helps to explain the great diversity of evangelicalism around the world.

A number of student ministries have also contributed greatly to the international circulation of evangelical personnel, ideas and programs. Perhaps the greatest sense of international cooperation has arisen from the interrelated movements connected to the movement that began in Britain, Australia, Canada and the United States as InterVarsity Christian Fellowship, but which have now evolved into a wide variety of local and regional organizations, like University and College Christian Fellowship (UK), Overseas Christian Fellowship (Asia), Comunidad Internacional de Estudiantes Evangélicos (Latin America) and the International Fellowship of Evangelical Students.

The narrative that follows will also draw attention to the role of international organizations such as the World Evangelical Alliance, the Lausanne Conference and its continuing committees, World Vision and others that have stimulated consciousness about the worldwide dimensions of evangelical movements. Such organizations, agencies and ministries highlight some of the important dimensions of recent evangelical history. Even more, however, are to be found in the local histories, regional associations and other initiatives that are touched on in the rest of this book. This makes it clear, at least, that an understanding of evangelical Christianity will not arise solely out of theological definitions. How it engages with the development of a global society, and how it emerges from its European cocoon will be developed in the following chapters.

FURTHER READING

Anderson, Allan. *An Introduction to Pentecostalism*. Cambridge: Cambridge University Press, 2006.

Case, Jay Riley. *An Unpredictable Gospel: American Evangelicals and World Christianity, 1812–1920*. New York: Oxford University Press, 2012.

Freston, Paul. *Evangelicals and Politics in Asia, Africa, and Latin America*. Cambridge: Cambridge University Press, 2001.

Haykin, Michael A. G., and Kenneth J. Stewart, eds. *The Emergence of Evangelicalism: Exploring Historical Continuities*. Nottingham: Inter-Varsity Press, 2008.

Hutchinson, Mark, and John Wolffe. *A Short History of Global Evangelicalism*. Cambridge: Cambridge University Press, 2012.

Larsen, Timothy, ed. *Biographical Dictionary of Evangelicals*. Downers Grove, IL: InterVarsity Press, 2003.

Lewis, Donald M., ed. *The Blackwell Dictionary of Evangelical Biography, 1735–1860*. 2 vols. Oxford: Blackwell, 1995.

———. *Christianity Reborn: Evangelicalism's Global Expansion in the Twentieth Century*. Grand Rapids: Eerdmans, 2004.

Marsden, George M. *Evangelicalism and Modern America*. Grand Rapids: Eerdmans, 1984.

Martin, David. *Pentecostalism: The World Their Parish*. Oxford: Wiley-Blackwell, 2008.

May, Cedrick. *Evangelism and Resistance in the Black Atlantic, 1760–1833*. Athens: University of Georgia Press, 2008.

Noll, Mark A. *The New Shape of Global Christianity*. Downers Grove, IL: InterVarsity Press, 2009.

Noll, Mark A., David W. Bebbington and George A. Rawlyk, eds. *Evangelicalism: Comparative Studies of Popular Protestantism in North America, the British Isles, and Beyond, 1700–1990*. New York: Oxford University Press, 1994.

Sanneh, Lamin. *Disciples of All Nations: Pillars of World Christianity*. New York: Oxford University Press, 2007.

Shaw, Mark. *Global Awakening: How 20th Century Revivals Triggered a Christian Revolution*. Downers Grove, IL: InterVarsity Press, 2010.

Ward, W. R. *Early Evangelicalism: A Global Intellectual History, 1670–1789*. Cambridge: Cambridge University Press, 2010.

———. *The Protestant Evangelical Awakening*. Cambridge: Cambridge University Press, 1992.

InterVarsity Press has an excellent (chronologically organized) five-volume series on the history of evangelicalism, four of which have been published to date (2014):

Noll, Mark A. *The Rise of Evangelicalism: The Age of Edwards, Whitefield and the Wesleys*. Downers Grove, IL: IVP Academic, 2003.

Wolffe, John. *The Expansion of Evangelicalism: The Age of Wilberforce, More, Chalmers and Finney*. Downers Grove, IL: IVP Academic, 2007.

Bebbington, David. *The Dominance of Evangelicalism: The Age of Spurgeon and Moody*. Downers Grove, IL: IVP Academic, 2005.

Stanley, Brian. *The Global Diffusion of Evangelicalism: The Age of Graham and Stott*. Downers Grove, IL: IVP Academic, 2013.

Treloar, Geoff. *The Disruption of Evangelicalism: The Age of Mott, Machen and McPherson* (forthcoming).

2

THE THEOLOGICAL IMPULSE OF
EVANGELICAL EXPANSION

Wilbert R. Shenk

As the momentous sixteenth century was drawing to a close, distressing signs appeared that the Reformation churches in Europe were mired in nominality. The theological training pastors received was dominated by an arid scholastic orthodoxy preoccupied with guarding doctrinal purity; but theologians were largely oblivious to the widespread listlessness among the masses. While wrestling with this reality in his own parish, German pastor Johann Arndt (1556–1621) discovered *Theologia Deutsch*, or *German Theology*, in 1597. These writings had been so crucial in Martin Luther's spiritual awakening that Luther arranged the printing of a new edition in 1518.[1] This work also lit a fire in Arndt.

In 1606 Arndt published his seminal treatise, *True Christianity*, a work that has been characterized as "at once protest and program."[2] As Arndt diagnosed the situation, he noted a deep separation between what people confessed when they recited the creed in the parish church and the way they lived their daily lives. The cultural norms by which people lived could not be reconciled with the gospel. He criticized theologians for failing to test formal scholarly knowledge against what has been called "practical wisdom," which is gained from life experience.[3] Each needed the other. Arndt was not promoting anti-intellectualism. He did not pit the mind against feeling.

---

[1]Printed by the Augustinian Monastery press at Wittenberg. It was reprinted many times.
[2]Heiko A. Oberman, preface to *True Christianity*, by Johann Arndt, trans. and ed. Peter Erb (New York: Paulist Press, 1979), p. xi.
[3]Ibid.

But if faith did not engage daily life, what use was it? If practical wisdom was not enriched by reflection, it inevitably became rigid and sterile.

Arndt's work proved to be seminal. He correctly identified tendencies inherent in the Christian movement and provided clues to renewal of Christian faith. Arndt's program marked "the path from faith and conversion toward rebirth and sanctification."[4] Shortly before he died, Arndt spoke about his purpose in writing *True Christianity*. He emphasized it was his desire to "lead believers in Christ out of dead belief to fruitful faith . . . [and] bring them from mere knowledge and theory to the real practice of faith . . . to show what genuine Christian life is."[5] The persistent dichotomy between faith and works could be overcome only by recovering a personal encounter with the fullness of the gospel. Living faith must be expressed in Christian service and witness.

Across the English Channel, Lewis Bayly, an Anglican pastor firmly committed to the Puritan vision, played a similar role. His book, *The Practice of Piety*, which by 1613 was in its third English edition, was motivated by the same concern as Arndt's. This was one of two books John Bunyan's wife gave her husband to read that led to his spiritual awakening. Arndt and Bayly influenced the development in the seventeenth century of a genre of literature that helped nurture and define the nascent evangelical movement. One measure of that influence is the publishing history of *True Christianity* and *The Practice of Piety*. Fifty-nine editions of Bayly's book were published in English, along with forty-five various European language editions, by 1740. Arndt's *True Christianity*, between 1605 and 1740, was reprinted ninety-five times in German, plus editions in Latin, English, Dutch, Danish, Swedish, French, Czech, Russian and Icelandic.[6] Arndt and Bayly were perhaps the best-known "spiritual" writers, but there were many others. Devotional writings became the staple of many Christian families throughout Europe, the British Isles and North America.

A subtle but decisive shift was taking place. Religious life and practice was inexorably being separated from the ecclesiastical life represented by the

---

[4]Ibid.

[5]David Tripp, "Arndt, Johan (1556-1621)," in *Encyclopedia of Protestantism*, ed. Hans J. Hillerbrand (New York: Routledge, 2004), p. 102.

[6]W. R. Ward, *The Protestant Evangelical Awakening* (Cambridge: Cambridge University Press, 1992), p. 48.

church.[7] This became formalized with the development of Pietism after 1675, spurred by the writings of Philipp Jakob Spener, a German pastor whose own faith was nurtured by Arndt's *True Christianity*. Spener was determined to restore the "priesthood of all believers" by making a place for laypeople in the life of the local congregation. He promoted small groups, or cells, where lay people read the Scriptures, prayed together and encouraged one another in practical ministry.

Beginning with Pietism in the seventeenth century, and followed by waves of evangelical revivals in succeeding centuries, the evangelical impulse has sustained a movement that has existed in tension with the organized churches. This stream of renewal has remained focused on conversion of the individual to vital faith in Jesus Christ; a warm personal piety nurtured through Bible reading, prayer and devotional literature; and active participation in witness and service. Much of this activism has been channeled through voluntary lay-led agencies outside of church sponsorship and control. The modern mission movement is the outstanding exhibit of the influence of the evangelical theological impulse over the past four centuries.

Contemporary evangelicalism, a burgeoning worldwide movement of almost confusing variety, is the direct descendant of these movements to renew Protestant Christianity in the seventeenth and eighteenth centuries. Rooted in Puritanism, European Pietism and the Anglo-American evangelical revivals, evangelicalism has been at the center of the revitalization and continuous spread of the Christian movement in the modern period.

PERSONAL RENEWAL

As noted, by the seventeenth century, Protestant Christianity was widely regarded as having lost its gospel vitality. Instead it was crippled by "formalism" in worship, daily life and doctrine. In response to these conditions, in 1675 a devout and energetic young German pastor and theologian, Philipp Jakob Spener (1635–1705), in his essay *Pia Desideria*,[8] urged the reform of the church through (a) intensive Bible study, both individually and in small groups; (b) recovery of the priesthood of all believers, thus emphasizing the

---

[7]Ibid., pp. 46-53.
[8]The full title in English: *Heartfelt Desire for a God-Pleasing Reform of the True Evangelical Church, Together with Several Simple Christian Proposals.*

ministry of the laity; (c) relating Christian faith to daily life; and (d) seeking to win unbelievers to faith through compassion and positive example rather than by coercion. Each of Spener's points responded to a perceived deficiency in the church of his day, and together they became the hallmarks of Pietism. Spener's answer to widespread nominalism in the Protestant church was a quickened and heartfelt Christian faith, nurtured and sustained by Scripture and actively applied in witness and service. Pietism emphasized the importance of personal conversion validated by the assurance of salvation and by active religious experience. From the foundation laid by Spener arose the works of August Hermann Francke (1663–1727), at Halle, and Count Nikolaus von Zinzendorf (1700–1760) of the Moravian Brethren.

Missions and evangelism soon became the hallmarks of Pietism and evangelicalism. Pioneer Protestant missiologist Gustav Warneck (1834–1910) observed, "It was in the age of Pietism that missions struck their first deep roots, and it is the spirit of Pietism which, after Rationalism had laid its hoar-frost on the first blossoming, again revived them, and has brought them to their present bloom."[9] Francke engaged in a lively correspondence with Cotton Mather (1663–1728), the leading New England Puritan pastor, about the work of missions. Mather had close knowledge of the missionary work of John Eliot and the Mayhew family among the Native Americans of Massachusetts, and Francke was developing his ideas about foreign missions. When King Frederik IV of Denmark initiated a mission to India in 1705, the first two missionaries were Francke's former students, Bartholomäus Ziegenbalg and Heinrich Plütschau. They arrived at Tranquebar, South India, in 1706, and Halle became the spiritual center of Pietist missions.

The evangelical revival that started in Great Britain and the United States in the 1730s drew inspiration from the Pietists. John Wesley (1703–1791) encountered Pietist missionaries while in Georgia (1735–1737), had his conversion experience in 1738 in a Moravian meeting at Aldersgate in London and later visited Zinzendorf in Germany. Pietists and evangelicals agreed on basic themes: renewal of the church starts with personal conversion, the theological core is justification by faith alone, Scripture is the indispensable guide in faith and doctrine, faith must be actively applied

---

[9]Gustav Warneck, *History of Protestant Missions* (Edinburgh and London: Oliphant, Anderson and Ferrier, 1901), p. 53.

in daily life and Christian witness will be expressed in evangelization and ministries of compassion.

A common criticism raised against the German Pietists and the evangelicals in the English-speaking world by the established churches was that they emphasized subjective personal experience at the expense of solid theology. But a leading New England pastor was also acknowledged to be a foremost theological influence in the eighteenth century. Jonathan Edwards (1703–1758) answered these criticisms in *The Distinguishing Marks of a Work of the Spirit of God* (1741). Edwards held that authentic revival (a) exalts Jesus Christ; (b) attacks the kingdom of darkness; (c) honors the Scriptures; (d) promotes sound doctrine; and (e) results in an outpouring of love toward God and others.[10] As he wrote, can anyone "deny that true religion consists in a great measure, in vigorous and lively actings of the inclination and will of the soul, or the fervent exercises of the heart?"[11]

THE LAITY AND THE VOLUNTARY SOCIETY

It is difficult from a twenty-first-century viewpoint to realize how intensely clergy-dominated Christianity was in the sixteenth century. The very fact that much of world missions is now performed by unordained people is a reflection of evangelicalism's success in mobilizing the whole people of God. As long as Protestantism stayed locked in the state churches of Europe, which reflected the hierarchical structures of their host societies, the rigid division between an acting clergy and a passive laity was bound to remain.

What was needed was a new form of organization that could maintain the churches but also provide legitimate outlets for lay energy. Around 1700 a new form of organization known as the "voluntary society" was introduced in Great Britain, and laws were enacted to give such organizations legal sanction.[12] This was a timely development. Before 1700 Protestant churches were not prepared to sponsor philanthropic or missionary activity, and neither did they have the religious orders that fuelled Catholic missions

---

[10]For discussion of the relationship between revival and theology in the thought of Jonathan Edwards, see Richard F. Lovelace, *Dynamics of Spiritual Life: An Evangelical Theology of Renewal* (Downers Grove, IL: InterVarsity Press, 1979), pp. 37-43.

[11]Jonathan Edwards, *Religious Affections*, section 2, part 1; in *The Works of Jonathan Edwards*, vol. 4, *The Great Awakening*, ed. C. C. Goen (New Haven: Yale University Press, 1972), pp. 213-88.

[12]Josiah Woodward, *Account of the Rise and Progress of the Religious Societies* (London, 1698).

with cheap labor and religious vision. Furthermore, church leaders resisted innovations. The voluntary society offered an alternative whereby a committed group could undertake such an initiative outside ecclesiastical channels. This legal device allowed members of a voluntary society to solicit funds and operate a program according to its stated purposes. This concept was immediately put to work in setting up missionary societies as voluntary associations of individuals committed to Christian missions. From the Moravian missions through the Baptist Missionary Society to the British and Foreign Bible Society, or further abroad, the Benevolent Funds, "ragged school" foundations, trade unions, political pressure groups, building societies and the like, voluntarism fuelled social change on a vast scale as evangelicals and others collected lay human energy and directed it toward single causes. The other side of Protestant mobilization through voluntary associations was the fact that the resources of states were not to be drawn upon. This put pressure both on evangelical sending organizations to rationalize their expenditures, and on evangelical theologians to develop new theologies that matched the voluntarist reality. The Enlightenment individualism of evangelical religion was equal to the task. One development that provided solutions to this problem was the evangelical tendency to mobilize nationals and to build toward indigenous churches. From the 1840s Henry Venn worked tirelessly to promote policies that would bring to birth national churches that were self-governing, self-propagating and self-supporting. A second development was the formation of "faith missions." This extended the sovereignty of God to the financing of the organization, in the belief that if one followed God's command to "Go," he would also provide the support. Both innovations increased the importance of lay involvement and made evangelical missions highly effective for their initial outlay. They also determined the nature of global evangelicalism as flexible in its form and multi-centered in its organization.

"JESUS SHALL REIGN": NINETEENTH-CENTURY DEVELOPMENTS

From the founders of Pietism and evangelicalism, evangelicals inherited their identity as an activist movement concerned with practical application of the gospel. In each generation the theological impulse of evangelicalism has had to be clarified and applied to the issues confronting

Christian conscience; evangelicals, however have often been impatient with academic theology.

From 1787 to 1833 the slave trade and slavery were the focal moral issues for British evangelicals, with such well-known evangelical laymen as William Wilberforce (1759–1833) and Thomas Fowell Buxton (1786–1845) at the forefront of the crusades. In 1797 Wilberforce wrote *A Practical View of the Prevailing Religious System of Professed Christians in the Higher and Middle Classes in This Country,* a book that was highly influential in setting the agenda for evangelicals in the first half of the nineteenth century. A member of the British parliament and already well established as leader of the campaign to end slavery, as well as the patron of numerous Christian philanthropic and missionary causes, Wilberforce was the very embodiment of activist evangelicalism. In his book he analyzed the tepid religiosity that characterized Protestant Christians and showed that genuine faith leads to the application of the gospel to every dimension of human experience, whether this be in matters of personal piety or public morality. By personal example and by precept Wilberforce encouraged evangelicals to embrace "experimental Christianity," a faith expression that emphasized *applied* Christianity.

In seeking a deeper obedience to Christ, these evangelicals found in Scripture the warrant for an "experimental Christianity" that enabled them to overcome the spiritual lethargy of the traditional church and make an impact on the world. The activist character of evangelicalism created an environment that fostered innovation. From evangelicalism sprang conceptual developments that led to a range of programmatic innovations in missions, revivalism, philanthropy and social policy, especially in the eighteenth and nineteenth centuries.[13]

MISSIONS

The successors to the leading Protestant Reformers of the sixteenth century—as well as Martin Luther, John Calvin and Ulrich Zwingli themselves—often did not advocate for missions. They argued that passages such as Matthew 28:18-20 and Acts 1:8 applied to the first-generation

---

[13]For one such account see Ernest Marshall Howse, *Saints in Politics: The "Clapham Sect" and the Growth of Freedom* (London: George Allen and Unwin, 1971).

church only. The seventeenth-century Protestant theologian Gisbertus Voetius (1589–1676), drawing on Roman Catholic teaching and example, promoted church planting as a response to the will of God. John Eliot (1604–1690), a seventeenth-century Puritan missionary to the Native Americans of Massachusetts, held that the basis for mission was the glory of God. In the eighteenth century, Samuel Hopkins (1721–1803), a disciple of Jonathan Edwards, developed a theology of "disinterested benevolence" that emphasized that personal regeneration resulted in selflessness and a strong commitment to social reform. Hopkins advocated missions as one way of carrying out this gospel mandate. Although most eighteenth-century Protestants did not agree that missions were a present Christian responsibility, this was about to change.

In 1792 a young English Baptist pastor published an eighty-seven-page book, *An Enquiry into the Obligation of Christians to Use Means for the Conversion of the Heathen.* In this book William Carey (1761–1834) examined the arguments used to strip the Mission Mandate of its authority for the post-apostolic church and then offered three reasons why this position must be rejected.[14] Carey's book is as important for what it tells us about the mentality of the churches of his day as it is for his critique. It was not an original work, but rather it sums up the increasing moderate Calvinist dissatisfaction with hyper-Calvinist inactivity, and as such it marks a turning point. Carey would become singularly important for the example provided by his career in India and his influence on the formation of the Baptist Missionary Society. His writing and work were persuasive: after 1800 most Protestants accepted the Mission Mandate as binding on the church in every generation. Without this consensus there would not have been a modern missionary movement. Emphasis on the Mission Mandate over the past two centuries has been essential to evangelical identity and has fostered and reinforced an activist understanding of the church.

---

[14]Carey's rebuttal: (1) If we say the command to "teach all nations" was for the first apostles only, then the injunction to baptize must also be set aside; (2) God promised the nations the blessings of the gospel but the traditional argument withholds authority from any minister who assists in conveying this message to the "heathens"; and (3) if Christ's command to "teach all nations" applied only to the first apostles, we cannot expect the presence of the Holy Spirit to be with us today. Carey, *An Enquiry into the Obligations of Christians to Use Means for the Conversion of the Heathens* (1792; London: Carey Kingsgate Press, 1961), pp. 8-9.

As evangelicals began organizing missionary societies and sending out missionaries from Europe and North America, it became evident that they needed to clarify the basis and motives of missions. Furthermore, the Second Great Awakening in North America (1785–1830) was raising a new set of questions concerning methods of evangelization.

A comprehensive gospel. It is essential to know how the gospel was understood in 1800. A critical feature of Carey's argument was that Christians should use all appropriate *means* in the cause of world evangelization. As Carey and his contemporaries analyzed their world, they spoke of human need in terms of the whole person—the material, spiritual and cultural needs of people they were encountering in other cultures—and the comprehensiveness of the gospel. The gospel is the biblical message that addresses every dimension of human experience and need. In the spirit of the apostle Paul, the missionaries were called to "become all things to all men so that by all possible means [they] might save some" (1 Cor 9:22 NIV). For example, Carey and his generation joined the rising chorus of criticism of slavery and the slave trade in which so-called Christian nations were participating. They identified with the antislavery movement. Over the next several generations, mission leaders and missionaries threw themselves into the struggle against the iniquitous slave trade.

Carey's writings reveal that his ideal was the missions model developed by the first Moravian missionaries. In the 1730s little companies of Moravians began going to far-flung places as self-sustaining communities. Each member would work at whatever menial tasks were available to support the missionary community from the local economy while evangelizing and establishing churches.

If the gospel addresses every dimension of human life, the *means* of witness must be flexible in order to enable the missionary to touch all aspects of life. Proclamation was important, yet it was but one of the means of missionary witness. In the first phase of the modern missionary movement the typical missionary team was comprised of the preacher, the teacher and the printer. After 1850 the concept was expanded to include ministries to women and children by women missionaries, the doctor, the agriculturalist and industrial missions. All of these activities involved building institutions for carrying out these ministries. And all were understood as responses to the Great Commission.

The basis of missions. After Carey helped to rescue the Christian mission from the prison of faulty interpretation of Scripture, the next step was to encourage ordinary Christians to become active participants by developing a clear and compelling basis for missions. The new missionary societies were eager to recruit missionaries and cultivate financial and moral support. To accomplish this goal, promoters of missions appealed to "motives for missions." The many missionary magazines that sprang up after 1800 became a major channel for circulating information and educating the Christian public concerning their missionary duty. Sermons preached on special occasions, and later printed as pamphlets, were a particularly powerful means of steering ministry toward missions.[15]

On February 6, 1812, an ordination service for the first five American missionaries commissioned by the American Board of Commissioners for Foreign Missions (ABCFM) for missionary service overseas was held at the Tabernacle in Salem, Massachusetts. The group included Adoniram and Ann Judson, Samuel and Harriett Newell, Gordon Hall, Samuel and Rosanna Nott, and Luther Rice. One of the two ordination sermons was preached on Psalm 67 by Dr. Leonard Woods, of Andover Theological Seminary. So long as there are people in the world who do not acknowledge Christ as Lord, he preached, the "fervent Christian cannot rest. His unalterable object is, *that the knowledge of the Lord may fill the earth. His heart beats high for the conversion of the world.*"[16] Woods developed his rationale for missions in terms of six motives that will "rouse you to benevolent exertion": (1) the worth of souls; (2) the ample provision Christ has made for the salvation of all people; (3) the Lord's command, "Go ye into all the world, and preach the gospel to every creature"; (4) the model established by the first apostles for us to go everywhere proclaiming the gospel and establishing the church in order that "God's way might be known upon the earth, and his salvation to all nations"; (5) the truth that, in contrast to the exclusivist attitude of Judaism, the Christian message is intended for all

---

[15]See, e.g., [Baptist Missionary Society], *Missionary Sermons: A Selection from the Discourses Delivered on Behalf of The Baptist Missionary Society on Various Occasions* (London: The Carey Press, 1924); R. Pierce Beaver, ed., *Pioneers in Mission: The Early Missionary Ordination Sermons, Charges, and Instructions* (Grand Rapids: Eerdmans, 1966).

[16]Beaver, *Pioneers in Mission*, pp. 257-58; emphasis in original.

people; and (6) the prophecy that indeed "all the ends of the earth shall see the salvation of God."[17]

As the nineteenth century progressed, several themes came to stand out in the evangelical understanding as to what should inspire people to go out on mission, themes that reflect the informing theologies of the movement. One major theme, the glory of God, is perhaps the earliest theme and is usually identified with the Puritan tradition. In the eighteenth century Jonathan Edwards and Samuel Hopkins had also urged "disinterested benevolence" as the motive for missions. How could one have the answer to humanity's ills and not be moved (like Christ himself) by humanitarian compassion? The evangelical contribution to the growing antislavery movement and a variety of philanthropic ministries at home are examples of this. Foreign missionaries and domestic reformers were often the same people. Some also advocated missions as a form of reparations that Europeans ought to undertake to atone for their role in the slave trade. From the 1820s millennialism grew in importance and would increasingly define conservative evangelical missions. After 1900 the Great Commission was embraced as the primary motive for mission. The Enlightenment also helped ingrain a general assumption that an important part of missionary work was to share the benefits of "civilization," such as science, technology, economic development and good manners. These "blessings" were to be shared primarily through education, though later medical and agricultural services were added. Imperialism, like the Enlightenment, was seldom appealed to directly. Despite its lack of biblical warrant, toward the end of the nineteenth century, missions were increasingly presented as holding in sacred trust guardianship over "the weaker people" of the world. By 1900, however, many of the peoples who had been colonized by European powers were growing restive and taking steps to organize movements of national independence. The missions with links to the imperial powers realized they had compromised themselves.[18] Having a "pure motive" was no longer enough, and so again evangelicalism needed to find new avenues of renewal.

---

[17]Ibid., pp. 258-63.
[18]For a balanced and insightful critique of this theme, see Brian Stanley, *The Bible and the Flag: Protestant Missions and British Imperialism in the Nineteenth and Twentieth Centuries* (Leicester, UK: Apollos, 1990).

PERSONAL RENEWAL AND LAY ENERGY IN REVIVALISM

The burden of Pietism and evangelicalism from the beginning was spiritual revival and renewal. It is no surprise then that evangelists, some of whom gained national and international reputations, played a dominant role in shaping evangelical identity, including its theological dimensions. In contrast to leaders of the First Evangelical Awakening in the eighteenth century (all of whom had formal training in theology), in the nineteenth century the most prominent revival preachers were largely self-taught in matters of theology.

Charles G. Finney (1792–1875) is often called the father of modern revivalism because of his bold innovations in methods and theology.[19] Prior to his conversion Finney had practiced law. On October 10, 1821, he experienced a dramatic conversion and immediately gave up his successful legal practice, believing he had "a retainer from the Lord Jesus Christ to plead his cause." He was ordained in the Presbyterian Church and accepted appointment as a missionary to the growing settler communities in western New York State in 1824. A forceful and dramatic speaker, revivals soon began to break out and Finney's reputation as an evangelist was established. Drawing on his experience in the courtroom, he introduced such new measures as the "anxious bench" and protracted meetings. These innovations brought praise, criticism—and a growing reputation. By 1827 Finney moved to the major East Coast cities of the United States where he conducted revivals. He visited Great Britain twice for extended preaching missions with widespread effect, first in 1849–1850 and then again in 1859–1860.

Finney's "new measures" would define evangelistic methods for several generations, and by his example he encouraged future evangelists to adopt the latest techniques for the revival cause. Finney viewed methods pragmatically. Theologically, he sought to combine a moderate "new school" Calvinism with elements of Wesleyan holiness teaching, thus allowing him to hold together the sovereignty of God and the human agency of his new methods. He advocated for the abolition of slavery, for temperance and other social reforms, such as equality of opportunity for women, as the fruit of revival. He was little interested in denominational loyalties.

---

[19]Keith J. Hardman, *Charles Grandison Finney, 1792–1875: Revivalist and Reformer* (Grand Rapids: Baker Books, 1987).

The rigors of evangelistic work took their toll on Finney's health, and in 1835 he accepted appointment as a teacher of theology in the new Oberlin Institute (later College) in Ohio. He developed and taught his own theological synthesis that has been called "Arminianized Calvinism." Finney's impact on nineteenth-century evangelicalism was to blur the lines separating Calvinists from Wesleyans and to emphasize the importance of a more pragmatic Christianity geared to producing results. This suited American—and indeed non-Western—situations rather more closely than the Old-World conditions of the state churches.

If Finney was the foremost evangelist in the first half of the nineteenth century, Dwight L. Moody (1837–1899) filled this role during the latter half of the nineteenth century. Moody was a salesman and businessman before he turned to revival work. Just as Finney's experience as a lawyer shaped his approach to evangelistic preaching, so Moody drew directly on his experience in business as he developed his methodology. He disliked sensationalism and was at home in the urban environment. Moody understood the importance of effective organization and insisted on careful preparation. He used advertising skillfully to promote his revivals.

Moody had no formal theological training. Unlike Finney, who became a teacher of theology later in life, Moody showed little interest in academic theology. He remained the quintessential layman throughout his life and used this to his advantage in communicating with his audiences. He was a shrewd judge of human nature and effectively appealed to people of all classes.

Yet Moody held an implicit theology representative of the evangelicalism of his day. He rejected hell-fire preaching, preferring to emphasize God's compassion for the sinner, redemption in Christ and regeneration through the work of the Holy Spirit.[20] Moody's evangelistic preaching was reinforced by the gospel songs that his associate, Ira D. Sankey, used in the campaigns. The gospel song— singable, sentimental, personal and in tune with musical tastes of the time— became the signature music of revival campaigns from the time of Moody. Its descendants—particularly in the charismatic and Pentecostal worship music produced by the Vineyard, Hillsong and Scripture in Song movements— continue to shape the global culture of evangelical churches to this day.

---

[20]Stanley N. Gundry, *Love Them In: The Proclamation Theology of D. L. Moody* (Chicago: Moody Press, 1976), chap. 2.

Moody was the first major American evangelist to include premillenni-alism in his message. Popularized by John Nelson Darby, the dispensational form of premillennialism resulted in intense debate among evangelicals. Given his aversion to controversy, Moody avoided Darbyist theories that were seen as combative and nonnegotiable. In an oft-quoted sermon passage, he reflected his view of the world and his responsibility there:

> I look on this world as a wrecked vessel. God has given me a life-boat, and said to me, "Moody, save all you can." God will come in judgment and burn up this world, but the children of God don't belong to this world; they are in it but not of it, like a ship in the water.[21]

In this sense, evangelicals had one duty—to reach as many as could be saved before the allotted space of God's mercy ran out. One popular conference speaker fuelled global student missions with the motto "evangelize to a finish to bring back the King." Although Moody himself took little interest in the intense debate about biblical prophecy toward the end of the nineteenth century, revival preaching was increasingly identified with premillennialism. This had a twofold effect on evangelical theology. On the one hand, it heightened the sense of urgency about the evangelistic task, and the premillennialist emphasis on the imminence of Christ's return became the hallmark of revival preaching. On the other, it undercut concern for social issues. If Christ's return was just about to happen, and the most important thing was the salvation of souls from hell, everything else was of secondary importance. This dichotomy polarized the evangelical impulse between the salvation of the soul and the message of compassion and social witness. Left to itself, such an emphasis could become abstract and sterile, but revivalism almost always resulted in more than merely personal change.

A balancing factor is that *revivalism* leaves itself open to *revival*, a broad-based process of change and renewal whose impact goes far beyond church walls. The East African Revival broke out in Rwanda in the 1930s and moved crossculturally into Kenya, Tanganyika, Uganda and elsewhere. Being contextually appropriate, the revivals embedded Christianity within the local social relationships. Through revival, the faith became truly indigenous, and missionaries found Africans to be their spiritual equals. A similar situation

---

[21]Ibid., p. 175.

emerged in the Elcho Island (Australia) and Chinese house church revivals.

Although not highly educated himself, Moody valued training and established several educational institutions. He also sponsored annual Bible conferences that were held in various places. These Bible conferences became particularly influential in promoting and sustaining a more conservative and premillennial (often dispensationalist) theology. In 1889 Moody founded the Bible Institute for Home and Foreign Missions in Chicago, which following his death in 1899 was renamed Moody Bible Institute.

The growing Bible institute movement would exert enormous influence on the evangelical movement after 1900 in two respects. First, Bible institutes geared themselves to the training of missionaries—for service both at home and abroad—and lay evangelists. Moody Bible Institute is reputed to have trained more Protestant missionaries than any other school. In the second place, these institutes emphasized practical training, were strong advocates of dispensational premillennialism, took a critical stance toward mainstream evangelicals and higher education, and helped form the foundation on which fundamentalism would be erected. The influence of these schools and their particular variety of evangelicalism was carried all over the world by the burgeoning missionary movement that would continue through most of the twentieth century.[22]

"We've a Story to Tell to the Nations": Twentieth-Century Developments

When the large Ecumenical Missionary Conference was held in New York City in 1900, the entire Protestant world missionary movement was represented. The venerable J. Hudson Taylor (1832–1905) had come from China to address the gathering, as did William McKinley (1843–1901), president of the United States and a devout Methodist layman. In 1896 the English hymn writer Henry Ernest Nichol, gripped by the vision of Christian missions, wrote "We've a Story to Tell," a song that captures the spirit of the surging Student Volunteer Movement and camaraderie of the mission movement:

---

[22]Joel A. Carpenter, "Propagating the Faith Once Delivered: The Fundamentalist Missionary Enterprise, 1920–1945," in *Earthen Vessels: American Evangelicals and Foreign Missions, 1880-1980*, ed. J. A. Carpenter and W. R. Shenk (Eugene, OR: Wipf and Stock, 2012), pp. 92-132.

We've a story to tell to the nations
That shall turn their hearts to the right,
A story of truth and mercy,
A story of peace and light.

The last line of the chorus underscores the millennial theme: "And Christ's great kingdom shall come to earth, the kingdom of love and light." Yet this façade of unity could not hide the fact that storm clouds were forming. The emerging struggle between modernists and fundamentalists was dividing Protestants, and divisions were appearing in evangelical ranks as well.

In 1886 Dwight L. Moody held a conference for university students at Northfield, Massachusetts. The success of this meeting led to the organization of the Student Volunteer Movement for Foreign Missions (SVM) in 1888 under the umbrella of the Young Men's Christian Association and the Young Women's Christian Association with John R. Mott (1865-1955) as chair. Among the regular speakers at SVM conventions were such prominent missions promoters as A. T. Pierson (1837-1911) and A. J. Gordon (1836-1895), both of whom had adopted premillennialism and espoused a theory of mission that emphasized the urgency of completing the task as rapidly as possible.[23] The SVM itself never took a position on millennialism, but its slogan, "The evangelization of the world in this generation," could readily be interpreted to suit a particular speaker's tastes. Gustav Warneck, German professor of missiology, called the slogan "dangerous" because "impatient pressing forward has led to the waste of much precious toil."[24] Warneck believed the force of the slogan was to encourage the continual occupation of new fields to the neglect of work already started.

The fragmenting of evangelicalism into various factions was symbolized by the emergence of new groupings and their agencies. J. Hudson Taylor, father of the "faith mission," was theologically conservative but irenic in spirit toward other missions. But from the 1880s on, under the influence of powerful missions advocates such as A. T. Pierson, A. J. Gordon and A. B. Simpson (1844-1919), the long-standing evangelical consensus broke down.

---

[23]For incisive studies of these developments and their consequences by the 1930s, see Joel A. Carpenter and Wilbert R. Shenk, eds., *Earthen Vessels: American Evangelicals and Foreign Missions, 1880-1980* (Grand Rapids: Eerdmans, 1990), chaps. 2-5.

[24]*Ecumenical Missions Conference, New York, 1900* (New York: American Tract Society, 1900), 1:290.

This was expressed in new mission theory based on dispensational pre-millennialism, the rise of new missionary training institutions, the establishment of the nondenominational faith missions and a new and separatist generation of leaders suspicious of higher education and committed to "defense of the faith." Initially, the nondenominational missions saw themselves filling a need the older missions were not prepared to do. The new missions were (1) ready to accept for missionary service people with a lower level of training and (2) would send them to work in the "interior" or "inland," occupying fields that hitherto had been neglected by the older missions. Naturally, the new missions were closely allied with the new Bible institutes that were training the missionary candidates in sound doctrine.

The nondenominational missions movement soon became an important worldwide force in evangelicalism in the twentieth century. It appealed to Matthew 24:14, linking the Great Commission and the return of Christ as the fundamental motive for mission: "This gospel of the kingdom will be preached in the whole world, . . . and then the end will come" (NIV). This movement forged an ideology that made preaching and evangelism the priority in missions, declined to have fellowship with those who differed with them doctrinally, and followed a conservative social ethic. In his reaction to the report of the Laymen's Foreign Missions Inquiry, *Re-Thinking Missions* (1932), Henry W. Frost (1858–1945), long-time North American director for the China Inland Mission, expressed this ideological viewpoint with clarity. The Laymen's Report had called on missions to emphasize social uplift as a main purpose in the future. Frost countered this, saying, "Social reform is good, but it is not the Gospel. Education is good, but it is not the Gospel. Medical work is good, but it is not the Gospel. Indeed, these matters, good as they are, may destroy the Gospel."[25]

Mainstream evangelicals found themselves overshadowed by the drama of the polarization between the social gospel of liberal Protestants and the evangelism-only rhetoric of the fundamentalists. Mainstream evangelicals never accepted either extreme and continued to follow a mission theory that William Carey would have approved. But the historic evangelical vision of a comprehensive gospel was obscured by the intense debate between the modernists and fundamentalists until after 1945.

---

[25]Cited in Carpenter and Shenk, *Earthen Vessels*, p. 55.

RECOVERY OF THE WHOLE GOSPEL?

Both theological modernists and theological fundamentalists were reacting to modernity. The modernist response was to accommodate as fully as possible to modern philosophy and values. The fundamentalist reacted by defending Christian faith but doing so using the rationalist categories of modernity. Modernist and fundamentalist alike read the Bible using modern perspectives, paying little attention to the cultural and historical context in which the Scriptures were originally written and overlooking the essentially narrative structure that conveys the life experiences of people in all their complexity. When read in this perspective, the Bible cannot so easily be reduced to propositions, on the one hand, or a social program, on the other. In the United States the social gospel as a movement largely disappeared by the 1920s, although some of its key ideas were incorporated into liberal Protestantism. Fundamentalism, on the other hand, remained strong throughout the twentieth century and maintained its emphasis on the gospel as proclamation.

By the 1940s evangelical leaders were increasingly troubled by the fact that fundamentalism had produced a reductionist understanding of the gospel. The pressure to challenge the modernist-fundamentalist dichotomy came from three sources: attempts to read the Scriptures more faithfully, the challenge of responding to tragic human need as the result of war and natural disasters, and international mission conferences.

The destruction caused by World War II, the delayed formation of evangelical leadership, and the massive blossoming of universities after the war, as the baby boom and government-funded retraining of demobilized soldiers took effect, attuned many evangelicals to social change and dislocation. There were many who returned from war determined to live lives of significance. Many found their way into missions, churches and work among children or the disadvantaged, as well as into secular alternatives such as the Peace Corps. Voluntary associations, long a hallmark of evangelicalism, again were formed to sponsor new ministries, especially those focused on youth. Examples include Youth for Christ and international bodies representing evangelical missions among students: the International Fellowship of Evangelical Students, Campus Crusade for Christ, Navigators, Student Life and many others. These overlapped with pre-War foundations such as the Children's Special Service Mission, Inter-Varsity Fellowship and

Scripture Union. For some of these people, as the rising nationalism of post-colonial nations was making traditional missions increasingly problematic, the new social emphasis of evangelicalism provided new outlets for lay energies, both at home and abroad. Surging new churches—such as the Pentecostal churches emerging in Latin America—saw social service as part of their core function. Others saw the need to refocus on redeeming the increasingly secular cultures of the West: the huge literatures on "culture wars," church growth principles and church planting have been one result of this, as has the emerging status of First-World countries as mission receiving cultures. As the centers of evangelical Christianity moved south and east, churches in the West struggled with their need to recognize that they had much to learn from their fellow Christians elsewhere in the world.

The Korean War in 1950–1953 was also a crucial turning point in evangelical awareness. Youth for Christ evangelist Bob Pierce (1914–1978) visited Korea during the war and saw human suffering on a massive scale. In response, he organized World Vision to mobilize Christian support for children's homes for the thousands of war orphans, for hospitals and relief aid. World Vision would become the largest Protestant agency in the world, responding to short-term emergencies and long-term development needs all over the globe and raising support for these programs in many countries. Numerous other evangelical agencies were established during this period dedicated to serving children, promoting community development, medical services and educational programs of various kinds. These agencies developed effective publicity that reached a large Christian public motivated by Christian compassion. Frequently, these agencies sought endorsements for their efforts by well-known evangelical leaders, including evangelists. Evangelicalism's shift away from fundamentalism is demonstrated by the decline of criticism of programs that focused primarily on ministering to the physical and emotional needs of people throughout the world.

By the 1950s evangelical biblical scholars and theologians were doing fresh work. New Testament scholar George Eldon Ladd (1911–1982) addressed a series of issues on which evangelicals disagreed, including millennialism, biblical hermeneutics and the kingdom of God. Other evangelical exegetes and theologians joined Ladd in reconsidering the way the Bible is to be read and applied in the world today. The modern penchant for taking the text apart and treating it piecemeal was—in some evangelical circles, at least—increasingly seen to be defective. Reading the text in light of the original context and with reverent attention to what the original writers were attempting to convey placed the Scriptures in a dynamic relationship with culture.

The third development after 1966 was the convening of a series of international evangelical missionary conferences. Several of these conferences were convened at the initiative of evangelist Billy Graham (1918–), who consistently promoted several concerns: (1) encouraging world evangelization, (2) fostering evangelical unity and (3) enabling non-Western evangelical leaders to contribute to world leadership. The 1974 International Congress on World Evangelization, held in Lausanne, Switzerland, stands out. One of the most important issues running through the Congress was how evangelicals would understand and interpret the gospel. Several of the plenary speakers from Latin America, Africa and Asia pleaded for a fully evangelical gospel, not one that forced one to choose between several ideological agendas. A representative voice from the non-Western world was that of Samuel Escobar of Peru. In his plenary address he argued:

> Evangelicals, seriously concerned with the integrity of the Gospel as well as with the proclamation of it unto the ends of the earth, must keep in mind the biblical pattern of evangelism and the biblical content of the Gospel. . . . The temptation for evangelicals today is to reduce the Gospel, to mutilate it, to eliminate any demands for the fruit of repentance. . . . The church . . . must stress the need for the whole Gospel of Jesus Christ as Savior and Lord whose demands cannot be cheapened. . . . The danger of evangelicalism is that it will present a saving work of Christ without the consequent ethical demands, that it will present a Savior who delivers from the bondage of spiritual slavery but not a model of the life that the Christians should live in the world.[26]

Escobar and his colleagues were speaking on behalf of the Majority World's peoples who were impoverished and frequently lived under repressive political systems.

Lausanne signaled that a new stage in the evangelical movement had arrived. By 1974 the trends in the growth of the Christian population worldwide

---

[26]Samuel Escobar, "Evangelism and Man's Search for Freedom, Justice and Fulfillment," in *Let the World Hear His Voice*, Official Reference Volume: Papers and Responses, ed. J. D. Douglas (Minneapolis: World Wide Publications, 1975), p. 310.

pointed to the fact that within ten years the majority of Christians would be in Asia, Africa and Latin America. From this point on, leaders from these continents would persistently challenge evangelicals to recover the *whole* gospel. By the end of the century, this was well and truly the case—not only were two-thirds of the world's Christians in the Two-Thirds World, but the majority of missionaries expressing the evangelical theological impulse were based in the Two-Thirds World and were both missionizing the Two-Thirds World and sending energetic tap roots back into the increasingly secularized First World. The original Lausanne Conference was followed by two important conferences: in Manila in 1989 and in Cape Town in 2010.

Relatively little attention has been paid to the wider impact of the modern missionary movement. One such line of investigation has been pursued by sociologist Robert D. Woodberry, through a large empirical study of the sources of the liberal democracy that has developed throughout the twentieth century in the non-Western world. Using sophisticated research methods and computer-assisted data analysis, Woodberry and his team have amassed impressive evidence that "conversionary Protestants" played a central role in introducing ideas about "religious liberty, mass education, mass printing, newspapers, voluntary organizations, most major colonial reforms, and the codification of legal protections for nonwhites in the nineteenth and early twentieth centuries."[27] The spread of democratic government around the world would have been quite impossible without these culture-transforming institutions, agencies and educational initiatives. No other Christian tradition has had comparable impact in non-Western cultures.[28] "Conversionary Protestants" were, of course, those motivated by what we here have called the evangelical impulse.

Elusive Consensus

In spite of the promise of initiatives such as the Lausanne movement to clarify and unify evangelicals theologically, the twenty-first century opened with no new consensus concerning the evangelical theological impulse. The sense of the integrity of the gospel that guided the movement prior to 1900 had not

---

[27]Robert D. Woodberry, "The Missionary Roots of Liberal Democracy," *American Political Science Review* 106, no. 2 (May 2012): 244.
[28]Ibid., p. 256.

been regained. Fundamentalists continued to assume as normative the modern worldview based on Enlightenment rationality. On the other hand, dynamic developments such as the emergence of the Pentecostal/charismatic churches were bringing into the evangelical movement fresh currents that required new wineskins. The emergence of significant scholarship from this movement (from thinkers such as Gordon Fee and Miroslav Volf) and the proliferation of increasing numbers of quality evangelical institutions of higher learning may be taken as yet another sign of the evangelical ability to adapt to the new circumstances presented by a global society.

FURTHER READING

Carpenter, Joel A., and Wilbert R. Shenk, eds. *Earthen Vessels: American Evangelicals and Foreign Missions, 1880–1980.* Grand Rapids: Eerdmans, 1990. Reprint, Eugene, OR: Wipf and Stock, 2012.

Elwell, Walter A., ed. *Evangelical Dictionary of Theology.* Grand Rapids: Baker Reference Library, 2001.

Escobar, Samuel. *The New Global Mission: The Gospel from Everywhere to Everyone.* Downers Grove, IL: InterVarsity Press, 2003.

Grenz, Stanley J. *Revisioning Evangelical Theology: A Fresh Agenda for the 21st Century.* Downers Grove, IL: InterVarsity Press, 1993.

Moreau, A. Scott, ed. *Evangelical Dictionary of World Missions.* Grand Rapids: Baker Books, 2000.

Nicholls, Bruce J. *In Word and Deed: Evangelism and Social Responsibility.* Grand Rapids: Eerdmans, 1986.

Ramm, Bernard L., and Kevin Vanhoozer. *The Evangelical Heritage: A Study in Historical Theology.* Waco, TX: Word Books, various editions.

Wells, David F. *No Place for Truth: Or, Whatever Happened to Evangelical Theology?* Grand Rapids: Eerdmans, 1993.

3

GLOBALIZATION, RELIGION AND EVANGELICALISM

Donald M. Lewis

THE THEOLOGICAL IMPULSES DISCUSSED in the previous chapter caused evangelicals to proclaim the Christian gospel throughout the world, and this proclamation had massive consequences. In making such a claim, it is important also to acknowledge that the expansion of evangelicalism beginning in the eighteenth century both coincided with and contributed to the global expansion of Western nations. This process of modernization and worldwide spread of a common culture is usually referred to by scholars as "globalization." Given that evangelicals were crisscrossing the world, how did their movement interact with or respond to this process? To understand this interaction, we need to examine the concept of globalization.

Globalization is a major theme in both popular and academic discussion. The term has ignited a highly complex debate that currently rages in books and journals, and given the nature of global politics, it is likely to continue for decades to come. The scholarly discussion of globalization is particularly difficult because it crosses a number of academic disciplines: sociology, anthropology, history, religion, economics and political science, to name a few. This chapter seeks to serve as a relatively simple introduction to a complex debate and to offer some observations on the way in which evangelicalism relates to these discussions.

What is surprising about this debate is the fact that the term *globalization* is so new. The word *global* is probably four hundred years old. The words *globalization, globalize* and *globalizing* were first used in English about 1960 and only became commonplace in the 1980s.

Marshall McLuhan (1911–1981) was the first person to popularize the idea when he coined the expression *global village* in his *Explorations in Communication* (1960). He invented the term as a way of conveying the effects of the communications revolution brought about by the widespread use of new technologies such as radio and television. Commercial radio stations began in the 1920s, but radio sets were bulky and relatively expensive. The advent of the transistor radio—only invented in the 1950s—made radio receivers portable and much cheaper and thus much more accessible to people throughout the world. Almost immediately the transistor radio began impacting remote societies, and perceptive scholars like McLuhan began to realize that something significant was happening. With the development of satellite television communications in the 1970s, not only were human events being listened to across the world, but also they were being seen and experienced by millions simultaneously. The widespread use of the personal computer and with it the popularity of the Internet and email in the 1990s enabled this communications revolution to jump to a much higher level. All of these factors have combined to "shrink" or "compress" the world, making it possible for people to be in contact with others (even many others) instantly across many miles. This is the core idea behind "globalization."

But *globalization* has become a much-contested term, with some suggesting it is a concept that can be employed as a tool to dominate, oppress and control. How one defines *globalization* is therefore important, because the definitions are often loaded with assumptions (such as implying the inevitable dominance of "the West" or the ultimate triumph of laissez-faire capitalism). Anthony Giddens offers the following definition: "Globalization can thus be defined as the intensification of worldwide social relations which link distant localities in such a way that local happenings are shaped by events occurring many miles away and vice versa."[1] Malcolm Waters suggests a similar definition: "[Globalization is] a social process in which the constraints of geography on economic, political, social and cultural arrangements recede, in which people become increasingly aware that they are receding and in which people act accordingly."[2] The common ground

---

[1]Anthony Giddens, *The Consequences of Modernity* (Cambridge: Polity Press, 1990), p. 64.
[2]Malcolm Waters, *Globalization* (London: Routledge, 1995), p. 3.

in these definitions includes an emphasis on rapid communication that makes geographical distance less and less important in how we live our lives, the availability of these means of communication to people throughout the world, and the increased awareness of other people and places in the world. The central idea is that the world is becoming more and more a single place, a single "village," with all the outcomes this has on human relations and the way we see the world.

Other definitions emphasize not so much the importance of mass communications (including travel) and the mass media (with its production of an international mass popular culture) but the global economic and political reach of multinational corporations, many of which are far more powerful than individual nation-states. The dismantling of national barriers to the operation of capital markets (the flow of money), which began in the early 1980s, and the demise of the Soviet Union, in 1989, both contributed to the apparent triumph of international capitalism in the economic domain. There have been violent protests by people whom the media have labeled as "antiglobalization" activists, and so for many the word *globalization* is a code word for an emerging and oppressive world economic order, along with instruments of that order such as the World Bank and the International Monetary Fund. In this chapter *globalization* is being defined more broadly, in that it includes the economic dimension but recognizes that there are other social, political, cultural and religious forces at work as well.

But "globalization" is more than just the idea that the world is becoming a smaller place, a worldwide village, because of the technological revolution. Key to the globalization debate is the idea that Western economic, political and cultural models are increasingly influencing this "global village." Some thinkers argue that globalization is a myth or lie that has been put forward to disguise the march of international capitalism, giving the impression that it is an unstoppable process that it is useless to resist. Others argue that globalization is merely a mask for Americanization: the world is becoming homogenized as all tastes are flattened and a single American flavor triumphs. Other theorists respond by saying the result of globalization is not that people want a single flavor but that it opens up a wide diversity of flavors to cater to individual tastes.

COMMON FEATURES

There are some common elements in scholarly thinking about globalization, with scholars generally agreeing on the following points: First, globalization is a cultural and economic phenomenon that is historically rooted in the expansion of European nations in what has been called the Vasco da Gama era (the period from 1497 to 1947). Vasco da Gama was the Portuguese explorer who pioneered global exploration in 1497 when he took the first Portuguese fleet across the Indian Ocean. The period is often seen as ending with Britain's granting of independence to its Indian territories in 1947, the first major step in the post–World War II relinquishing by European powers of their overseas holdings.

The Portuguese were primarily interested in establishing trading posts for commercial purposes and were not particularly interested in settling the lands that they visited (with the exception of Brazil). The Spanish and the French were major players in the colonial enterprise; Holland, Belgium, Italy and Denmark were much more minor players. But it was the British (especially after their defeat of Napoleon in 1815) who began to acquire a far-flung empire, parts of which (the United States, Canada, New Zealand and Australia) they populated with English-speaking immigrants. Important for the global spread of Christianity is the fact that all of these European nations were self-consciously Christian with established state churches. These churches were transplanted to their colonies, and often the impulse to explore and expand political and economic power beyond Europe was closely linked to a desire for Christian expansion. To what extent this link helped or hindered the global growth of Christianity is a matter of much ongoing debate.

Second, many theorists see globalization as closely linked to the rise of modern capitalism in the eighteenth and nineteenth centuries. A new group of businessmen emerged who became wealthy through their ability to work successfully in the marketplace; with their new wealth they challenged the old ways of doing things and the old elites whose authority was based on family status or inherited wealth or land. The old "establishment" was challenged by the *nouveau riche* (newly rich). The newly rich wanted freer trade instead of the monopolies favored under the old economy, as well as exploration and military adventure to expand markets abroad. In the late nineteenth century many nation-states became more powerful as they sought to control their expanding economies and provide for their workers who were demanding more state services and a social safety net.

Third, although theorists may disagree as to its effects, they do agree that international capitalism has triumphed (for better or ill) as an economic system that seems to be almost unstoppable. (Although perhaps historians are more likely to be aware of the tendency for majority cultural forces to create the circumstances for minority oppositions to arise; success can breed the conditions for eventual failure.) We now live in a world economy made possible by better communications, cheap transport, new divisions of labor and the free flow of money. All of these factors have facilitated the growth of transnational corporations, many of which are economically more powerful than numerous countries belonging to the United Nations.

Fourth, there is a level of agreement among theorists that globalization involves

1. a process of contraction or the diminishing of the importance of barriers of distance and geography;

2. the disembedding of people from their received traditions—people tend to move beyond their tribal allegiances in a globalized world;

3. people, companies and even nations reorienting themselves to the wider world, which is now having more and more impact on them;

4. the undermining of universal claims and particular identities.

All of these assertions, however, can be and have been called into question when applied to particular conditions.

Fifth, the future of the nation-state is a key issue of debate. Some theorists speculate that the nation-state is being undermined or "relativized." Wallerstein sees them as creations of the modern era that will become obsolete or simply dissolve under global pressures.[3] Various solvents are suggested by different theorists. Given the communications revolution, people (especially the poor) have rising expectations of their governments that most modern states are unable to fulfill adequately. In a globalizing world national identities (and boundaries) are harder to retain given the international flows of

---

[3]See Immanuel Wallerstein, *The Modern World-System*, 4 vols. (1974, 1980, 1989 and 2011).

money, people and culture. Or perhaps the free flow of information means that it is more difficult for nation-states to control their people. Some think that regional alliances of states (such as the European Community) will be the trend of the future, leading perhaps to a unified world. Balanced against such claims are other theorists who believe that nation-states have the capacity to adapt and change their functions so as to be more, rather than less effective in the international arena.

Moreover, many globalization theorists think that a global culture will not emerge in any meaningful sense, but rather that geographical location will not be a basis on which to predict how people will act. Islam in a globalized world, for instance, would be practiced throughout the world rather than be localized in the geographical band in which it has traditionally operated (from North Africa and the Middle East to Pakistan, India and parts of Southeast Asia). It would be globally available with differing degrees of orthodoxy.

Finally, globalization theorists agree that academic analysis now needs to operate, not at the level of the nation-state, but at the global level. The context for cultural, political, economic and social analysis is now global, and discussions of the contemporary world can no longer operate within the restrictions of a single nation or continent. Unless the larger context is taken into consideration one will never be able to understand the changes occurring in the world today. It is in this context that a number of Christian historians are calling for a rethinking of Christian history in the context of the global expansion of the faith, particularly with regard to the eclipsing of Christianity in traditional areas of Christendom.

GLOBALIZATION AS DESCRIPTION VERSUS GLOBALIZATION AS PREDICTION

One has to be careful, however, to distinguish between "globalization" as a description of *what is happening*, the various theories advanced by scholars about *why* it is happening and, finally, *the impact that it may it have*. There are several cautions that need to be heeded.

First, we need to think of globalization in terms of "what is happening." Perhaps it would be better to say "in terms of what *appears* to be happening," because in a world where many people are still so poor that they have never used a telephone, the extent of the reach of high-tech revolution is at least debatable. This has been called "the digital divide." As the use of radio in the fight against disease in Africa has shown, perhaps the low-tech transistor radio has been more significant in "shrinking" the world than the high-tech Internet.

We have to be careful, moreover, to identify assumptions that people import into discussions about globalization. For instance, theorists often imply that globalization is an inevitable and irreversible process. Sometimes writers use *globalization* like a code word to suggest that there is an emerging global culture that cannot be resisted, and that this process of "globalization" involves both Westernization and the inevitable triumph of capitalism. (It may, on the other hand, be the case that Western values and international capitalism are only incidental to this stage of the development of "globalization" and that further down the line the dominant "globalized" values will be quite different.)

Third, we need to distinguish between *description* and *prediction*. People writing about globalization often move from description to prediction without distinguishing between the two. Observing the impact that globalization has had in one area of the world does not mean that a similar impact will be felt in another area. It is easy to generate generalizations about the impact of globalization and create scary scenarios about the future. So we have to be very careful to distinguish between *what* is happening, *why* these things are happening and theories about *where* globalization may lead.

We also have to realize that those who theorize about globalization express a range of views. There have been three main "schools" of globalization theorists. One group (including Waters, Giddens and Robertson) emphasizes the cultural aspects of globalization (although they disagree on a number of points of interpretation). Because Robertson has taught at the University of Pittsburgh for many years, he and his followers are often labeled the "Pittsburgh School." Another group focuses on economic factors (the key figure here on the "left" of the political spectrum is Immanuel Wallerstein, who has developed his "World System theory") and on the dominance and impact of international capitalism. A third school offers a sociopolitical analysis that centers on the impact of globalization on international relations. Again, it is important to acknowledge the wide variety of scholarly opinion concerning both the nature of globalization and its effects upon the world.

Fifth, it is important to realize that scholars are very aware that globalization can produce powerful countertendencies. Talk of globalization often brings a local reaction against it. While there may be tendencies working toward a single global identity, these frequently produce or heighten the desire of some to retain a separate, often exclusive identity. People who feel threatened that impersonal forces (as implied by the term *globalization*) are robbing them of important aspects of their identity may react negatively and reverse the process. Local reactions could take the forms of strident nationalism, exclusive ethnic identities, religious extremism, sexism, racism or other specific forms of social exclusion.

Some also acknowledge understandings that globalization may allow for some local differences—that global trends may be adapted in different ways in different places. Roland Robertson has invented the concept of *glocalization* to describe this process. This word combines *global* with *local* to convey the idea that global outlooks can be adapted to local conditions. The word originally referred to a business strategy developed in Japan that took a global business plan but has adapted its expression to different locations. It may also describe local appropriations of global phenomena, sometimes for subversive or other meanings originally not intended by the global originator.

Finally, it is important to recognize that the concepts of globalization and glocalization are both often related to the concept of *postmodernism*, a broad term characterizing the cultural shifts associated with the proliferation of cultural contacts that lead to a questioning of traditional ways of doing things. Boundaries (religious, political and cultural) are blurred or marginalized as ideas, people and commodities travel the whole world at will. The key assumption of postmodernism is that there is no ultimate universal truth to be attained; all one can hope for is a particular set of "truths" that "work for me," and it is the individual's responsibility to determine what these "truths" are.

RELIGION AND GLOBALIZATION

Many globalization theorists are virtually silent about the role of religion in globalization. Others argue that the idea that the world was created by a single God and that all people are related to God and thereby share a common humanity is a primary long-run driving force in the direction of globalization. The two most effective globalizing religions are acknowledged to be Christianity and Islam, both of which are rooted in Judaism. In the period following the adoption of Christianity as the official religion of the Roman Empire in the late fourth century A.D., Christianity became closely entangled with the politics of Western Europe and from the seventh century became hemmed in by the rise of Islam. Islam came to dominate North Africa and much of the Middle East, thereby isolating Christian Europe from India and the East. There is mounting evidence that Christian missions managed to percolate through this barrier, planting churches in modern-day India, China and parts of Russia. These remained largely cut off from a continuous Christian culture until the sixteenth century, however, when European Catholicism became expansive again with the rise of the Portuguese and Spanish colonial empires.

Pietism's and evangelicalism's emphasis on the direct relationship of individuals to God through personal faith created the conditions in which personal faith and not membership in a state church came to be seen as vital. This eventually led to the separation of the church from the state (most notably in America but eventually in most of Western Europe) and therefore from "place." This made it possible for Christianity to realize the global aspirations that were inherent in its founder's vision.

Roland Robertson—who is widely regarded as the most important and creative globalization theorist—has argued that the "take-off phase" of globalization really comes in the fifty-year period between 1875 and 1925 when two factors combined to spread European values throughout the world. Expansive Western capitalism pushed European merchants and traders to all corners of the globe in the search for new markets and raw materials. Alongside them (sometimes preceding them, sometimes following in their wake) were Christian missionaries.

Robertson (who conceives of culture having a more central role in globalization than many economists would appreciate) argues that the missionaries—and not just merchants—were important to this phase of globalization. Wherever the missionaries went they sought to establish schools, which helped to create Western educational systems in nations that had never known them, and sought to educate people (including females) to read and write. The long-term cultural impact of these Christian educational efforts is still being felt.

Even today many of the Christian schools that were founded in the late nine-teenth century remain important in countries that only have small Christian minorities. Some of those who attended these schools went on to receive their university educations in Western countries. The net effect, Robertson reasons, is that the elites in many non-Western countries now function with (Western European) assumptions and worldviews that are widespread throughout the world and are, in effect, global citizens. As will be noted later in this book, this was particularly the case for that generation of leaders of new nations who emerged through the 1920s and 1930s.

Perhaps, as noted above, it is only a coincidence that globalization was largely driven from a continent that once identified itself as "Christian." Some (like Weber, the father of modern sociology) have speculated that there is historically a close link between the rise of modern capitalism and Calvinistic forms of Protestantism.[4] Weber argued that Calvinism helped to focus people on this world rather than on the world to come— on material things, rather than spiritual ones. Calvinism (in Weber's view) reinforced and ignited capitalism as an expansive, international force. Crucial to Weber's view is his argument that Calvinism produced both character and anxiety—it produced sober, serious and disciplined people who worked hard and, anxious to demonstrate to themselves that they were among God's chosen people, they accumulated wealth as a sign that reassured them that they were among the elect. Closely linked with this was their concept of *calling* or *vocation*. Being good Calvinists, they did not believe that God spoke to people directly (as did the Anabaptists— the charismatics of their day); rather they came to equate the idea of *calling* with a *career*. It was in one's career (calling) that one brought glory to God.

Closely linked with this idea is the suggestion (again from Weber) that the basic assumptions of modern capitalism are a legacy of this Calvinistic impact. Weber's summary word for these processes is *rationalization*. Ration-alization involves the depersonalizing of relationships (people are viewed as consumers or mere barcodes); the refining of techniques of calculation (as

---

[4]Max Weber's *The Protestant Ethic and the Spirit of Capitalism* was written 1904–1905 in German and only translated into English in 1930. It is regarded as one of the founding works in the field of sociology.

in the Vietnam War, during which the Pentagon issued "kill-ratios" as a means of assessing the effectiveness of battles); the enhancement of the importance of specialized knowledge; and the extending of technically rational control over nature (chicken farms where the chickens never see the light of day) as well as social processes (statisticians decide who will or will not receive public health care depending on their mathematical calculations).

All of this leads, in Weber's view, to a demystifying of the universe, whereby the magical mindset that had prevailed in the Middle Ages was overthrown and the world became "disenchanted." In time, this "disenchanted universe" came to be replaced with a lonely universe, one in which humans have become locked into an "iron cage" of rationalism. For Weber, "rationalization" is the solvent that dissolves borders and homogenizes culture. Weber, however, did not think that all societies would be affected by this process because he believed that societies with strong religious traditions (India and China for instance) would resist the Western trend. In this he perhaps underestimated the power of cultural globalization.

Other social theorists have come up with their own explanations of the impact of modern capitalism: Emile Durkheim used the term *differentiation*, and Karl Marx developed his own deterministic economic explanation. Unlike Weber and current globalization theorists, these theorists held that the social and economic processes at work throughout the world are likely to affect all societies.

Modernization is a specialized term used to describe the social process involved in capitalist development (with its end being the creation of a global consumer culture). Theorists like Robertson see globalization as the internationalizing of the key features of this process. Many sociologists have linked the process of modernization with that of secularization—arguing that the "this-worldly" focus of capitalism marginalizes religion, inevitably leading to the decline of its importance and practice. This suggests a bias toward the view that religion is irrational and would be tamed by enlightened modernity. However, neither Weber nor Robertson agree that religion can be so domesticated, while more recent studies have tended toward exploring the "rational choices" that underlie religious faith. Some have argued that there may be a new period in which important religious movements may arise again, led either by new prophets or by old religious traditions experiencing a resurgence. Thus, a number of theorists see religion as the potential spoiler of globalization.

But more needs to be said about the historical role of Protestantism in globalization than these analyses account for. While Robertson acknowledges the impact of nineteenth-century missions in the "take-off" phase of globalization, he does not pay attention to their *motivation*. Here another Protestant understanding of "calling" comes into play. In the late seventeenth century, German Pietists questioned the received Lutheran understanding of "calling" and argued that God can still speak to people individually, returning to a more fully biblical understanding of the "vocation" or "calling" of every believer. This sense of calling pushed believers out into mission. As noted elsewhere in this book, German Pietists were thus the first mainstream Protestants to really do anything significant about crosscultural mission work, for example, in India (1706) and with the international expansion of the Moravian Brethren. By the 1790s these Pietist ideas were being picked up by evangelicals in the English-speaking world, leading to the nineteenth century eventually becoming known as the "great century of Protestant missions." These Protestants were not locked into Weber's "iron cage of rationalism"; rather, they demonstrated innovation in creating new voluntary societies that broke with the territorially based state-church model of Western European Christendom.

Another important point related to Christian missions needs to be made: in addition to making available Western education throughout many areas of the world in the nineteenth and early twentieth centuries, Christian missionaries also did much to provide the tools that national Christians could use in the twentieth century to shape their own forms of Christianity. Catechisms, hymnbooks, teaching materials and above all Bibles were made available to peoples throughout the world in their own languages. These resources enabled them to establish their own ways of being Christian in the twentieth century. In the 1930s, perceptive observers were noticing the rise of two parallel phenomena: the growth of strident (often anti-Western) nationalism and the rapid expansion of Christian movements that were independent of Western missions. Both were indebted to the missionary legacy.

It would seem logical to say that scholarly theories about globalization need to be tethered to facts on the ground. However, surprisingly little attention has

been given by scholars (including Robertson) to what has actually been happening to Christianity in the past few decades, and in particular to evangelical
Christianity. Yet according to the *Encyclopaedia Britannica* (2010), at the start
of the new millennium Christianity was the religion of about 2.28 billion
people, or 33 percent (one-third) of the world's population. David Barrett's
World Christian Encyclopaedia (2001), puts the Christian population at 2
billion (34 percent of the world's population), followed by Islam at 1.18 billion
(20 percent) and then Hinduism at 0.8 billion (13.6 percent). According to the
Encyclopaedia Britannica, about 16.7 percent of the world's population are
Roman Catholic, 3.9 percent are Eastern Orthodox, and the remainder (11.9
percent) are Protestant or belong to various independent Christian groups.

Table 3.1. Percentages of Followers of Major Religions

Source	Global Population	Christian	Muslim	Hindu
Encyclopaedia Britannica (2010)	6.909 billion	2.281 billion (33.0%)	1.553 billion (22.5%)	0.943 billion (13.6%)
Barrett's *Christian Encyclopedia* (2001)	5.882 billion	2 billion (34.0%)	1.18 billion (20.0%)	0.8 billion (13.6%)

Table 3.2. Percentages of Christian Groups

Source	Christian	Roman Catholic	Orthodox	Protestant	Other
Encyclopaedia Britannica	2.281 billion*	1.151 billion (50.5%)	0.270 billion (11.8%)	0.416 billion (21.1%)	0.506 billion (25.6%)

*The figures add up to more than 100 percent because many of the "others" have dual allegiance to
both traditional denominations and new independent churches.

In the twentieth century Christianity underwent enormous changes in
its makeup. In 1900 only 19 percent of Christians were nonwhite, but by 2001
Barrett claimed that non-Anglos formed 55 percent of Christianity. Outside
of the West, Christianity and Islam appear virtually equal in numbers, as the
Christian population at the end of the twentieth century outside the West
had grown to over 1.1 billion. It is now a much more widespread faith than
in 1900, and is now the most truly globalized religion in the sense that its
followers are to be found spread throughout the whole world.

    Establishing what portion of Christians could be considered evangelical
is highly problematic and depends a great deal on which definition one uses.
A careful scholarly attempt to arrive at estimates of the numbers of evan-

gelicals and Pentecostals/neo-Pentecostals has been made by John Wolffe and Mark Hutchinson in a chapter of their recent book titled "'The Actual Arithmetic': A Survey of Contemporary Global Evangelicalism." Their estimates by continent are as follows:

Table 3.3. Distribution of Evangelical Communities by Continent (in millions)

	2010 Population	Evangelicals, including denominational charismatics	Pentecostals/ Neo-Pentecostals*
Asia	3,879.00	65.94	135.77
Caribbean	40.81	3.26	4.08
Latin America	580.09	29.00	58.01
North America	340.75	4.79	17.04
Europe	831.00	8.31	8.31
Africa	1,000.01	150.00**	250.00
Oceania***	35.67	3.57	3.57
	6,707.32	344.88	476.77

*Not including denominational charismatics. Gross population figures extracted from Organization for Economic Co-operation and Development reports, 2007–2010; evangelical and charismatic figures from projection (2000–2010) based on reconciliation of figures provided by *World Christian Encyclopedia* and Burgess (2002).

**Estimated division of evangelicals (15%) and Pentecostals (30%).

***Including New Zealand.

Source: John Wolffe and Mark Hutchinson, *A Short History of Global Evangelicalism* (Cambridge: Cambridge University Press, 2012), p. 242. Approximate figures only.

Clearly much of Christianity's growth in the second half of the twentieth century was due to the expansion of evangelicalism in its Pentecostal or charismatic forms in the non-Western world. While Christianity in Europe and North America suffers defections at a rate of about 2 million a year, Latin America and South America have seen a rapid expansion of Pentecostalism (largely at the cost of nominal Roman Catholicism), and sub-Saharan Africa and parts of Asia (China, India and Korea) now boast considerable numbers of evangelicals.

Evangelicalism's ability to harness lay initiative is probably the single most important factor behind the statistic that 79 percent of the 2.3 million Christian congregations in the world today are non-Catholic congregations—that is, they are Orthodox, Protestant or independent congregations, the bulk of which appear to be evangelical—both Pentecostal or charismatic and traditional Protestants. With initiative breaking forth from multiple centers, it can be argued that evangelicalism in its many forms is well suited for expansion in the twenty-first century.

The way in which evangelicalism has grown has led one scholar to speak of its expansion as an instance of "globalization from below," as it has not depended primarily on Western missionaries nor has it benefited from close association with the West's economic advances. Rather, it has grown rapidly because it has been embraced by many of the world's poor and adapted to their settings and needs, as the growing edge of Christianity has been among poor, nonwhite urban dwellers attracted to Pentecostal and charismatic versions of evangelicalism. Much of evangelicalism therefore typifies unplanned religious glocalization—it is a global religious movement that has managed time and again to adapt to local situations and develop independent, indigenous leadership. It has created a form of popular Christianity that is culturally diverse and centered on an infinite number of localities (in sociological language, it is "culturally diverse and polycentric"). It is important to underline the fact that by its ability to localize and embed itself in new forms in diverse cultures, evangelicalism represents a powerful force resisting the homogenizing tendencies of globalization.

This countercultural dynamic is important in understanding the amazing growth of Pentecostalism, which first emerged among America's underclass— notably among poor blacks and women—and was often carried abroad by immigrants, artisans and others associated with counterestablishment religion. These carriers bypassed the wealth and power of traditional religion and created their own informal but highly effective networks to communicate their message. As in the early church, it was those on the periphery—those whom the world regarded as powerless—who turned the world upside down. This confirms Weber's observation that new religious perceptions usually emerge among those on the periphery of civilizations, as they are the people who are often willing to question received ways of operating.

The result has been similar to what has happened several times in the history of Christianity: the faith is undergoing both a major expansion while at the same time virtually reinventing itself in new forms. Unlike Islam, Christianity has not spread from one geographical center to another from a central heartland, and its Scriptures can potentially be translated into every language known to humankind. Islam's spread, on the other hand, has been limited by its reliance on a holy text that is understood to have been dictated directly by Allah in seventh-century Arabic: it can only be paraphrased, not translated, and the text is to be memorized in its original language. Further "localizing" Islam is the *hajj*, the pilgrimage that the faithful are to undertake to Mecca, the holiest site of Islam, located in modern Saudi Arabia. (The real globalizing forces behind Islam, ironically, are the identification of Islam with the global struggle *against* globalization, and international migration patterns.) The lack of a single holy language and a specific holy space are important factors in enabling the globalization of Christianity.

Following on from this, Christianity's attitude to indigenous cultures has differed significantly from that of Islam. Indigenous names for God found in tribal cultures have been embraced by Christians but rejected by Muslims who insist that all must worship God as "Allah." In Africa, it has been found that in areas where the indigenous names for God have been forgotten or displaced, Islam has prospered. In areas where indigenous names have survived, these areas have welcomed forms of Christianity that embraced the use of these names, thereby enabling people to incorporate their religious traditions into Christianity. Thus in the twentieth century, Islam grew tenfold in Africa while Christianity grew thirty-eight-fold. In other places such as Burma, Christianity has also become identified (among the Karen people, for instance) as a bulwark against cultural annihilation by a majority, non-Christian culture tied to the state.

Unlike Islam's linear history of growth and spread, Christianity has grown and flourished in different civilizations at different times, sometimes eventually declining and virtually dying out, only to spring up in a new culture in very different forms. Thus it shifted from a Jewish, Jerusalem-centered religion to a Greco-Roman culture (focused on Constantinople and Rome), and then to the barbarian tribes of Northern Europe who had little in common with either the Jewish or Greco-Roman worlds. In the last two centuries its heartland has shifted again: this time to the non-Western world, particularly to the south and east, where the majority of its adherents now live. For many the word *missionary* still conjures up pictures of nineteenth-century white Westerners going from Britain or the United States to share their faith with people of color in Africa or Asia. This popular understanding obscures the fact that a large percentage—probably the majority—of Christian missionaries today come from non-Western churches and go to non-Western countries.

Whether another religious tradition might have been the seedbed of globalization is an interesting question, but all religions now have to deal with the fact that history has unfolded in a particular way and that the Christian heritage through its association with Western colonial powers has profoundly shaped the modern world, although in ways that are not entirely clear. It could be that in the future the forces of globalization will be associated with a different religion, or no religion; but globalization as historically experienced in the past five centuries has been significantly enmeshed with the history of Christianity, while at the same time evangelicalism offers a counternarrative to the homogenizing effects of globalization.

EVANGELICALISM'S FUTURE IN A GLOBALIZING WORLD

There are at least three observable trends that need to be considered in relation to the future of evangelicalism:

1. *Continued international migration.* International migrations have been important for the globalization of evangelicalism. In the eighteenth and nineteenth centuries, the sustained flow of immigrants from Britain and Europe created evangelical diasporas in places such as Canada, the United States, Australia and New Zealand. But in the twenty-first century, new patterns are affecting evangelicalism's spread. Different ethnic groups have been significant for this, such as West Indians in Britain and Europe, Chinese in Malaysia and Indonesia, and Latin Americans in the United States. Diasporas in the twentieth century tended to be into traditionally Christian areas of the world (Europe and America), and diasporas of non-Christians had little impact in terms of conversion to other religions. Thus, while there are many Muslims in Europe, to date there have been comparatively few conversions to Islam among the Europeans. Evangelical growth, by contrast, has occurred in many parts of the world that are not traditionally Christian; it now exists in virtually every region where religious freedom is allowed, and has done well even in some areas where it is has been actively suppressed (as in China under Mao). Globalization by means of diasporas is not the same as globalization by means of conversion,

and it is the latter rather than the former that has been most important to evangelical growth. That said, continued international migration is likely to be a significant factor in evangelicalism's spread.

Encouraged by increasing ease of travel—or forced migration—people are likely to continue to cross borders, some to emigrate, others to live abroad for part of their lives, whether to study or work. Permanent residence in other countries may result from these migrations. This means that unexpected people will keep turning up in unexpected places. A practical real-life example: Christian missionaries from (Muslim) Indonesia turn up in Pakistan (a fellow Muslim nation) and end up working with Chinese engineers who have embraced Christianity under a nominally Marxist regime, and their efforts are encouraged by Korean-speaking missionaries whose sermons are translated into English and Urdu.

2. *The importance of "global cities."* Key or "global cities" (notably London, Shanghai, Beijing, New York and Tokyo) that are multiethnic and multicultural are likely to continue to be central to the emerging world economy. These cities host the headquarters of important transnational corporations and feed their needs for access to advertising, legal expertise, financial markets, multilingual staff and political decision makers. Within these "global cities" are often huge numbers of temporary foreign residents. In London, for instance, there are reportedly some 90,000 Japanese nationals who work in Britain's capital but live, move and have their being in a Japanese cultural enclave of their own. Shanghai, the banking capital of China, has reputedly over 200,000 foreign passport holders living within its bounds. This pattern is repeated throughout the world. Large multicultural cities are crucial centers of transnational corporate power, global transport and international communications. The key cities are in turn closely linked into one another and come to resemble each other in terms of having high concentrations of professionals, business people, bankers, media and information personnel, leaders of the fashion industry and among them a high number of privileged foreigners. These cities present unique opportunities for multicultural and multiethnic churches that can demonstrate the power of the Christian message to transcend barriers that have kept people in closed societies from encountering the Christian message. Global cities are thus likely to see the growth of ethnically based evangelical congregations, as evangeli-

calism's strength is among the underclass of the world and these churches are likely to be strongest among marginalized minorities within these cities.

3. *Protests against the dark sides of globalization will continue.* Concerns for social justice in the face of powerful economic and political pressures to capitulate before the juggernaut of a new world order need to be both heard and heeded. Antiglobalization protests both in the West and the Two-Thirds World are likely to increase, and thoughtful Christian critiques must be developed against the dark sides of globalization, such as the expansion of the international sex trade or the further impoverishment of marginal countries and regions. There are many legitimate reasons to be concerned with the negative effects of globalization, especially on the part of thoughtful, socially conscious Christians.

Alongside the calls for justice, evangelicals need to aware of the impact of social dislocation accompanying these global trends. When local identities (whether ethnic, racial, national or religious) are eroded or marginalized, people often experience identity crises. Identity crises can produce strong reactions that are difficult to predict or control. New leaders could emerge to express the rage and frustration of those who feel powerless in the face of forces that they believe are overwhelming them, and some of that frustration may well be aimed at Christians whom they perceive as aligned with these disruptive forces. Such leaders might well articulate new visions of society that are exclusive, reactionary and particularly hostile to evangelical Christianity.

Evangelicalism has undoubtedly benefited from the growing attention to human rights that has made evangelization much easier in areas where only a single religion was traditionally approved of and promoted. For instance, Latin American evangelical growth only really took off following the Universal Declaration of Human Rights, which the Roman Catholic Church endorsed in 1965 as part of the Second Vatican Council. Similarly, in Eastern Europe the demise of Marxist regimes that sought to exercise strict control over religion has in many cases enabled significant evangelical growth. Conversely, political realities in many other parts of the world still hinder evangelical growth, particularly in Muslim countries and in some strongly centralized societies such as China. In other words, a free market of ideas aids in the growth of evangelical Christianity.

It is, however, important to realize that in spite of the growth of human rights and an awareness on the part of many that there are in theory different religious options, perhaps as many as half of the world's people live in societies in which traditional forms of authority (parental, family or society-wide) put such choices beyond reach. In the late twentieth century, the global trend was often away from, rather than toward, religious liberty. So what the globalization theorists have been saying—that globalization leads to deterritorialization and increased freedom of the individual—has not always been true in the area of religious liberty. If globalization does eventually lead to increased freedom of choice in religion and more openness to individual initiative, then it is likely that evangelicalism will grow in societies that have traditionally shut it down.

The strongly indigenous flavor of evangelicalism has been a great secret of its strength; however, this is often unacknowledged by contemporary scholarship, which often portrays evangelical growth outside the West as the product of "globalization from above." Time and again the charge is made that evangelicalism's strength in the non-Western world is the result of an alliance with American power and culture. It is a charge not supported by experience in many parts of the world. Indeed, there is evidence that in Brazil, close association with Western culture and even with Western missions has been counterproductive to evangelical growth. The more indigenous and distant from foreign influence, the faster evangelicalism has grown.[5] Lamin Sanneh has recently argued that the ending of traditional forms of Western imperialism has brought about, not the expected collapse of Christianity in former colonial lands, but rather the explosion of indigenous forms of Christianity.[6]

Conclusion

Evangelicalism began as a European variant of a Middle Eastern religion, and now it is a truly global expression of Christian experience, theology and spirituality. Its heartland is now in the Majority World and its leadership

---

[5]This is borne out by Paul Freston's summary: "The general picture, therefore, is that most Latin American Pentecostal churches (unlike their historical [mainline Protestant] counterparts) were founded either by Latin Americans who broke with an existing Protestant denomination or by independent missionaries, and only rarely by a foreign Pentecostal denomination." Paul Freston, "Contours of Latin American Pentecostalism," in *Christianity Reborn: The Global Expansion of Evangelicalism in the Twentieth Century*, ed. Donald M. Lewis (Grand Rapids: Eerdmans, 2004), p. 244.
[6]Lamin Sanneh, *Disciples of All Nations: Pillars of World Christianity* (New York: Oxford University Press, 2007).

now firmly in the hands of indigenous believers outside of the West. It has contributed to globalization through its interests in missions, in calling and in education. It has opposed globalization through its tendency to embed itself in local cultures and enrich local conceptions of God. As an active participant in the emerging global culture it should be taken seriously as a vital and creative religious movement in a globalized world.

Further Reading

Carey, Hilary. *God's Empire: Religion and Colonialism in the British World, c. 1801–1908.* New York: Cambridge University Press, 2011.

Freston, Paul. *Evangelicals and Politics in Asia, Africa and Latin America.* Cambridge: Cambridge University Press, 2001.

Giddens, Anthony. *The Consequences of Modernity.* Cambridge: Polity Press, 1990.

Gilley, Sheridan, and Brian Stanley, eds. *World Christianities, c. 1815–1914.* Cambridge: Cambridge University Press, 2006.

Kim, Sebastian C. H. *Christianity as a World Religion.* London: Continuum, 2008.

Lewis, Donald M., ed. *Christianity Reborn: The Global Expansion of Evangelicalism in the Twentieth Century.* Grand Rapids: Eerdmans, 2004.

Martin, David. *Pentecostalism: The World Their Parish.* Cambridge: Blackwell, 2001.

McLeod, Hugh, ed. *World Christianities, c. 1914–2000.* Cambridge: Cambridge University Press, 2006.

Robertson, Roland, and William R. Garrett, eds. *Religion and Global Order.* New York: Paragon House, 1991.

Rosenberg, Justin. *The Follies of Globalisation Theory.* London: Verso Books, 2001.

Sanneh, Lamin. *Disciples of All Nations: Pillars of World Christianity.* New York: Oxford University Press, 2007.

Sanneh, Lamin, and Joel A. Carpenter, eds. *The Changing Face of Christianity: Africa, the West, and the World.* New York: Oxford University Press, 2005.

Wallerstein, Immanuel. *The Modern World-System.*

    Vol. 1, *Capitalist Agriculture and the Origins of the European World-Economy in the Sixteenth Century.* New York: Academic Press, 1974.

    Vol. 2, *Mercantilism and the Consolidation of the European World-Economy, 1600–1750.* New York: Academic Press, 1980.

Vol. 3, *The Second Era of Great Expansion of the Capitalist World-Economy, 1730s–1840s*. San Diego: Academic Press, 1989.

Vol. 4, *Centrist Liberalism Triumphant, 1789–1914*. Berkeley: University of California Press, 2011.

Waters, Malcolm. *Globalization*. 2nd ed. New York: Routledge, 2001.

Weber, Max. *The Protestant Ethic and the Spirit of Capitalism*. New York: Scribner, 1958.

PART TWO

EVANGELICALISM
AT GROUND LEVEL

Regional Case Studies

$$\binom{4}{}$$

EUROPE AND NORTH AMERICA

John Wolffe and Richard V. Pierard

MODERN EVANGELICALISM EMERGED out of movements in the seventeenth century that challenged the status quo of the Protestant state churches in Western Europe. Reformation had happened but many—both in the pews and the pulpits—were dissatisfied with the results. In England a group of serious-minded Christians had argued from the 1550s that the Reformation had not gone far enough; they were nicknamed "Puritans" because they wanted a pure Church of England. They became a major religious force that eventually revolutionized church and state in the middle of the seventeenth century, resulting in the overthrow of King Charles I and the establishment of a Puritan commonwealth (1649–1660). Other English Christians moved out of the state church into separate churches outside of government control (thus they were called "Separatists"). The English Puritan and Separatist movements emphasized simplicity of worship, freedom from control by the bishops of the Anglican state church and, in some quarters, speculation about the future kingdom of Christ. The Quaker (Society of Friends) movement was a prominent separatist group in the seventeenth century and contributed the idea of a mystical experience with Christ or the "inner light." Some Puritans desiring freedom from the state church migrated to New England and in the Massachusetts Bay Colony experimented with the creation of a righteous society through a covenant community of believers.

The same dissatisfaction could be seen in seventeenth-century French Catholicism, where the Jansenists (Catholics with a particular Augustinian leaning) emphasized personal experience with Christ and were persecuted by the Jesuits, often in alliance with the French monarch. (The most notable figure among these was the scientist and philosopher Blaise Pascal.) French Calvinists (known as Huguenots), although granted a modicum of toleration in the Edict of Nantes (1598), continued to experience the persecuting power of the state and the state church. When the Edict was revoked in 1685, large numbers of them fled France and found refuge in Protestant countries. Like so many other dissenters, the Huguenots manifested an experiential, otherworldly faith and the formation of small groups of dedicated believers. In Germany popular devotional writers like Johann Arndt and Jakob Boehme advocated mystical experience, and English Puritan devotional literature enjoyed a wide readership in Protestant areas of Europe. In short, many people were looking to a spiritual tradition common to Catholicism and Protestantism for sustenance during a time of bloody wars and continual uncertainty. The evangelical revivals that soon would sweep the Western world arose from the lack of spiritual vitality in the established churches and were rooted in forms of popular piety that existed in spite of official disapproval.

THE PIETIST AWAKENING

The resurgence of the kind of evangelical fervor that had animated the early Protestant Reformation was labeled by its eighteenth-century critics as "Pietism," but its adherents and subsequent commentators alike accepted the term as an identification of the new religious outlook. Bible-centered in its approach, Pietism emphasized personal conviction of sin, repentance, conversion and the new life in Christ. The forgiven Christian was to manifest the Savior through personal holiness and concern for the needs of others. Worship focused more on the emotions than it did in previous generations, and religious behavior was highly personal and expressive of inward feeling. Pietism involved a reaction against intellectualism, religious authoritarianism and formalistic creeds.

Pietism first gained public attention through the ministry of Lutheran pastor Philipp Jakob Spener in Frankfurt am Main. A dedicated churchman who recognized the need for church renewal, he came to see that a conversion experience—a second birth—was necessary for the Christian life. From the beginning point of faith, a process of growth followed in which one's existence came increasingly to reflect Jesus Christ. This process of sanctification would lead to victory over temptation, sin and even Satan himself. The church could be improved by better religious instruction of the children, individual study and family reading of Scripture, combating ignorance and moral defects among the clergy, encouraging heartfelt preaching and admonition, a reform of pastoral training, and fostering lay involvement in religious activity. To achieve the latter, Spener held small group meetings (called *collegia pietatis*) in his home, where participants discussed the Sunday sermon or passages from a devotional book and thereby were brought nearer to God. The idea of these "little churches within the church" spread to other congregations and became a means to assist the pastor in his spiritual duties and to return church life to what it was in the New Testament Christian community. Spener's ideas received wide currency in a small book published in 1675, *Pia Desideria*—in English: *Pious Desires, or Heartfelt Longing for a God-Pleasing Reform of the True Evangelical Church.*

Spener's work was simply a response from within the church to a clearly felt spiritual need, but the Orthodox Lutherans strongly reacted to his suggestions and accused him of substituting piety for faith. Although controversy swirled around him, his fame grew so rapidly that he was appointed court chaplain to the Elector of Saxony at Dresden in 1686. Five years later he moved to Berlin at the invitation of the Brandenburg ruler, where he became the main preacher at the prestigious St. Nicholas Church. He also encouraged the ruler to found a new university at Halle, which quickly became the academic and pastoral center of Pietism, and he published a four-volume exposition of his theological views.

Spener's protégé, August Hermann Francke, was the practical, organizing genius of Pietism. From a devout home, he was a student of biblical languages at Leipzig University and taught there as well. In 1686 he and a friend formed a small group called *Collegium Philobiblicum*, "the study circle of those who love the Scriptures." The following year he had a crisis experience that led to a deepening of his faith, and Spener soon took him under his wing. Controversy subsequently arose at the university, and in 1690 the authorities banned all Pietist group meetings. Francke then took a pastorate in Erfurt, from which he soon was dismissed for his Pietist views, and Spener helped him find a new charge: the struggling congregation in Glaucha, an impoverished village on the outskirts of Halle. He was appointed as a teacher of Greek in the new university, where within a few years he had advanced to professor of theology and helped to orient the institution in a Pietist direction.

Pietism's social concern. Francke became concerned about the physical needs of people in his community, a matter that he regarded as inseparable from conversion and revival. He began giving bread to the starving youths in his catechism class and in 1695 opened a school for poor children in his parsonage. So many came that he soon had to find another facility, and in 1698 he constructed the first of what would be a huge complex of buildings just outside the Halle city wall. Largely due to his efforts, the sleepy town on the Saale River became the international center of Pietism. Gifted with limitless energy and enthusiasm, organizational skill, and a keen eye for public relations, his humble institution grew into a small city that accommodated three thousand people. From his position at the university he inspired untold numbers of students to serve God as pastors in Germany and as missionaries in distant corners of the earth, and he helped raise funds for their support. Francke was the first "ecumenist," in the sense that he had broad interdenominational sympathies and he carried on extensive correspondence with people throughout the Western world from different denominational backgrounds, and through this means his reforming ideas were transmitted to many countries. He even fostered linguistic research to facilitate the study and translation of the Bible, and Halle became a center for the publication and distribution of the Scriptures. The geographical outreach of Halle Pietism contributed enormously to the eventual worldwide spread of Protestant Christianity. In fact, the globalization of evangelicalism in the nineteenth century finds its roots in the universal goals of German Pietism as they emerged at Halle.

Social concern was a hallmark of Pietism. Spener encouraged the founding of a residential workshop in Frankfurt to provide shelter and employment for needy people, and several German cities established similar institutions based on this model. Francke went even further, as his vision of a better world involved not only changes in the church but also the reordering of human structures to provide a more just society. He created various levels of schools at his foundation, and orphans and the poorest children were actually housed on the premises. He employed university students as teachers and residential overseers—which reflected his conviction that they should live as well as study the Christian faith—and he introduced the first organized program of teacher training in Germany. He intended to train both good teachers and theologians who would spread his theory that the goal of education was the development of godly character.

Francke also opened a residence for widows where they could live in comfort and dignity, created a pharmaceutical dispensary that produced standardized medicines on a commercial basis and marketed its wares through catalogues in various languages, and provided a hospital where medical students could receive clinical instruction. There was a library open to the general public and a press that produced Bibles and religious literature. A subsidiary organization, the Canstein Bible Society, printed and distributed over 2.5 million copies of the Scriptures—by far the largest enterprise of this type in the eighteenth century.

Pietism and missions. Besides the orphanage and schools, the Francke foundation was a beehive of other philanthropic activities. Halle was a training and sending center for foreign missions, and at least fifty-six missionaries went out to other parts of the world during the eighteenth century, beginning with Bartholomäus Ziegenbalg in 1706. The best known were Christian Friedrich Schwartz in India and Henry Melchior Muhlenberg in North America. Some at Halle were interested in reaching Muslims and Jews with the gospel, and they studied Arabic, Persian, Turkish and Hebrew, prepared and circulated Christian literature in these languages, and sent out evangelists to the Jews of Europe. Correspondence flowed into Halle from the various missionaries, and their activities were publicized through a bulletin that circulated widely in Europe and even Britain.

The long-term connection of Halle with the movements of religious revival elsewhere in Europe was crucial. Halle-trained preachers worked in Silesia, Württemberg, Switzerland, the Rhineland and Prussia, as well as some places in Western Russia and the Baltic area, and centers of Pietist activity emerged in several of these regions. An important development in the realm of scholarship occurred in Swabia (Württemberg), where Johann Albrecht Bengel, who had studied under Pietist teachers, became a distinguished scholar of biblical exegesis and textual criticism. His critical Greek New Testament is still widely used. Moreover, Joachim Neander and Gerhard Tersteegen, the leading German hymn writers of the time, were Pietists.

Pietism and the Moravian Brethren. A significant offshoot of Pietism that emerged in the 1720s was the movement known as the Unity of the Brethren, the Moravian Brethren, or today, the Moravian Church. A remnant of the old Hussite church from the early 1400s in Bohemia-Moravia sought asylum from Catholic Hapsburg persecution on the estate of Count Nikolaus von Zinzendorf in Saxony. A deeply devout young man who had been influenced by Spener and studied in Francke's preparatory school in Halle, Zinzendorf became a court official in Dresden. In the early 1720s he resettled the refugees and founded a village called Herrnhut ("Watched over by the Lord"). They adopted a modified communitarian lifestyle and Zinzendorf left his government post to become the colony's full-time leader. As his faith matured, he moved away from the Halle Pietists somewhat with his peculiar and extreme emphasis on "heart religion"—a deeply mystical and experiential faith—as well as Christian community. Zinzendorf and the Pietists were of one mind, however, on the necessity for worldwide evangelism and the forming of ecumenical relationships. Although he received Lutheran ordination, circumstances in Germany eventually forced Zinzendorf and his followers to form a separate organization.

The church that emerged under Zinzendorf's direction was service-oriented and based on a common experience of salvation, mutual love and emotional religious expression. His global vision led the Moravians to undertake the most extensive Protestant missionary operation in the eighteenth century, beginning with the dispatch of the first two workers to the Danish Virgin Islands in 1732. Soon other mission outposts were established in Greenland, Suriname, West and South Africa, Estonia, the Nicobar Islands and North America. They founded thriving churches in England and Holland, which provided yet more funds and workers for missions, and by 1782 some 175 Moravian missionaries were working in twenty-seven places.

Particularly notable was their endeavor in the North American colonies. They attempted to develop a station in Georgia from 1735 to 1736 but it fared poorly, and George Whitefield invited them to help out in a venture he was planning in Pennsylvania. Although theological differences soon led them to part company with Whitefield, the Moravians went on to establish a "new Herrnhut" in America named Bethlehem. Zinzendorf came to Pennsylvania in 1741 in an ecumenical effort to unite all the German sects on the frontier, but this failed. The Moravian Church then took on a denominational character and founded other settlements in Pennsylvania and North Carolina. Clearly their most noteworthy achievement was the Native American mission. The leading figure in this enterprise was David Zeisberger, who gained the confidence of tribal leaders and founded a number of peaceful Christian communities, but his work suffered irreparable harm from the attacks of white settlers and their continuing frontier wars with the Indians.

While this brief survey can only highlight a few details of the Pietist awakening and its effects, it reveals that Pietism was significant because it released the Protestant faith from the bonds of tradition and restored the primacy of personal decision in spiritual matters, thus contributing to the growth of human freedom. It avoided an anti-institutional religiosity that could have been directed against the church, while transcending the constrictions of the narrowly defined state church orthodoxy. By renewing and strengthening the ideal of primitive Christianity as relevant for the present, it laid the foundation for the evangelical revival movement. Finally, with their consciousness of geography and intense desire to spread the gospel beyond their immediate locality, the Pietists launched the first truly global movement in the history of the Protestant church.

EVANGELICALISM IN THE BRITISH ISLES

On May 24, 1738, the Church of England clergyman John Wesley attended a small Moravian religious meeting in Aldersgate Street in the city of London. Wesley's account of his experience that evening is one of the most widely quoted passages in the history of Christianity. Someone was reading aloud from Martin Luther's *Preface to the Epistle to the Romans*, and he recalled as the reading proceeded,

> I felt my heart strangely warmed. I felt I did trust in Christ, Christ alone, for salvation, and an assurance was given me that He had taken away my sins, even mine, and saved me from the law of sin and death.[1]

Some regard this event as his conversion, others his coming to full assurance in his faith. Whatever the case may be, this is traditionally regarded as the symbolic beginning of evangelicalism in Britain. Like any other historical "turning point," however, it needs to be viewed in a wider context.

---

[1]John Wesley, *The Journal of John Wesley* (Chicago: Moody Press, 1951), p. 55.

Much of Wesley's own life linked him with earlier traditions of Christian piety. There were more indications of continuity than change in the immediate circumstances of his conversion experience. This was not the resolution of adolescent emotional turmoil but a reflective change of heart in a mature thirty-five-year-old man, who could even recall the exact time it took place. It was stirred not by any big new idea but by the words of Martin Luther, a man dead for nearly two centuries, who was not the representative of a radical sect but of mainstream European Protestantism. It occurred not on a remote frontier, but in the heart of the English capital.

Born in 1703, Wesley was the son of a high-church Anglican clergyman who sought to uphold the spiritual status of the church against the state's attempts at political control. John's mother was also a deeply committed Christian, whose formative experiences lay in the Puritan and Dissenting movements of the previous century. While a student at Oxford he was a leading figure in the Holy Club, one of several small societies in the Church of England at the time that sought to encourage more faithful and rigorous practice of Christian devotion. In the 1730s he set out to express his sense of religious obligation by being a missionary in remote Georgia, Britain's newest North American colony, and on his journey he was influenced and inspired by the Moravians.

Stepping back from Wesley and viewing the wider picture of early evangelicalism in Britain and Ireland, one is struck by the number of diverse and complex influences that came together to bring it about. Space does not permit a detailed analysis of all of these, but the most important factors can be pointed out. First was the impact of Continental Pietism, as mediated both through Francke and Zinzendorf, and through British travelers in Europe. It is noteworthy that immediately after his Aldersgate experience, Wesley journeyed to Germany to visit Halle and Herrnhut. The presence of numerous Protestant refugees from religious persecution, particularly French Huguenots, provided a further link to the wider European movement. Second was the indigenous tradition of an intensely Protestant lifestyle and devotion flowing from seventeenth-century Puritanism. Although this had receded, its imprint on national religious culture could still be felt. Third was the spiritual renewal that was stirring within the Church of England, nurtured by small societies such as Wesley's Holy Club and by much larger voluntary organizations like the Society for Promoting Christian Knowledge and the Society for the Propagation of the Gospel. Fourth were the simultaneous currents of revival elsewhere in the British Isles, linked in Wales to a renaissance of the language, and in Scotland and Northern Ireland to the distinctively Reformed (Calvinistic) heritage of the Presbyterian tradition. The report of the revival in New England from 1734 to 1735 that centered on the ministry of Jonathan Edwards added further to the sense of spiritual ferment throughout the North Atlantic world.

The early evangelicals could draw on many threads of Christian tradition, and they began weaving them together in the 1730s to produce a distinctively new religious movement. Yet from the outset its variegated origins were reflected in its internal diversity, and this was augmented by the contrasting personalities and strategies of the leaders. By the time of Wesley's defining experience, the open air preaching so characteristic of the revival was already well underway, exemplified by Howell Harris, a key figure in Wales, and George Whitefield, a passionate and powerful orator. In 1735 both were converted and began itinerant ministries. In summer 1742 Whitefield's preaching provided one of the high points in early evangelical history, the revival at Cambuslang in Scotland, which drew crowds numbering in the tens of thousands and saw many professions of conversion. While Whitefield was the master of spectacular and often short-lived mass evangelism, the more methodical and authoritarian Wesley was the architect of the enduring Methodist movement, with its class meetings, circuits and disciplined groups of itinerant preachers.

At the time of the emergence of evangelicalism (and until the mid-nineteenth century), British religious life was dominated by what essentially were state churches—Anglican in England, Wales and Ireland, and Presbyterian in Scotland. This is particularly apparent in the case of John Wesley, who (being the devout Anglican that he was) conceived of the Methodist movement as a society *within* the Church of England that would renew the devotional life of its adherents and broaden the popular appeal of the church. In fact, the institutional dynamic of Methodism and the refusal of Anglican bishops to ordain Wesley's preachers set it on a course that would lead inexorably to separation. Other evangelical Anglican clergy included the former slave ship captain and hymn writer John Newton, and William Romaine, the leading preacher in London; although sympathetic to Methodism, they exercised their ministry through the established structures of the Church of England and enhanced their appeal and effectiveness. At the same time, the evangelical impulse led to a recovery of momentum in the Dissenting or Nonconforming groups (primarily the Congregationalists, Baptists and Quakers) that had left the Church of England in the seventeenth century, either because they perceived it as insufficiently Protestant or as disastrously compromised by its connection with the state. Wales in particular experienced a great upsurge in religious dissent. In the north a similar ambivalence was apparent, with the growth of a vigorous evangelical movement within the Church of Scotland, but also the stimulation of secessions from it. Thus British evangelicalism simultaneously renewed state churches and strengthened the tide of opposition to them. However, the common perception that evangelicalism was inherently hostile to connections between church and state is an oversimplification of its history in Britain.

It should be noted that the early decades of British evangelical history were characterized more by slow, steady progress than by rapid advance. Anglican evangelicals, such as Samuel Walker at Truro in Cornwall and Henry Venn at Huddersfield in Yorkshire, had a substantial impact on the spiritual lives of their parishes and made them notable centers of renewal. While the euphoria of revivals like Cambuslang in Scotland could not be sustained indefinitely, Methodism had a lasting appeal to the humble people for whom conversion had given their lives meaning and purpose. In the villages and towns of the early Industrial Revolution it provided an attractive alternative structure of community, one sustained by the vision of Christian fellowship and given devotional focus by the hymns of John's brother, Charles. Methodist membership had reached 22,410 in 1767 and more than doubled to 56,605 by the time of John Wesley's death in 1791. Evangelicals were still a small minority, but they clearly were one with a secure position and future.

Early Evangelicalism in North America

Varying levels of religiosity marked seventeenth- and early eighteenth-century settlements in North America. The colonies from Virginia southward possessed Anglican establishments largely lacking in spiritual vigor. Internal dissent, political changes and growing indifference were eroding the vitality of the Puritan Congregationalist communities in New England. The middle colonies were the most religiously diverse, with Roman Catholicism tolerated in Maryland, a lethargic Dutch Reformed church in the Hudson River valley, the Quaker settlement in Pennsylvania coexisting with a variety of German Mennonite, Lutheran, Reformed and Pietist sects there and in New Jersey, and Scotch-Irish Presbyterians in the Appalachian frontier. French Canada was dominated by Roman Catholicism, but Scottish Presbyterians were filtering into the Atlantic region. The Society for Promoting Christian Knowledge (SPCK) and the Society for the Propagation of the Gospel (SPG) devoted their attention to fostering Anglicanism among the colonial residents and some evangelism of Native Americans. Noteworthy also was David Brainerd's mission to the Delaware Indians.

The winds of the evangelical revival began to sweep through America as in Britain. The beginnings of the "Great Awakening" are dated to the preaching of Theodore Frelinghuysen, a Dutch Reformed minister inspired by Continental Pietism, in New Jersey in the 1720s. His movement was aided by the family of William Tennant, Scottish Presbyterians who fostered an experiential form of evangelical Protestantism and trained revival preachers. Farther north, in 1734 the young Congregationalist pastor Jonathan Edwards saw the outbreak of revival in his ministry in Northampton, Massachusetts. Through his preaching, a sense of anxiety and fear of God's wrath gripped the community, and the movement spread rapidly through the Connecticut River valley.

Edwards's account of this, *A Faithful Narrative of the Surprising Work of God in the Conversion of Many Hundred Souls in Northampton* (1737), had a deep impact in Britain, especially on John Wesley, and it became for all practical purposes the prescription for revival. The connection between the colonial awakening and the English one was fully established by George Whitefield's missionary tour of 1739–1740. His preaching at Northampton deeply moved Edwards and his congregation, and a new wave of revival spread. In two years, out of a total population of 300,000, some twenty-five to fifty thousand members were added to the New England churches. Whitefield returned repeatedly to evangelize in America, where he died in 1770, while Edwards went on to become an educator and today is recognized as the most significant theologian and thinker of early America. He devoted much of his writings to reconciling the revival with traditional Calvinism.

Although the Great Awakening had run its course in the north by the late 1740s, it spread into the southern regions through Baptist preachers and the actions of the Methodist "circuit riders," itinerant lay preachers who traveled on horseback through the back country and engaged in open air preaching. The awakening was carried to maritime Canada by the evangelist Henry Alline in the 1770s and gave the English-speaking settlers in British Nova Scotia a new sense of identity.

Because the colonial clergy were deeply divided about the value of the spiritual awakening with its emphasis on sin, salvation and a distinct conversion experience, lay people began to take much more initiative in religious life. This was a major step in the democratization of American Protestantism. To train the swelling number of ministerial recruits, the revivalists founded new colleges, several of which are now major universities. Moreover, because the cooperation among the itinerant evangelists cut across regional, ethnic and denominational boundaries, the Great Awakening was the first truly national experience for Americans. This opened the way for the political cooperation that culminated in the movement for independence from Britain.

Evangelicals in the United Kingdom, 1791–1914

In the half century after Wesley's death, British evangelicalism moved from a marginal position to one of considerable prominence. In fact, evangelical doctrines had a widespread ideological and cultural influence on British history between 1790 and 1860. There were four aspects to its success.

First, Wesleyan Methodism greatly expanded, and by the 1840s its adherents exceeded the 300,000 mark. In addition, three smaller groups were founded: the Methodist New Connexion in 1797, the Primitive Methodists in 1811 and the Bible Christians in 1815. These bodies rejected the conservative politics of the Wesleyan leadership and possessed a more populist and less centralized ethos. Adding these numbers, Methodist membership as a whole approached the half-million mark by midcentury, with attendance at services substantially higher. The Primitive Methodists and Bible Christians were especially successful in rural communities, thus complementing the strength of the Wesleyans in the more urbanized and industrialized districts. Thus the Methodist advance was related quite closely to the advent of industrialism and the concomitant rapid growth in population.

In England and Wales the rigid structures of the Anglican Church could not respond effectively to the pastoral demands of the age, and so the Methodists moved in to fill the gaps. They began class meetings and eventually set up chapels in burgeoning settlements that were often remote from the nearest parish church. They were also well placed to respond to the psychological and spiritual stresses of working-class life. Communal experiences of revival and conversion were widespread, often stirred by visits from itinerant preachers. Hence Methodists grew both in numbers and as a proportion of the overall total, being 1.6 percent of the adult English population in 1801 and 4.5 percent in 1841. The trend was even more pronounced in Wales, where the Calvinistic Methodists (later the Presbyterian Church of Wales) gathered considerable momentum. Even among the Protestant population of Northern Ireland there were around 25,000 Methodists out of a population of 1.65 million. Only in Scotland did it fail to grow, as the evangelical impulse there was contained primarily within Presbyterianism.

Second, evangelical influence increasingly permeated the existing denominations. A steady consolidation of influence in the Church of England took place, especially as a result of the half-century ministry of Charles Simeon at Holy Trinity Church in Cambridge. He had a pivotal influence on the students at Cambridge University, helping to spread evangelical beliefs among over two generations of future clergymen. Many of them entered foreign missionary service and spread the evangelical message throughout the world. The main strength of the evangelicals lay in the middle and lower ranks of the church where they occupied many important parish ministries. At first the appointments to key positions were minimal, with only three named to bishoprics before the 1830s. However, after J. B. Sumner became Archbishop of Canterbury in 1848, the number of evangelical bishops soon increased substantially. Evangelicals were also influential in the (Anglican) Church of Ireland, but their involvement in the self-defeating militancy of the "Second Reformation" movement of the 1820s that sought large-scale conversion of Roman Catholics diluted their effectiveness.

In the Church of Scotland the evangelical party also grew in strength. It was led by Thomas Chalmers, who served as a parish minister in Glasgow in the 1810s. He promoted evangelical Christianity as the means of spiritual salvation for the urban poor as well as communal social responsibility to relieve their material needs. In the 1830s the evangelicals gained control of the Church's General Assembly, but they were frustrated in their efforts to create new parishes to care for the growing population and unhappy with the role of lay patronage in the appointment of ministers. Governmental interference in the internal operations of the church resulted in a third of the ministers of the church seceding in 1843 to form the Free Church of Scotland.

The evangelical influence also expanded in the Dissenting denominations (that is, those outside of the state churches), especially the Baptists and Congregationalists. Significant figures were the Baptist Robert Hall and Congregationalist John Angell James. The autonomy of local churches meant that new ideas could be absorbed relatively easily, but they could be divisive. However, both experienced rapid numerical growth by responding to the needs of an industrializing society and the gaps in pastoral provision by the Anglicans. Even the relatively small Society of Friends (Quakers) proved receptive to evangelical influence.

Third, evangelicalism had a growing impact on social, cultural and political ideas. In the 1780s and 1790s a generation of educated and influential evangelicals emerged who sought not merely to convert individuals and sustain local churches and Christian communities, but also to transform the spiritual state of the nation as a whole. In 1788 the well-known playwright and poet Hannah More, who had become an evangelical, published *Thoughts on the Importance of the Manners of the Great to General Society*, in which she urged the wealthy to reflect on the quality of their religious and moral lives and the impact they had on poorer people. Between 1795 and 1798 she penned a series of "Cheap Repository Tracts," simple stories with a strong religious moral that were aimed at elevating the poor and that sold in the millions.

Equally important was William Wilberforce, Member of Parliament for Yorkshire, who was converted to evangelical convictions in 1785 and in 1797 published the influential *Practical View of the Prevailing Religious System of Professed Christians in the Higher and Middle Classes of This Country Contrasted with Real Christianity*. Wilberforce's effectiveness as an advocate of evangelicalism derived from his position in the social and political elite—he was a close friend of the prime minister William Pitt—and from his personal charm, enormous wealth and ability to present deeply held convictions in a nonconfrontational manner. He was the leading figure in the "Clapham Sect," a group of wealthy evangelical laymen centered in the village of Clapham on the outskirts of London. Other prominent members included Henry Thornton, Charles Grant, Zachary Macaulay and James Stephen. In Parliament Wilberforce led a loosely associated group of evangelicals jokingly called the "Saints," who advanced their Christian beliefs and a host of reform endeavors that followed from them. Their most significant achievement was the campaign against slavery, supported by the many evangelical individuals and congregations across the country. The slave trade was abolished in 1807, and legislation emancipating slaves in the British Empire passed in 1833. Meanwhile, numerous voluntary societies came into being, such as the British and Foreign Bible Society (1804), the London City Mission (1835) and the Church Pastoral Aid Society (1836), which provided a focus for evangelistic and philanthropic endeavors.

Finally, and most importantly, the formation of missionary societies represented the strand of global consciousness in British evangelicalism. The impulse to engage with a wider world was present from the beginning. Wesley wrote that "I look upon all the world as my parish,"[2] and Whitefield repeatedly crossed the Atlantic in his preaching tours. Other travelers, correspondence networks and publishing enterprises defied the slow pace of communications to maintain far-flung contacts and uphold the common cause in the work of the gospel. The campaign against slavery drew upon and further reinforced this worldwide awareness. This global vision, however, needed to develop an action agenda. A stimulus was the publication of William Carey's *Enquiry into the Obligation of Christians to Use Means for the Conversion of the Heathen* in 1792, followed by the formation of the Baptist Missionary Society in the same year. The Congregationalists formed the London Missionary Society in 1795, and evangelical Anglicans, the Church Missionary Society in 1799. Overseas mission work began from Scotland in the 1790s, and the Methodist Wesleyan Missionary Society was founded in 1813. In that

---

[2]Nehemiah Curnock, ed., *The Journal of the Rev John Wesley*, 8 vols. (London: Epworth, 1938), 2.218.

landmark year Wilberforce and his Clapham allies secured the opening of the British East India Company domains to Protestant missions.

The creation of voluntary societies to carry out missionary work reflected the evangelical understanding of the kingdom of God, namely, that the task was much too important to wait for the sluggish state and its established church to begin doing something. Thus, while British missionary endeavor initially was on a small scale, it expanded steadily as the nineteenth century progressed. It was inevitably compromised by its association, whether apparent or real, with Western imperialism, but the seeds it sowed eventually germinated in the development of truly indigenous churches. The reports from the mission field did much to shape British attitudes toward the wider world, and, among evangelicals, to foster a sense of engaging in a worldwide rather than merely a local and national endeavor.

At the same time, the journalistic side of evangelicalism took on a broadly international character, and such magazines as the *Evangelical Magazine*, *Evangelical Christendom* (Evangelical Alliance) and *Christian Observer* (Anglican evangelical) were read widely at home and abroad. This stimulated evangelical awareness of the wider world, while enabling some communication of ideas from afar to the home base.

Meanwhile, the current of Romanticism, with its emphasis on history, nature, emotion and supernaturalism, stirred many evangelicals into more intense worship and expectation of Christ's second advent, and followers of Edward Irving in London even began speaking in tongues long before the Pentecostal movement of the twentieth century. The ferment in British evangelicalism resulted in the formation of two new groups, the Catholic Apostolic Church, which later impacted German free church life, and the Christian or Plymouth Brethren. The dispensationalist system popularized by Brethren leader J. N. Darby figured prominently in prophetic thinking on both sides of the Atlantic, and the group contributed to the shaping of evangelical piety and fostering overseas missions. The Keswick movement with its emphasis on sanctification and the "deeper life" animated evangelicalism in the latter decades of the century, and its influence spread far beyond Britain through its ties with Holiness movements in North America and Germany.

At the same time, evangelicalism contributed much to the ethos of the Victorian era. The novelist George Eliot attributed to it the development of the "idea of duty, that recognition of something to be lived for beyond the mere satisfaction of self."[3] The wide diffusion of such a spirit of conscientious service characterized Victorian Britain, as did other practices that owed much to evangelicals, notably the upholding of strong personal morality and family life and the keeping of Sunday as a day for rest and Christian worship. Such social customs tended to characterize middle class rather than working class behavior, but their prominence as a norm to which conformity was expected in "respectable" society testified to the extent of evangelical influence.

Evangelicalism in Britain contributed to a weakening of the historic ties between church and state. Although the movement was strong in the Church of England, it also thrived in the Nonconformist churches, resulting in substantial membership increases. According to the religious census in 1851, there were almost as many Nonconformists as Anglicans. A series of legislative changes in the mid-nineteenth century that greatly reduced Anglican privileges recognized this trend. A similar process occurred with respect to the Church of Scotland, while the Church of Ireland was formally disestablished in 1870 in response to Roman Catholic demands and the presence of evangelical Presbyterianism in Ulster. The disestablishment of the Anglican Church in Wales in 1921 was due largely to pressure from evangelical Nonconformists. The 1870s and 1880s were the heyday of the "Nonconformist conscience"—which insisted that British government policy at home and abroad should be congruent with Christian values—when their thriving congregations, animated by evangelical beliefs and values, exercised a strong influence on politics and social behavior.

Revivalism brought ongoing renewal to the spiritual force of evangelicalism. The long-range trend in revivals was a change from localized and spontaneous outbreaks to more coordinated and controlled nationwide movements, reflected above all in the campaigns by the Americans Charles G. Finney in 1849–1851 and 1859–1860, and Dwight L. Moody in the 1870s. An important new form of revivalism was the Salvation Army (an offshoot of Methodism) under the leadership of William and Catherine Booth, which focused on the spiritual needs of the urban poor. Such grassroots revivals as those originating in Ulster in 1859 and Wales in 1904–

---

[3]George Eliot, *Scenes of Clerical Life* [1858], ed. G. Handley (London: J. M. Dent, 1994), p. 264.

1905 quickly assumed a transatlantic character and their effects were felt around the world.

An important example of the international connections among believers was the Evangelical Alliance, formed in 1846 at a conference in London attended by many Americans and Continental Europeans. The intention was to create an umbrella organization for worldwide evangelicalism, but the venture never achieved as much as its founders had hoped because of internal dissension over such matters as slavery in the United States. Still, it played a role in sustaining interdenominational networks between the English-speaking world and the heartland of Continental Pietism, and it promoted religious liberty for free churches in Europe.

Despite the appearance of evangelical success in later nineteenth-century Britain, trends that presaged decline were evident. The publication of Charles Darwin's *Origin of Species* in 1859, which challenged preconceived understandings of Scripture's account of origins, and the book *Essays and Reviews* in 1860, which argued for applying the historical-critical method to the study of Scripture, would both eventually shake the evangelical world: while the initial response to Darwin was somewhat ambivalent, as Social Darwinism gained momentum evangelicals became more critical. Although neither work was intended to weaken traditional belief, they had the effect of weakening evangelicalism. This was due both to the attempts at compromise with the new views that seemed to subvert the integrity of the Christian message and the hard-line reaction that appeared irrational to the public. Many Anglican evangelicals also became so obsessed with resisting the advance of Catholic and ritualistic tendencies in the Church of England that their actions merely confirmed the impression of the movement as negative and reactionary.

Wider cultural and social changes worked against British evangelicals. As the early phase of rapid industrialization gave way to the mature, better-organized urban society, the role of churches as focal points for community diminished. In this new age, evangelical churches and chapels found themselves in competition with other organizations that provided social support and leisure opportunities. As living standards and life expectancy increased, preachers were no longer speaking into a context of immediate insecurity and fear of death. Once the momentum began to falter, evangelical churches were increasingly burdened by the financial pressure of paying for and maintaining overly large buildings, and by elaborate organizational structures that could not easily be scaled back. A movement whose initial growth had owed much to its spontaneity and lack of material "baggage" was now a victim of its own success. From the 1880s it began to lose ground in its proportion of the population, and by 1914 the numbers were in absolute decline.

EVANGELICALS IN NINETEENTH-CENTURY NORTH AMERICA

Most American church figures supported the War of Independence from Great Britain, while those in the peace churches—Mennonites and Quakers, along with the Moravians who tried to preserve their Indian missions— suffered for their convictions. Even evangelicals commonly sanctified the American Revolution with biblical imagery and ascribed sacredness and purity of purpose to the struggle with Britain. Christians regarded the outcome as a sign of God's special affection for America, and elevated George Washington, the army leader and the new republic's first president, to the status of civil sainthood. From this point forward many Americans viewed their country as a chosen nation, the object of divine favor, with a special providential mission to spread evangelical Christianity and democracy.

This mixing of religion and nationalism, called by some historians the "American democratic faith," held that society was underlaid by a basic moral law, constitutional government was necessary for the restraint of evil, individual responsibility must be affirmed, progress was the ongoing hope of the future, and America's mission was to save the world from both autocracy and satanic governance. Most Americans came to assume this ideology, and it remained the central feature of the civil religion that persisted in the country long after the evangelical consensus of the nineteenth century had passed away.

However, this idolizing of America did not occur overnight. The disestablishment of those churches with ties to the colonial governments as well as Enlightenment ideas that encouraged theological liberalism led to a decline in religious zeal and church membership. But other forces were at work in the new nation that resulted in the "Second Great Awakening." A quiet and orderly movement of awakening began in some colleges, while itinerant Methodists worked in the rural areas of New England and central and western New York. Then a revival marked by emotional outpourings and dramatic conversions exploded along the western frontier. The intensity of the spiritual movement was such that churches could not contain the masses, and outdoor camp meetings resulted. The revivals led to spectacular growth among the Methodists and Baptists and to the formation of a new denomination, the Christian Church (Disciples of Christ).

By far the most important figure in the revivals was Charles Grandison Finney, a lawyer and self-educated preacher who combined the scholarly and measured character of the East and the emotional enthusiasm of the West. As a traveling evangelist, he introduced so-called new measures into revivalism, such as singling out sinners by name while preaching, encouraging those "under conviction" to come forward for counseling, allowing women to testify and pray in the services, and holding "protracted meetings" that might last for weeks or months at a time. In his *Lectures on Revival* (1835) Finney wrote about his use of human measures and declared frankly that "a revival is not a miracle, or dependent on a miracle in any sense." Rather it is purely the scientific result "of the right use of the constituted means."[4]

Moreover, Finney urged his converts to become involved in social reform efforts. Like others of his time, he believed that the way to transform society was through the conversion of individuals. They would then channel their energies through voluntary societies into doing good for the whole country, and through this means achieve the moral Christian society. Revival preachers across the young nation adopted Finney's measures, thereby bringing to evangelical Christianity an emphasis on activism, pragmatism and measurable results. Other revivals took place from time to time in the pre–Civil War era, with the last one being the "Prayer Meeting Revival" of 1857–1858, a largely lay-led movement by businessmen in response to the financial crash that had ruined many of them.

For evangelicals the awakenings had unexpected consequences. Some denominations, including the Presbyterians and Lutherans, divided over how to respond to revivalism. Radically new denominations that diverged from evangelical teaching in important aspects, such as Seventh-day

---

[4]Charles G. Finney, *Lectures on Revivals of Religion* (New York: Fleming H. Revell, 1868), p. 11.

Adventism and the Jehovah's Witnesses, and a completely new religious movement—Joseph Smith's Church of Jesus Christ of Latter-day Saints (or Mormons)—sprang from revivalist roots. The major failure of revivalistic evangelical social reform was the treatment of the Indians or Native Americans. Evangelical missionaries working among the Cherokees in the southern Appalachians had won many of them to the Christian faith and encouraged them to accept American democratic political institutions and the doctrine of self-reliance. But when the federal government brutally removed the Cherokees from their lands and gave it to white settlers, most missionaries simply accepted what had happened, although a few did protest and even engaged in acts of civil disobedience.

Evangelicals in the North and the South clashed over the issue of slavery. Many Northerners insisted that Christianity mandated the elimination of slavery, and believed firmly that if the power of the gospel were unleashed, slavery would end in America as it had in the British Empire. However, the continuing growth of the slave population in the South and escalating political crises ensured that such would not be the case. The struggle between the Northern abolitionists and Southern defenders of slavery (whether they were slaveholders or not) led to schisms in the Baptist, Methodist and Presbyterian churches. Southern Protestants used the Scriptures to defend the slave system and even prevented the development of black churches among the unfree population, while many cautious evangelicals in the North were uneasy about the strident demands for immediate abolition, fearing the social consequences of such a radical move for blacks and whites. Northern evangelical religious leaders lost all hope of "converting" the nation to their antislavery message, as the initiative for resolving the slavery issue passed from their hands to the politicians. The nation's fragmented churches were unable to halt the inexorable drift toward war.

Still, Protestant evangelicals dominated public life in America at mid-century, and they resisted the demands of the Irish and German Roman Catholic immigrants for equal rights. The United States also engaged in a wave of expansion that extended its rule from coast to coast, thus fulfilling the political sentiment expressed in 1845 by journalist John L. O'Sullivan: "Our manifest destiny [is] to overspread and possess the whole of the continent which Providence has given us for the development of the great ex-

periment and federative self government entrusted to us."[5] Most Protestants embraced this outlook and regarded their country as a "redeemer
nation" whose mission was to save the world by creating a new humanity
based on evangelical religion and democratic institutions. And some of this
thinking seeped into American overseas missionary work.

These views were to be put to the test in the Civil War. Although the
conflict began in 1861 over the secession of the southern states from the
Union, it is now widely recognized that the division between the North and
the South had been happening for some time. It has also become increasingly evident that although the apparent or presenting issues were the issue
of slavery and the South's desire to preserve its own way of life against
outside encroachment, the struggle was in large measure an economic one.
The Civil War proved to be the bloodiest war in American history. Each side
strongly couched its position in religious language, and the churches gave
their full support to the conflict. Both North and South felt the war was just
and that God was on their side. Many if not most political and military
leaders professed an evangelical faith of sorts, and ministers were welcomed
into the camps and encouraged to hold prayer meetings. Chaplains served
in the field, organized regimental churches and conducted revival services.
It was estimated that between one and two hundred thousand men in both
armies were converted during the war. Even President Abraham Lincoln—
by no means an evangelical—interpreted the war in theological terms in his
Gettysburg Address and Second Inaugural Address.

The fractured nation would not easily come back together after such a
brutal war. There was no hope of church reunification; the southern churches
adopted a separate, sectional identity marked by revivalism, orthodoxy and
upholding the local culture and values. Only in the twentieth century did the
Lutherans, Methodists and Presbyterians from North and South come back
together, and the Baptist schism was never healed. Northern denominations
provided much of the idealistic support for the reconstruction program in
the South, a reform effort that took place in the presence of an occupation
army. The former slaves were given substantial rights, and northern churches
engaged in a generous outpouring of philanthropy. Home missionaries and

---

[5]John L. O' Sullivan, "Manifest Destiny," editorial, *New York Morning News,* December 27, 1845.

teachers, many of whom were evangelicals, labored under conditions of ridicule and economic privation to bring education and opportunity to the blacks.

Unfortunately, interest in the plight of the freedmen soon waned, and American society did not rise to the moral challenge presented by emancipation. After withdrawal of the federal troops, southern blacks were disenfranchised, marginalized and subjected to brutal and unjust rule. They were excluded from nearly all white churches, evangelical or not, but within their own totally self-governing churches they determined their own spiritual future. The spirit of evangelical revivalism survived in these Christian communities, which put the emphasis on divine immediacy, on the Bible as the sole source of religious truth, on spontaneity and individual response to the gospel message, on a quest for personal holiness and on the certain hope that present injustices would be redressed.

In the post–Civil War period, American evangelicals faced unprecedented challenges as the "new" immigrants (from the areas of Europe where Roman Catholicism, Judaism and Eastern Orthodoxy were strong), poured into the country to work in factories, mills, railroads and mines. The immigrants settled in cities where churches and synagogues representing their various religious beliefs and ethnicities abounded, and assisted them in getting established. The old evangelical consensus was supplanted by the new religious pluralism, and Protestants now faced the unpleasant prospect of having to share power with those of different faiths.

At the same time, the concentration of upwardly mobile churchgoers in affluent city congregations led to a new respectability and genteel piety in such groups as the Methodists and Baptists. Robed choirs performed sophisticated music and the clergy were noted for pulpit oratory. Wealthy laymen provided the funding and assumed the initiative in leading congregational affairs.

Since the need for an evangelical conversion experience and a pure Christian life continued to mark the Protestant ideal, a new breed of urban revivalist took center stage, typified above all by Dwight L. Moody. After a successful two-year campaign in Britain in the mid-1870s, he emerged as the leading mass evangelist in America. His meetings were organized in a businesslike manner, and committees of prominent ministers and wealthy laymen took charge of planning and finance. On the platform Moody spoke like the salesman of salvation, and the audiences were moved by his simple, unsophisticated message and the sentimental music of his song leader, Ira D. Sankey. Moody appealed especially to the displaced country folk who had come to the city to find work, and his promise of salvation and eternal life through simple faith in Christ provided stability and comfort to thousands of converts. And like his early nineteenth-century forebears, he believed that individual conversions would lead to the improvement of society.

Parallel to the urban revivals was the Holiness movement. Drawing on John Wesley's teachings, it emphasized moving on to a "second blessing" of entire sanctification where all temptation to sin would be conquered and removed, thereby achieving a state of "sinless perfection." In American Methodism the Holiness revival sought to relieve the spiritual stagnation that had set in during the post–Civil War era. The American Holiness movement had links with the Keswick Holiness movement in England, although the latter stressed the deeper life, not eradication of the sinful nature. By the 1890s many of Holiness persuasion had left the Methodist Church in despair of achieving the renewal they sought and formed new denominations—the Free Methodists, Pilgrim Holiness, Church of the Nazarene, Christian and Missionary Alliance, Church of God (Anderson, Indiana, and Cleveland, Tennessee)—or joined holiness groups such as the Salvation Army.

From the Holiness movement emerged Pentecostalism, which identified the gift of speaking in tongues as the sign of the Holy Spirit's infilling. Its American origins are often traced to two related events at the opening of the twentieth century. At his small Bible school in Topeka, Kansas, Charles Fox Parham taught that those who had gone on to perfect holiness should expect a baptism of "the Holy Ghost and fire," and in 1901 this was fulfilled when several students began speaking in sounds they could not understand. Influenced by Parham was William J. Seymour, a black Holiness preacher, who in 1906 founded the Azusa Street Mission in Los Angeles. The first full-fledged Pentecostal revival occurred there, marked by fervent prayer, ecstatic spiritual speech and healing of the sick; women and racial minorities (blacks and Hispanics) were involved from the outset. Within a short time came new Pentecostal denominations such as the Assemblies of God.

An ominous threat to evangelicalism was the influx of new ideas from abroad: Darwinism, Marxism and biblical criticism. The theory of evolution seemed to challenge the biblical story of creation and, by inference, the entire authority of Scripture. In areas where evangelicals were strong, laws were adopted banning the teaching of evolution. Marxist socialism denied spiritual values and portrayed religion merely as an opiate used by the bourgeois ruling class to dull the senses of the workers. The new "higher criticism" from Germany cast doubt on the Mosaic authorship of the Pentateuch and taught the evolutionary development of the Old Testament from primitive polytheism to ethical monotheism. Evangelical scholars reacted by affirming the plenary inspiration and inerrancy of Scripture.

The emphasis upon reason, science, evolution, biblical criticism and divine immanence in the world that marked the progress of theological liberalism, also known as "modernism," led to bitter controversies in the divinity schools and seminaries that had once been strongholds of evangelicalism. One effort to counter this development was the series of twelve booklets called *The Fundamentals: A Testimony to the Truth*. Written by noted American and British evangelical scholars between 1910 and 1915, with the costs underwritten by wealthy California oilmen, they reasserted traditional Protestant theology. Probably more than anything else, this collection would provide the theoretical grounding for the future liberal-conservative struggle.

In terms of ongoing social engagement, many evangelicals saw the need to help to combat the evils of the urban industrial system. Among these were rescue missions to assist the down and out, shelters for homeless women and unwed mothers, urban endeavors such as the Salvation Army and Volunteers of America and Evangelical Alliance associate Josiah Strong's call for an evangelical social regeneration. Some felt that individual piety was not enough to improve society; capitalism itself must be reformed. The best-known spokesman of this "social gospel" movement, Walter Rauschenbusch, insisted on a new idea of the kingdom of God as a counterfoil to the ethic of rugged individualism. He called for the spread of the spirit of Christ in political, industrial and social life, by which means society could be redeemed.

Some evangelicals met at prophecy conferences in the 1870s and 1880s and discussed ideas associated with "dispensational premillennialism." They searched out God's "pattern for the ages" and concluded they were living in the time of apostasy immediately preceding the return of Christ. Bible teacher

C. I. Scofield set forth a full-blown dispensationalist scheme in his popular *Scofield Reference Bible* (1909), and many evangelicals saw in the scenarios contained there an explanation of what was happening around them.

THE INTERNATIONALIZATION OF EVANGELICALISM

The transatlantic links among evangelicals in Britain and North America were numerous, since they shared so many common features, especially in the realm of hymnody, theology and denominational development. All emphasized the importance of the Bible, personal conversion and Christian social action through voluntary societies. Since the legal structures permitted a large measure of religious freedom, there was little hindrance to evangelical activity.

Canada occupied an important place in this network even as it endeavored to achieve its own identity. The residents of the maritime region did not join the American Revolution partly because of the apolitical pietism of Henry Alline and other "New Light" revivalists. During the War of 1812 Canadian ministers hailed God's providential rescue of his people from the despotic designs of the American "democratic mob," and the rejection of revolution by the United Empire Loyalists and their descendents encouraged an incipient sense of Canadian nationalism. When the Dominion of Canada was formed in 1867, New Brunswick Methodist preacher Leonard Tilley saw his country as the fulfillment of Psalm 72:8 ("He shall have dominion also from sea to sea" [KJV]). Churches received much more support from the state than their counterparts to the south, and some Christians were active participants in Canadian public life, even though a smaller percentage of the population belonged to evangelical Protestant congregations than in the United States (due in part to the large French Roman Catholic population in Canada).

In spite of cultural differences, the Anglo-Saxon evangelicals interacted closely with their counterparts on the European continent. Out of south German Pietism emerged a movement known as the *Erweckung* (revival or awakening). Its first institutional form was the German Christianity Society, founded in 1780 by Pastor Johann Urlsperger of Augsburg. Modeled on the English Society for Promoting Christian Knowledge, it carried out its work through a widely circulated magazine, personal contacts and correspondence. Within a few years it had facilitated the formation of missionary,

Bible and tract societies across Europe. Its secretary in London, Pastor Karl F. A. Steinkopf, spread news about the London Missionary Society in Germany and was a cofounder of the British and Foreign Bible Society (BFBS). He established BFBS branches in Germany, encouraged his countrymen to donate to British foreign missions and helped to organize German mission enterprises as well.

Revival preachers crisscrossed Germany, and some regions (such as Swabia in the south and Wuppertal and the Siegerland in the west) became centers of evangelical piety, a situation that has remained to the present. Johann Evangelista Gossner—a Catholic priest who preached evangelistic sermons in his parish church, held Bible studies and prayer meetings in his home and was involved in activities of the Christianity Society—finally became a Lutheran and founded a mission society. Another revivalist was Ludwig Hofacker, who died at the age of thirty and whose posthumously published sermons became a classic in popular Christian literature. Johann Christoph Blumhardt, a pastor in Württemberg, gained distinction as a revivalist and faith healer. He left the pastorate in 1852 and opened a center for evangelism and international missionary work. He deeply longed for the coming of Christ, and believed that a new Pentecost with the return of the spiritual gifts would open the way for the Second Advent. Many regard Blumhardt as a major precursor of Pentecostalism.

One result of the *Erweckung* was the founding of specialized schools for missionaries in Berlin (1800), Basel (1815) and St. Chrischona (1840). The Berlin school was founded by Pastor Johannes Jänicke in his church, and many of its graduates served under British boards. The Basel mission school prepared workers both for the local society of the same name and for the Church Missionary Society in Britain. St. Chrischona in Switzerland, the creation of Christian Friedrich Spittler, secretary of the Christianity Society, trained skilled tradesmen as evangelists and sent them out as self-supporting workers for whatever church or mission society that would accept them.

A good example of evangelical cooperation was Johann Gerhard Oncken. Born a Lutheran in Germany, he worked for a tradesman in Scotland, was converted in a Methodist chapel in London and returned to his native land as a Bible society agent. He became convinced that believer's baptism was correct and founded the first Baptist church in Hamburg in 1834. Operating on the principle "Every Baptist a Missionary," Oncken trained journeymen craftsmen to go out as evangelists and start churches throughout Germany, Scandinavia and Eastern Europe, and he himself traveled as far as Russia to assist his workers. He received financial aid from the American Baptist mission society and visited Britain and the United States to strengthen his support base.

Evangelicals in Germany engaged in a wide range of social ministries, including Baron von Kottwitz's workshop for the unemployed of Berlin during the Napoleonic occupation; Theodor Fliedner's "deaconess" movement, which opened to women the field of philanthropic work in the Protestant church (and had a formative influence on Florence Nightingale, the pioneer of modern nursing); Johann Heinrich Wichern's training schools for destitute youths in Hamburg, which developed into the Inner Mission, the most influential social service institution in Protestant Germany; and Friedrich von Bodelschwingh's Bethel Institution in Bielefeld, an integrated system of schools, hospital facilities and workshops for the mentally handicapped. Also products of the *Erweckung* were the two most important evangelical theologians of the nineteenth century, Johann August Neander of Berlin and Friedrich August Tholuck of Halle.

The evangelical awakening spread north and east. In Denmark Nikolai Grundtvig promoted revival in the Lutheran church, while Karl Olof Rosenius, influenced by English Methodism, proclaimed the message of God's grace in Christ and unmerited forgiveness of sins in the Swedish Lutheran Church. Various groups emerged in the wake of his endeavors, including the Swedish Mission Covenant of 1878. Baptists in Denmark and Sweden had close links with their counterparts in Germany and North America. In Norway evangelist Hans Nielsen Hauge initiated a popular religious movement within the state church of self-supporting lay preachers who proclaimed salvation and personal holiness. They suffered persecution and imprisonment at the hands of a hostile Lutheran state church that objected to any religious activities outside of its direct control. In Russia, Prince Golitsyn founded a Bible society in 1812, which the reactionary Tsar Nicholas I eventually closed. By the 1860s Lutheran Pietists in southern Russia known as Stundists were holding Bible studies and Baptists were engaging in illegal evangelism. F. W. Baedeker, a German evangelist with Brethren connections, began holding Bible studies in St. Petersburg in 1875 and had some success in reaching upper-class people. His associate there, Lord Radstock from Britain, was instrumental in the conversion of army colonel Vasilii Pashkov, who then became the leader of the "revival" in the Russian capital. Baptist figures Vasillii Pavlov and Ivan Prokhanov lived abroad at various times and were involved in the nascent Baptist World Alliance (founded in 1905) that encouraged and supported their efforts.

Similarly, a significant renewal movement called the *Réveil* (awakening) took place in the Swiss and French Protestant churches during this period. From 1816 to 1819 the Scottish lay evangelist Robert Haldane visited Geneva and various places in France where he held meetings in homes, taught the plenary inspiration and infallibility of the Bible, and won many converts. Among those touched by Haldane's message was César Malan, who became an evangelist in Geneva and undertook numerous preaching missions throughout Western Europe and Britain. Another was J. H. Merle d'Aubigné, who was affected by the revival as a student in Geneva. After serving churches for a time, he returned to his hometown in 1831 and with François Gaussen founded the Evangelical Society of Geneva. To promote the spread of sound doctrine, they founded an independent theological school and supported missionaries, pastors and Christian literature distribution. Also influenced by Haldane was Frédéric Monod, who became a noted defender of Christian orthodoxy. In 1849 he broke with the French Reformed Church over liberalism and started the Free Evangelical Church.

The cross-fertilization between the *Réveil* and British evangelicalism was remarkable. The French preachers traveled to Britain and their works were translated and widely read there. The British and Foreign Bible Society helped found the Protestant Bible Society of Paris in 1818, and four years later the French followed the example of their British and German counterparts in the foreign mission movement by forming the Paris Evangelical Missionary Society.

The impact of the French awakening was felt in the Netherlands, where Guillaume Groen van Prinsterer came to know Christ through the ministry of Merle d'Aubigné in 1828. He was a strong critic of the enthronement of reason and argued that it must be opposed with the gospel. He also called for the recognition of God's sovereignty in the political sphere as well as all other areas. He founded a political movement called the Antirevolutionary Party to oppose the ideas he felt had come from the French Revolution. Groen's protégé was Abraham Kuyper, Holland's best-known Christian politician. A Dutch Reformed minister, Kuyper became convinced that the way to combat liberalism was to form separate political, economic and educational institutions that would enable one to confront every aspect of the society and culture with a distinctly Christian perspective. He eventually became leader of the party and even served a term as prime minister.

Many of these elements joined together in the Evangelical Alliance, founded in London in 1846. The major effort at ecumenism by evangelicals, its purpose was to promote communication and fellowship throughout the world and assist in spreading the gospel. Unfortunately, as noted above (p. 102), the aspirations of the Evangelical Alliance to form a united front were frustrated by American objections to its refusal to admit slave owners, and the delegates decided to encourage each country to have its own Alliance. Still, periodic conventions were held in major cities (including Berlin in 1857), and the various national groups cooperated in such matters as defending religious freedom for evangelicals, supporting evangelistic endeavors, encouraging missionary work and sponsoring a Universal Week of Prayer. The most effective organizations were in Britain and Germany, and these are still quite active. The American Alliance never amounted to much and virtually passed from the scene by 1900. After World War II (1951) the Evangelical Alliance was revitalized as the World Evangelical Fellowship and reclaimed its original name of World Evangelical Alliance in 2002.

Among the most important achievements of the European and North American evangelicals were in the area of overseas missions. As mentioned above, the major British societies originated between 1792 and 1813. The Netherlands Missionary Society was created in 1797, while in the United States the Congregationalist American Board of Commissioners for Foreign Missions was founded in 1810 and the Baptists' Triennial Convention in 1814. Within a few decades, every sizeable American denomination had its own separate mission board. The Swiss-German Basel Mission was established in 1815, and the Germans followed with the Berlin Society in 1824, the Rhenish or Barmen Mission Society in 1828, and over a dozen more in the next few years. Other mission society foundings in this era included the Danish in

1821, the French in 1822, the Church of Scotland in 1824, the Brethren in Britain in 1829, the Swedish in 1835, the Norwegian in 1842, the Scottish Free Church in 1843 and the Finnish in 1859.

These were primarily voluntary societies, meaning that the mission agency was autonomous, engaged in public relations to call attention to its work, raised its own funds and recruited and sent out workers to the field. A few of them, particularly in the United States, were program boards of denominations, which supervised their work and placed some limitations on their freedom of action. Societies and boards were necessary as missionaries seldom could be self-supporting on the field. However, the China Inland Mission (founded in 1865) introduced a new approach to the support question, namely, the "faith mission." This society had no church or denomination behind it, and the workers did not receive a fixed salary but instead trusted God to supply their needs. Friends of the enterprise were to pray for missionaries and the funds they needed for travel and support, but no direct appeals for this would be made, nor would the society borrow money to assist its workers. The faith model was adopted by many new societies in the years prior to World War I, including the Evangelical Alliance Mission (1890), Sudan Interior Mission (1893), African Inland Mission (1895), Liebenzell Mission (1899), Oriental Mission Society (1901), Worldwide Evangelisation Crusade (1914) and several others.

Several features characterized the evangelical missionary enterprise. One was the emphasis upon the indigenous principle: the idea that the churches founded by the mission should be "self-governing, self-supporting and self-propagating." Another was the remarkable contribution to social progress in the areas where the missionaries worked—establishment of educational institutions at all levels, medical facilities and the treatment of endemic diseases, translation work that preserved and revitalized the vernacular languages and the cultures associated with them, and combating barbaric and inhumane practices (such as foot binding of girls in China, burning of widows on their husband's funeral pyres in India, female circumcision in Africa, and slavery).

Missions was *the* area of church ministry most open to women, and by the end of the nineteenth century females comprised about two-thirds of the entire missionary force. Here they could preach, evangelize, plant churches, educate national leaders and carry on humanitarian works. Although they lacked clerical ordination, they functioned on their own, far from the critical eyes of males in Europe or North America. Well-organized women's societies in the sending countries publicized mission works, raised large amounts of money and sent out and supported female missionaries.

Also noteworthy were youth missionary movements. The Young Men's Christian Association, founded in England in 1844 and brought to North America in 1851, soon had college chapters in Canada and the United States that emphasized Bible study, worship and personal evangelism. Equally significant was its female counterpart, the Young Women's Christian Association. In Britain, the Cambridge Inter-Collegiate Christian Union founded in 1877 was the nucleus for a vigorous interdenominational network of student-led Christian Unions throughout Britain, which in the 1920s regrouped as Inter-Varsity Fellowship. As a result of one of Moody's missions to Cambridge in 1882, the famous "Cambridge Seven" volunteered for missionary work with the China Inland Mission; this group included several leading athletes and did much to promote missions awareness. During a student gathering at D. L. Moody's Massachusetts home in 1886, revival broke out and one hundred youths pledged themselves to missionary service. One was John R. Mott, who two years later formed the Student Volunteer Movement for Foreign Missions (SVM). With the watchword "The Evangelization of the World in This Generation," the SVM was the foremost organization engaged in recruiting young people for missionary service. Mott was to spend his life in ceaseless travel and organizational labor on behalf of student work, missions and Christian cooperation.

The ecumenical movement originated in the evangelical missionary advance. As Christians from many denominations and countries engaged in the common effort of preaching the gospel, they discovered that the differences among them were not all that great. Cooperative ventures began on the fields in the form of regional consultations and general conferences. A variety of missionary conferences took place in Germany and Britain in the late nineteenth century, culminating in large gatherings in London in 1888 and New York in 1900 that called for greater unity. Cooperative organizations were formed in the major sending countries—the Standing Committee of German Protestant Missions (1885), Foreign Missions Conference of North America (1911) and Conference of Missionary Societies of Great Britain and Ireland (1913).

The culminating event of these ecumenical efforts was the World Missionary Conference at Edinburgh in 1910. The prime mover was the indefatigable Mott. The conference was organized by an international committee, and 1,200 delegates represented 159 mission societies and boards. Seventeen Asian churchmen were present. The focus of the plenary discussions and commission meetings was missions. A Continuation Committee was named to follow up on the topics investigated and prepare the way for a permanent international missionary council, but its work was interrupted by World War I.

THE WEST IN THE TWENTIETH CENTURY

At the dawn of the new century two scenarios of the future presented themselves to evangelicals. One was postmillennialism, which had been the mainstream view of the future held at the beginning of the nineteenth century. By the start of the twentieth, the postmillennial view had come to assume that because living standards had reached unprecedented heights, an integrated global economy based on capitalism and the gold standard now existed, Western power and influence were transforming the whole world, and the gospel was being preached around the globe, thus Christ's kingdom would gradually be established on earth. Postmillenialism was inherently optimistic about the future; its challenger, premillennialism, was not. Premillennialism pointed to the political uncertainty in Eastern Europe, the spiraling arms race, labor unrest and the spread of Marxist doctrines, declining church attendance figures, the modernist threat to traditional evangelical beliefs, and the growing Roman Catholic influence as evidence that conditions in the world were steadily worsening. In this view things were not slowly getting better, but worse, and the coming of Christ would bring cataclysmic judgment—a judgment that could occur at any moment.

World War I dealt the death blow to postmillennial optimism, but the premillennialists' hopes were not fulfilled either. They perceived the signs of Christ's return at every juncture, yet he failed to appear. Moreover, as the West squandered its human and economic resources and its accumulated moral capital in a titanic but futile struggle, its vulnerability was exposed for all in the non-West to see. The "great crusade" to cleanse the world of militarism and despotism and make it safe for democracy achieved neither, while the self-inflicted wounds in this internecine struggle, aptly labeled the "civil war of the West," would call into question the West's dominance. From the standpoint of world history, this marked a turning point of modern times. It empowered anticolonial forces that would continue to undermine Western political dominance and accelerate the process of globalization.

The postwar decade was a period of disillusionment and decline in religious fervor. The onset of secularism, a worldview that stressed the material over the spiritual, and the ideologies that accompanied it—fascism, communism and individualism—enormously impacted Christianity in the West. Even as theologians adjusted to the new thought, church attendance and membership declined. In Britain evangelicals were divided and polarized over whether to accommodate to contemporary intellectual and cultural trends. Conservatives seemed overly dependent on the leadership of elderly men and relied too much on the writings and inspiration of earlier generations. They tended to turn their backs on the strong social activism and political involvement that had characterized the movement in the nineteenth century and to concentrate on more narrowly spiritual concerns, even as North American fundamentalism did not appeal to them.

In America, social-gospel modernists and evangelical churchmen achieved their long-held dream of securing an end to the manufacture and sale of alcoholic beverages, but they failed to win the support of the entire nation. The result was widespread lawlessness as many evaded Prohibition through bootlegging and secret drinking clubs, and its eventual repeal was a stunning defeat. Also undermining their public influence was the bitter struggle between the liberal "modernists," mentioned above, and the "fundamentalists," who emerged at the end of the Great War. Taking their name from *The Fundamentals*, they insisted on upholding the cardinal beliefs of historic Christianity, defined as biblical inspiration and inerrancy, the virgin birth, substitutionary atonement, the bodily resurrection of Christ, and his imminent return.

The battle was fought on two fronts—the churches and the culture at large—and the fundamentalists lost on both. In an effort to combat liberalism in the major denominations and their missionary agencies (Northern Baptist Convention, Presbyterian Church in the U.S.A. and Christian Church [Disciples of Christ]), fundamentalists pressured officials to commit themselves to traditional doctrines but they were unable to capture control of the ecclesiastical machinery that would have made this possible. In the cultural realm the endeavor focused on saving American civilization from the baneful influence of Darwinism, which they charged with causing the current revolution in morals and threatening the foundations of democracy. In 1925 a Tennessee law forbidding the teaching of evolution in the public schools was challenged, and the resulting trial (popularly known as the Scopes Monkey Trial) was a media circus where the ridicule heaped on the fundamentalists contributed to their decline.

The confessionalist Lutheran churches and the black churches, most of which were solidly evangelical in their core beliefs, were hardly aware of the conflict, and many if not most of the rank and file members in the strife-torn churches continued to hold to a simple evangelical faith. Meanwhile, fundamentalism quietly underwent an institutional transformation into a popular religion through the creation of a complex interlocking network of Bible institutes, theological seminaries, summer Bible conferences and camps, radio broadcasting efforts, and faith missionary societies. These enabled conservatives to emerge in the 1940s with renewed vigor.

Also untouched by the struggle were the Holiness and Pentecostals on both sides of the Atlantic, and their movements thrived largely unnoticed. In Europe the German Gnadauer Bund and Blankenburg conferences were centers of holiness and deeper life piety, while Pentecostalism spread outward from various centers. The Baptists, heretofore an insignificant minority in Germany, gained public attention when the Baptist World Congress took place in Berlin in 1934. In its proceedings, searching questions were raised about Nazi ideology, with the result that never again would an international church meeting take place in Nazi Germany. During the 1920s and 1930s in Britain a movement that emphasized the direct personal experience of God called the "Oxford Group" (later Moral Rearmament), led by the American Lutheran Frank Buchman, gained a significant following, especially among educated younger people.

The missionary leaders who played such a key role at Edinburgh in 1910 restarted the ecumenical process after the war, and one major accomplishment was saving the German mission works from being destroyed in the World War I peace treaty. They founded the International Missionary

Council in 1921 that, along with the Faith and Order and Life and Work movements in the interwar years, laid the groundwork for the World Council of Churches. Founded in 1948, the WCC became the primary ecumenical organization. Although the IMC promoted cooperation among the Western missions and the younger churches of Asia and Africa, missionary enthusiasm was falling off. Attendance at the Student Volunteer Movement quadrennial rallies declined, as did the number of new missionaries going to the field. The controversial report of the Laymen's Foreign Missions Inquiry in 1932, chaired by W. E. Hocking of Harvard University, even questioned whether foreign missions had a future. At the same time, many evangelicals retained their strong commitment to international work, which was reflected in the Inter-Varsity Fellowship in Britain and the emergence of the Student Foreign Missions Fellowship in North American that supplanted the increasingly ineffective Student Volunteer Movement.

The major resurgence in evangelicalism came in the wake of World War II. In Britain a new generation of evangelicals emerged who occupied key positions in churches and academic life. Anglican John Stott became rector of All Souls Church in London in 1945, and that same year Church of Scotland minister William Still assumed the pulpit at Gilcomston South Church in Aberdeen. In 1938 Martyn Lloyd-Jones, the leading representative of the Welsh Nonconformist tradition in evangelicalism, was called to the pastorate of Westminster Chapel in London, the capital's most prominent independent church. Among the respected academics were theologians F. F. Bruce and J. I. Packer, lawyer Norman Anderson, and Assyriologist Donald Wiseman, while the career of C. S. Lewis as a literary apologist for orthodox Christianity was flourishing. Symbolic for this resurgence was the National Evangelical Anglican Conference at Keele in 1967, where the evangelical movement demonstrated its aspirations to reshape British Christianity as a whole and to reengage with social and political issues.

In North America the fundamentalists resurfaced in the early 1940s in two rival associations. The American Council of Churches, created by militant separatist Carl McIntire, attacked the ecumenical organizations but never had much of a following. The moderates led by Harold J. Ockenga and others organized the more inclusive National Association of Evangelicals, but with a few exceptions it did not attract evangelicals in the mainline and black churches, or from the three largest conservative denominations: the Southern Baptist Convention, Lutheran Church–Missouri Synod, and the Churches of Christ. At the same time, many former fundamentalists began to define themselves as "new" or "neo" evangelicals. They rejected anti-intellectualism, negativism and compartmentalizing of one's faith, and they called for cooperative effort by like-minded people in such areas as evangelism, education and social action. Its scholarly center was Fuller Theological Seminary, opened in 1947, and its principal organ, *Christianity Today*, founded in 1956 and edited by the theologian-journalist Carl F. H. Henry, the evangelical counterpart to the ecumenical *Christian Century*. Henry was the foremost spokesperson for the new evangelicalism.

In World War II, many evangelicals who served overseas as chaplains or simply in the rank and file of the armed forces were animated by the vision of returning to labor among the peoples where they had fought or of entering full-time Christian service at home. Veterans thronged into evangelical colleges and seminaries after the war, bringing with them maturity and a vital sense of commitment to God's work. The evangelistic ministry of Youth for Christ, founded early in the war years, and Inter-Varsity Christian Fellowship, transplanted from England to Canada in 1928 and then to the United States in 1940, also contributed to mobilizing the younger generation. The result was that in the postwar years many existing mission boards and evangelistic agencies, both denominational and interdenominational, expanded their operations and major new ones were formed, such as the Far Eastern Gospel Crusade (now Send International), Greater Europe Mission, Missionary Aviation Fellowship, Campus Crusade for Christ (now CRU) and World Vision.

By far the most important personality in the globalization of evangelicalism was Billy Graham. He was only thirty-one when successful evangelistic "crusades" in Los Angeles and Boston in 1949–1950 catapulted him to national fame, and he gained international renown with his London campaign in 1954 and Asian tour in 1956. Although at first he manifested the characteristic traits of one nurtured in American fundamentalism, he demonstrated remarkable flexibility and changed with the times. His contacts with the highest figures in government and business broadened his understanding of the world, and his emphasis on "cooperative evangelism"—local level ecumenical support for his campaigns while keeping the machinery firmly in the hands of his organization—contributed immensely to their success. He also matured in his grasp of social issues, first rejecting racial segregation, then moving away from anticommunism after visits to Eastern Europe, and finally calling for nuclear disarmament. Most importantly, he was able to bridge the chasm that separated evangelicals from other expressions of the Christian faith by appearing at World Council of Churches functions and forming a cordial relationship with Pope John Paul II.

The Graham organization played a pivotal role in fostering greater cooperation among evangelicals. It facilitated the Berlin Congress on Evangelism in 1966, the first major meeting that brought European evangelicals together, and then the globally oriented Lausanne Congress on World Evangelism in 1974, with a follow-up convention in Manila in 1989 and Cape Town in 2010. It also sponsored regional consultations on various topics and several training conferences for itinerant evangelists in Amsterdam. These gatherings emphasized the importance of cooperative effort on a worldwide scale to reach men and women for Christ, and they involved non-Western leaders both in the planning process and as major speakers.

With the relative decline of the established churches in postwar Germany, the free churches had much more space to minister and evangelize, while an evangelical renewal in the mainline churches, the pietistic "Fellowship Movement," whose roots go back to the late nineteenth century, attracted a wide following. Some evangelists were internationally known figures, such as Reinhard Bonnke, who held large meetings in Africa. The Germans also maintained a loose network of Bible schools, evangelistic organizations, social service agencies, missionary societies and publishing enterprises. To distinguish themselves from the existing Protestant (*evangelisch*) church, these new evangelicals took the label of *Evangelikale*.

Pentecostalism occupied an increasingly prominent place in North American evangelicalism in the postwar period, even as it did in Britain, Germany, Russia and virtually everywhere else in the world, especially in Latin America, Africa, and several Asia and Pacific countries. In the United States it not only was a significant force in the black, Hispanic and Asian churches, but also in the white community, where remarkable growth occurred both in the traditional Pentecostal denominations and independent churches. Examples of its influence include the healing ministries of Oral Roberts, Benny Hinn and others; the world's largest congregation, the Yoido Full Gospel Church in Korea (David Yonggi Cho was its long-time pastor); and the Full Gospel Business Men's Fellowship, founded by Demos Shakarian.

Equally important was the closely related charismatic renewal that began in the late 1950s. This included a mixture of such things as personal conversion, emphasis on individual or self needs, small group fellowships, physical healing, speaking in tongues, emotional expression in worship, freshly written songs utilizing a wide range of pop, folk and rock styles (with guitars, drums and synthesizers replacing the organ in church services), and music projected on a screen to enable worshipers to lift their hands while singing. Many Roman Catholic, mainline Protestant and traditionally evangelical congregations adopted charismatic worship styles, while new fellowships of charismatic churches came into existence, such as the network of Calvary Chapels under the leadership of Chuck Smith and John Wimber's Association of Vineyard Churches. The 1994 meetings at the Toronto Airport Vineyard Fellowship where people broke out in "holy laughter" and were "slain in the Spirit" illustrate the intense religious experience that can occur in such contexts.

Charismatics became a substantial force in the Church of England under the leadership of such figures as Michael Harper, who set up the Fountain Trust specifically to disseminate charismatic teachings, and David Watson, who had a most successful ministry in York. The impulse also gave rise to the "house churches," which tended to group together in wider networks like Covenant Ministries and Newfrontiers. John Wimber was closely associated with Anglican charismatics and made numerous visits to Britain to advance his concept of "power evangelism," linking the preaching of the gospel to manifestations of the Holy Spirit.

The evangelical churches in the Soviet Union were virtually wiped out in the Stalin era, but the Baptists were allowed to resume their existence in 1944. They and other evangelical churches suffered varying degrees of persecution in the subsequent years, and Billy Graham's visits to Moscow in the early 1980s called attention to their plight. With the fall of communism and end of the Soviet Union, both the Pentecostals and the Baptists in Russia and the

Ukraine began aggressive programs of evangelism and training Christian workers. At the same time, evangelical missionaries swarmed into the former Soviet territories, leading to tensions with the Russian Orthodox Church, which regarded them as foreign interlopers.

Conclusion

This brief historical sketch has tried to show that Western evangelicals are a highly complex grouping. They differ in their social and political attitudes, worship styles, and theological views, and of course in their diverse racial, ethnic and socioeconomic standings. The one common element is their commitment to evangelism and missionary outreach, both at home and abroad. Although the Westerners took the lead in conceptualizing and propagating modern evangelicalism, the movement spread so widely throughout the world that they are now a numerical minority in that vast company of faithful followers of Jesus Christ.

Further Reading

Europe

Bebbington, D. W. *Evangelicalism in Modern Britain: A History from the 1730s to the 1980s.* London: Unwin Hyman, 1989.

Ganiel, Gladys. *Evangelicalism and Conflict in Northern Ireland.* New York: Palgrave Macmillan, 2008.

Hempton, David, and Myrtle Hill. *Evangelical Protestantism in Ulster Society, 1740–1890.* London: Routledge, 1992.

Hindmarsh, D. Bruce. *The Evangelical Conversion Narrative: Spiritual Autobiography in Early Modern England.* New York: Oxford University Press, 2005.

———. *John Newton and the English Evangelical Tradition: Between the Conversions of Wesley and Wilberforce.* Oxford: Clarendon, 1996.

Railton, Nicholas. *No North Sea: The Anglo-German Evangelical Network in the Middle of the Nineteenth Century.* Leiden: Brill, 1996.

Warner, Rob. *Reinventing English Evangelicalism, 1966–2001: A Theological and Sociological Study.* Milton Keynes: Paternoster, 2007.

The works of W. R. Ward cited in chapter one are important for understanding the development of international networks among evangelicals and for appreciating the key role that German Pietism played in influencing evangelicalism in the English-speaking world.

North America

Brint, Steven, and Jean Reith Schroedel, eds. *Evangelicals and Democracy in America, Vol. 1: Religion and Society.* New York: Russell Sage Foundation, 2009.

Case, Jay Riley. *An Unpredictable Gospel: American Evangelicals and World Christianity, 1820–1900.* New York: Oxford University Press, 2012.

Christie, Nancy, and Michael Gauvreau. *The Christian Churches and Their Peoples, 1840–1965: A Social History of Religion in Canada.* Toronto: University of Toronto Press, 2010.

Eskridge, Larry. *God's Forever Family: The Jesus People Movement in America.* New York: Oxford University Press, 2013.

Gauvreau, Michael. *The Evangelical Century: College and Creed in English Canada from the Great Revival to the Great Depression.* Montreal and Kingston: McGill-Queen's University Press, 1991.

Marsden, George. *Fundamentalism and American Culture.* 2nd ed. New York: Oxford University Press, 2006.

Noll, Mark A. *American Evangelical Christianity: An Introduction.* Oxford: Blackwell, 2001.

Noll, Mark A., and Luke E. Harlow. *Religion and American Politics: From the Colonial Period to the Present.* New York: Oxford University Press, 2007.

Stackhouse, John G. *Canadian Evangelicalism in the Twentieth Century.* Toronto: University of Toronto Press, 1993.

$$5$$

AFRICA

Ogbu Kalu

THE STORY OF CHRISTIANITY IN AFRICA is as complex as the continent itself. It was a center of Christian enterprise in the early centuries—significant doctrinal and monastic development occurred in Egypt; the center of the Donatist controversy was in North Africa; and the greatest patristic theologian, Augustine, lived and worked in Hippo (Tunisia)—but the seventh-century Islamic conquests reduced Christian influence in Africa to that of the Coptic minority in Egypt, the upper Nile Valley and the Ethiopian plateau. Centuries later the slave trade ravaged Africa, bringing about the involuntary removal of an estimated twenty million people—half taken by Europeans to the Western Hemisphere and the other by Muslim traders to western Asia (the Middle East), Persia and India. During the age of European imperialism the continent's development was both disrupted as well as advanced, while simultaneously Christianity sank deep roots in this vast region.

It is helpful to begin with the big picture. The most recent demographic figures classify as Christians 503 million of the 973 million people living in Africa. About 36.9 percent of them are regarded as traditional Protestants (188 million, including 51 million Anglicans); another 33.4 percent as Roman Catholics (170 million); 19.4 percent identified as belonging to African independent (or initiated) churches (99 million); and 9.4 percent come under the category of Eastern Orthodox (48 million, mainly Coptic communities). The remaining 4 million, less than 1 percent, were lumped into a "marginal" class.[1] It is obviously difficult to determine the precise number of evangel-

---

[1]Todd M. Johnson and Kenneth W. Ross, eds., *Atlas of Global Christianity* (Edinburgh: Edinburgh University Press, 2009), chap 1.

icals within these various groupings, but among scholars of African Christianity there is little doubt that a large percentage of the African Protestants and many members of the African independent churches fit under the label "evangelical," if one utilizes David Bebbington's widely accepted definition of evangelicals as being conversionist, biblicist, crucicentric and activist.[2]

THE INTRODUCTION OF WESTERN CHRISTIANITY INTO AFRICA

As mentioned above, the African encounter with the Christian gospel reaches back to the earliest years of the church, but its demographic strength retreated under the Muslim conquest. The Portuguese and Spanish advance into the coastal regions of sub-Saharan Africa in the fifteenth and sixteenth centuries, and in some places even into the interior, was mainly for commercial reasons—the quest for gold, lucrative tropical products and slaves for their Western Hemisphere colonies—while the simultaneous introduction of Christianity was essentially a rationalization for and byproduct of their economic and geopolitical aims. Catholic missionaries who accompanied the Spanish and Portuguese did achieve some significant breakthroughs, the most noteworthy being the conversion of the ruler of the Kongo kingdom in west-central Africa in the sixteenth century. These missionaries were active in the Atlantic island settlements, in the Indian Ocean coastal towns and in various areas of Angola and Mozambique, where they were complicit in the Portuguese advance. At the Cape of Good Hope, where the Dutch established a way station to India, Protestant Christianity was provided for the European residents but no missionary effort was directed toward the indigenous peoples.

As the transatlantic slave trade intensified in the seventeenth and eighteenth centuries, various Western and Northern European powers established twenty or so "forts" (trading stations) along the West African coast to facilitate their side of the commercial enterprise. In this, African rulers were equal partners and many enhanced their political positions through their involvement, even though the trade generally disrupted African societies. The forts were run by nationally chartered trading companies, and the church in the home country assigned "chaplains" to minister to the Euro-

---

[2]David W. Bebbington, *Evangelicalism in Modern Britain* (London: Unwin Hyman, 1989), p. 3.

peans living there. A few companies actually employed African chaplains at their forts. Such individuals were converted to Christianity, given a new "Christian" baptismal name and then trained in Europe for this purpose. The best known of these were Christian Protten, Philip Quaque and Jacobus Capitein—but they achieved little in terms of evangelism.

The abolitionist impulse in the eighteenth century converged with and was indebted to the evangelical revival. The spiritual movement inspired a network of motivated people in North America, Britain and Europe to concentrate on the issue of slavery. These abolitionists touched people's consciences and inspired philanthropic efforts, creating a sensitivity that impacted the existing black population in England, which numbered about fifteen thousand in 1772, and included some free blacks and others of slave status. In a celebrated court case that year dealing with the status of American slaves who had run away after their owners had brought them to England, Chief Justice Lord Mansfield handed down a judgment that profoundly affected the abolitionist cause. Dealing with the slave James Somersett, who had escaped from his Massachusetts owner but was caught and placed on a ship slated to go to Jamaica where he would be resold, the jurist ruled that English law had never allowed for a slave to be recaptured and resold anywhere. Therefore the person concerned had to be set free. Although it did not formally outlaw slavery in England, the ruling acknowledged that neither the common law nor any specific parliamentary legislation recognized slavery's existence there. Slavery was, in effect, illegal in England.

At the time, popular interest arose in the accounts of exslaves about the ordeals and evils of human trafficking. In 1787 a Fanti man from West Africa named Ottobah Cuguano published *Thoughts and Sentiments on the Evil and Wicked Traffic of the Slavery and Commerce of the Human Species*. More significant was the bestselling autobiography *The Life of Olaudah Equiano* (1789), which was intended to address Christian issues. An Igbo from southern Nigeria, Equiano had purchased his freedom from servitude and devoted his energy to promoting the antislavery cause. His aggressive approach, high profile and personal independence symbolized the solution to slavery. Quite important was his networking with groups and individuals in North America at a period when the relationship between Britain and its former American colonies was in tatters. Ironically, more poor blacks arrived in England in the 1780s as a result of the American war of independence.

Between 1770 and 1783 the question of slavery increasingly gained attention in England. Educated free blacks designed projects to raise consciousness and agitated for the liberation of their race. Quakers protested about the immorality of slavery but, as they were social and political outsiders, their efforts were not particularly effective. However, the American Quakers John Woolman and Anthony Benezet achieved notoriety as the first whites in the colonies to publicly denounce slavery. In 1784 the Reverend James Ramsey published a pamphlet in England titled "Essay on the Treatment and Conversion of the African Slaves in the Sugar Colonies." Ramsey was a surgeon on a British naval vessel who settled in the West Indies as an Anglican minister, and he observed the growth of evangelicalism among the slave population resulting from the work of Moravian missionaries. His tract argued that the enslavement of the blacks was unchristian, the Africans were responsive to the gospel message and British Christians were duty bound to take seriously the need to evangelize Africa. In effect, Ramsey set the moral and missionary agenda for the next half century for British evangelicals. His former ship captain and old friend was Lord Middleton, an ardent abolitionist who circulated his tract among the British political elite, including William Wilberforce and British Prime Minister William Pitt the Younger. Then, in 1787, the most important organization in the slavery debate, the Society for the Abolition of the Slave Trade, was formed by Granville Sharp and Thomas Clarkson.

The American Revolution helped bring matters to a head when the British offered to grant freedom and land to slaves who would desert their masters and join the loyalist cause. Many blacks accepted the offer, and the British felt obligated to keep their word even though they had lost the war. Some freed slaves were sent to the West Indies, others to England, but most to Nova Scotia. Those who went to England added to the number of blacks in poverty whose fate aroused philanthropic consciences. The Committee for the Relief of the Black Poor (founded in 1786) provided help for these destitute people. Blacks in the new United States of America quickly learned that the principles of equality before the law stated in the American Constitution did not apply to them. The document allowed slavery to continue to exist, and its provisions applied mainly to white males. Although legislative seats were apportioned on a population basis, women were not allowed to vote and black slaves were counted as three-fifths of a person for apportionment purposes.

The blacks relocated to Nova Scotia in 1783 upheld the ideal of equality that the United States had ignored. They had absorbed the idea of progress and its potential for social, political and economic redemption, but their experience in the harsh Nova Scotia climate belied the rosy promises and ignited agitation for redress. Thomas Peters, a Yoruba exslave born about 1740 and captured in Africa in 1760, took the British freedom offer seriously and found his way to Nova Scotia. There he became a social activist, and in 1789 he eloquently took the petition of the now destitute exslaves to London.

In England the evangelical abolitionists realized that their efforts could only succeed if Africa was involved in the solution, and that the use of force to restrain the slavers must have local support. The result was the Sierra Leone settlement project, initially supervised by the Committee for the Relief of the Black Poor. Forming the community of Freetown, the project bypassed the compromised traditional rulers and created a local, supportive civil society that would use "legitimate" economic enterprise to undercut and destroy the slave system. In 1787 the first contingent of London-based blacks, many of whom were British loyalists who had fled America, left England to start the experiment. The initiators, led by Granville Sharp, had underestimated the power of the chiefs who had colluded and profited in the slave trade, and their opposition along with tropical diseases soon ruined the colony. In 1791 abolitionists Sharp and banker Henry Thornton obtained a commercial company charter from Parliament for a new Sierra Leone Company. Thomas Peters returned to Nova Scotia and helped to organize a second emigration to Africa in association with the Sierra Leone Company to rescue the Freetown enterprise. This action brought an evangelical dimension to the fore, as both Peters and black Baptist preacher David George accompanied the expedition to Africa and provided leadership to the community.

The antislavery cause now had a strong evangelical Christian rhetorical overlay. Most denominations grounded their recognition of slavery in the Bible, but the evangelical revival introduced the emphasis on a personal relationship with Christ, a different kind of biblicism and an activism that applied to social problems (including slavery) the ethical implications of the equality of all human beings before God. The "Clapham Sect" (further discussed in chapter four) exemplified the new brand of spirituality, and its prominent political and business figures were people central to the antislavery movement: William Wilberforce, Granville Sharp, Henry Thornton, Charles Simeon and Thomas Clarkson.

Evangelicalism was subversive. Its preaching built on voluntarist principles, elevated the speech of God above that of men, and downplayed pomp and the powerful. In England this spirit suffused the thinking of a humble Baptist, William Carey, who in 1792 urged his fellow Baptists to obey the Great Commission and mobilize for crosscultural mission. He called for formation of a voluntary society to sponsor missionaries to such places as Sierra Leone and India. Soon Christians in various church communities in Britain, Europe and the United States caught the vision and formed missionary societies—some denominational, others interdenominational.

An important personality in the new age of Protestant missions was Henry Venn, who became secretary of the (Anglican) Church Missionary Society (CMS) in 1841. Through his "three-self" strategy (churches must be self-supporting, self-governing and self-propagating), he gave primacy to what came to be known in Africa as "native agency." These were the seeds that would nurture healthy growth and expansion of the indigenous church. Venn's counterpart in the United States, Rufus Anderson of the American Board of Commissioners for Foreign Missions, shared the same strategy and goals, as did other theorists later in the century.

African American blacks formed their own churches. They functioned as highly visible centers of Afro-cultural presence in the United States that were firmly rooted in evangelical Christianity. As the only form of organized communal life available to African Americans, evangelical institutions were places where people of African origin developed a sense of belonging and asserted a cultural presence. In the nineteenth century, most black Christians were Baptists or Methodists.

Some of them were strongly motivated to evangelize Africa. Lott Carey, a black Baptist in Virginia who had bought his freedom, in 1821 went to serve as a missionary in Liberia. This enterprise was a scheme to "repatriate" free blacks to West Africa that had the support of abolitionists and slave-holders alike, who regarded the presence of such people as an anomaly in white America. The colonization effort had only limited success and required US government backing to preserve the political independence of Liberia. Like white abolitionists, the early black missionaries stamped evangelicalism in Africa with an indelible imprint—the quest for a new identity through a fervent gospel message and responsible citizenship. These African Americans returning "home" hoped to redeem the motherland through the gospel, regain freedom and dignity for all blacks, prove they could build a civil society based on the ideals espoused in Europe and America, and wipe out the stigma of the slave trade. Over the years African American missionary work in the ancestral homeland increased and spread to areas far beyond Liberia.

Baptist work in the West Indies was very significant. African American preacher George Liele went from Georgia to Jamaica after the Revolution to begin a ministry there, and the early nineteenth-century English Baptist missionaries William Knibb, Thomas Burtchell and James Phillippo did much to light revival fires in the island. The Christmas rebellion of 1831, led by black Baptist preacher Sam Sharpe, convinced the colonial authorities that Christianized slaves were subversive. Ironically, this fueled abolitionist protests and helped advance the process of emancipation.

With its noteworthy black Christian population, Jamaica soon became a center for sending missionaries to other islands and then to West Africa, with workers going to the island of Fernando Po, Cameroon, Nigeria and the Gold Coast. Afro-Caribbeans sought to evangelize the area whose climate had made it the proverbial "white man's grave." Others trained "recaptives," people rescued from slave ships, for service in various African locations.

The most significant recaptive was Samuel Adjai Crowther, a liberated Yoruba who became an Anglican minister. Born around 1809, he was baptized in 1825 and educated in England. He set the tone of Christian presence in the early period—one marked by an evangelical temper, strenuous evangelization of the interior, reasoned dialogues with Muslims, vernacular Bible translation and the maintaining of schools, hospitals and other charitable institutions. In 1864 he was the first African to be consecrated an Anglican bishop. His diocese lay in the Niger River region distant from his ancestral home. Many white missionaries opposed the appointment, fearing that giving authority to Africans would diminish their own status, and the younger university-trained whites did their best to marginalize him. Upon his death in 1891 he was replaced by an Englishman, as were other black Anglican bishops in Liberia and Nigeria by the end of the century.

The evangelization of Africa in this time period was very uneven. The denominations working in Liberia were locked in competition and did not pursue evangelization of the interior. In Sierra Leone, the Gold Coast and Nigeria, where opportunities were more promising, few missionaries were available. The ongoing expansion of Islam in West Africa prevented several planned missions from getting off the ground.

As European colonial authorities increasingly established their power, they had no clear policy regarding Islam. First they considered it a false religion, but opinions mellowed over time because, unlike African primal religions, Islam taught the existence of only one God. Further, some argued from an evolutionary standpoint that Islam might be beneficial for "less-advanced" races. Some colonial governments actually prevented Christian missionaries from working in Muslim areas as a way of keeping order. Another factor was the moral effect of the trade in alcoholic drinks. Some suggested that Islam, a religion that prohibited liquor, was a solution to the gin problem; the counterargument offered was that Muslims supported the ongoing slave trade. Together, the lack of a functional evangelical strategy to reach Muslims and the hindrance of colonial governments combined to contribute to the Islamic numerical superiority existing today in most of West Africa.

In Eastern and Southern Africa a somewhat more hospitable climate and the discovery of valuable mineral resources made white settlement more attractive, and these factors shaped the pattern of Christian presence. White missionaries generally had a higher profile than the indigenous Christian leaders, with the result that the settler community set the cultural agenda. On the other hand, some so-called Christians operated plantations employing Africans and even slaves, while along the eastern coast Europeans competed with Arab and Indian traders. Such Europeans strongly opposed any missionary presence and hindered the growth of the faith in every way possible.

Also noteworthy were missionaries from the European continent— French, German, Norwegian and Danish—who had their own forms of evangelicalism and theories of mission that differed from the British and

American models. They felt the Venn/Anderson "three-self" formula for missions was too Anglo-American and voluntarist in its approach and placed too much emphasis on the free agency of the indigenous peoples. German theorists in particular saw mission as the task of the church (carried out on its behalf by voluntary societies) and the goal as the planting of a folk or people's church (*Volkskirche*) among the non-Christian populace. From Gustav Warneck (1834–1910) to Hendrik Kraemer (1888–1965), Continental thinkers rejected "three-self" Anglo-American missiology. The Continental scholars tended to promote a moralism that valued top-down control by the missionaries. Although organizationally centered around the mission, Westernization of the peoples was to be avoided. "Native" social institutions were viewed positively, and the "tribes" were to be evangelized within their cultural context. They would function indigenously and not adopt foreign practices. The church would be their church, not a Western implant.

A good example of this Continental missiological approach was Albert Schweitzer's hospital at Lambaréné, Gabon. He insisted that the indigenous people come to a hospital that felt akin to their huts. Another was the German Leipzig Mission worker Bruno Gutmann's positive approach to the Chagga people and their customs. Some alleged that he even wanted his mission in Tanganyika (modern-day Tanzania) to accept polygamy. When the Germans were expelled during World War I, indigenous workers provided the leadership to keep the work going until the missionaries could return. This happened in other places as well when the displacement of Germans made room for indigenous leadership.

Elsewhere in East Africa dedicated efforts by Africans bore fruit. Some have dubbed the experience of the region of Buganda (present-day Uganda) as a "Christian Revolution" because of the way Christianity sank such deep roots there. During the 1880s, the ruler Mutesa first welcomed Christians as a counterfoil to Muslim intrigues, but then, as Christian numbers increased, he began a vigorous persecution and many were martyred. But thanks to the work of indigenous catechists, the faith spread so widely that a wave of spiritual revival swept the region in 1893–1894. Ganda missionaries soon established the first Christian communities, and their Bible and language predominated in Christian usage. Many Luo people from Kenya who were migrant workers in Buganda became Christians. They in turn evangelized their villages, similar to the way migrants from southeastern Africa who labored in the South African mines and embraced Christianity later returned to evangelize their people back home.

EVANGELICAL PRESENCE AND INDIGENOUS RESPONSES DURING THE AGE OF HIGH IMPERIALISM

Characterizing the early nineteenth-century European involvement in Africa was the struggle against the slave trade, expanding commercial activities and outposts of political control in coastal enclaves populated by settlers and merchants. Over the course of the century, European powers expanded into the interior for political, economic and religious purposes. Britain and France nibbled away at the coastal areas, while Portugal continued its retrogressive rule in Mozambique and Angola—with the latter linked closely to Brazil, Portugal's colony across the Atlantic. In the south, competition between the small Dutch-speaking Boer or "Afrikaner" population and English-speaking immigrants marked European activity. To escape growing British cultural influence, the Afrikaners withdrew into the isolated interior (the "Great Trek" of the 1830s). After 1870 the "scramble for Africa," a phrase from the era of imperialism, replaced this modest beginning.

1. *The Berlin Congress of 1884–1885.* Touching off the heightened tempo of expansionism was the personal commercial enterprise of King Leopold II of Belgium in the Congo basin and the action of the German Empire, which had been newly created in 1871, in declaring "protectorates" over Southwest Africa, Cameroon and Togo. An international conference met in Berlin in 1884–1885 to resolve the issues arising from the heightened competition in Africa. The diplomats allowed Leopold to have his "Congo Free State" and drafted procedures to regulate future expansion. Countries could not simply "annex" areas by drawing lines on a map, but were required to "effectively occupy" them, that is, they had to have their people on the ground—colonial troops, administrators and residents—and notify the other powers of what had been done. This meant that in theory missionaries would essentially became part of the colonial establishment. On the ground, however, this was not always the case. For instance, mission interests opposed the abuses in Leopold's Congo State, while Lutheran workers criticized the brutal suppression of the Herero uprising in German Southwest

Africa. African Christians also resisted by creating their own indigenous expressions of evangelicalism.

In the far south, the British won out in the long power struggle against their Dutch-speaking rivals in the Boer War (1899–1902) and reorganized the territories into the Union of South Africa, a "dominion" that functioned as an autonomous state within the British Empire. Possessing extensive gold and diamond mining operations, it was the wealthiest area in the continent, and to exploit this wealth, the British drew heavily on indigenous labor. South Africa also had the largest white population, and adopted segregation policies that became increasingly harsh over time.

The partition of the continent introduced competing European nationalisms into Africa, and this competition was reflected in the denominations. Africans were forced to speak in various foreign tongues, although Swahili rescued the eastern coast from the worst effects of this phenomenon. The Berlin Act's stipulation of physical presence rather than mere declarations of intent increased the incentive for missionary work in the interior. The missionaries, who now had the backing of colonial authority, also had less respect for African chiefs and vernacular tongues. As the scale of Christian work enlarged, competition and rivalries were rife. Catholics not only contended against Protestants, but also Catholic orders that had their seats in various countries competed with one another. Similar rivalries bedeviled the witness of Protestant denominations and negatively influenced the direction and nature of the Christian presence.

2. *Missions and the colonial enterprise.* The relationship of missions to the colonial enterprise seriously affected the evangelical spirit animating the endeavor. Allegations of collusion between missionaries and the colonial governments abounded, as did conflicts over cultural policy, educational curricula and the moral character of colonial governance. Since most missionaries shared the Western worldview and with it a low esteem for African culture, mission educational policy was intended to create a black cadre to assist in carrying the gospel to their people. Whites had little interest in producing "black Europeans," an ideal to which many Africans ironically aspired.

What left the missionary enterprise with such a negative image in the postcolonial era was its association with European imperialism and its psychological and physical dominance. Various reasons have been offered for this: white racialism, evangelical biblical literalism and Protestant missionary organization as a top-down structure stressing principles of hierarchy, discipline and control. Although some missionaries and colonial officials admired aspects of African society, the ties between Christianity and white settler communities—especially in southern Africa—generally were harmful. South African culture implicated all whites in a system that erected social and geographical boundaries between them and the indigenous people. White civilization allegedly envisioned the spiritual redemption of Africans, but in fact held them back and frustrated their desire for self-expression.

3. *Initial responses to missionary imperialism.* Two examples from East and West Africa illustrate the early pattern of African response to missionary control. From 1895 the African Inland Mission, a faith mission, worked among the Kikuyu of Kenya. Strong piety and a passion for evangelism distinguished its recruits; unfortunately, their beliefs demonized the local cultures and encouraged tightly knit communities of believers set apart from the other people. The resulting tensions prompted the twentieth-century Kenyan novelist Ngugi wa Thiong'o to describe this type of Christianity as *The River Between*; instead of being a water of life, it fostered division. Missionary cultural policy further divided African communities by excluding those who practiced polygamy and female circumcision or refused to take a loyalty oath to the colonial regime. In effect, evangelical religiosity splintered the community into various "Christianities." Some have argued that this splintering eventually provided a religious groundwork for the Mau Mau uprising that ravaged Kenya in the 1950s. A more immediate consequence was that the Kikuyu, while not rejecting Christianity per se, rejected the mode of evangelization practiced. Some Kenyan nationalists contended the spiritual "liberation" offered was less than that found in the Bible. Missionaries accepted the validity of colonial rule, and like most whites, they feared the African—his dark skin, large population and culture steeped in traditional religion.

The second example was the wave of "Ethiopianism" that swept West Africa between 1860 and 1900 and emphasized African Christian identity over against missionary Christianity. In his analysis of the forms of Ethiopianism that enabled many Africans to adjust to the cultural realities of the age, historian Adrian Hastings argued the movement drew upon four sources.[3] One was biblical, following Psalm 68:31: "Princes shall come out of Egypt; Ethiopia shall soon stretch out her hands unto God" (KJV); or "Envoys will come from Egypt; Cush will submit herself to God" (NIV). This was seen as a prophecy of the destiny of the black race. Added to this was the conversion of the Ethiopian eunuch in Acts 8. A second was intellectual: the Western ideals of freedom, as expressed in American revolutionary rhetoric, had inspired African American returnees to the motherland. These ideals were linked with antislavery values and promoted the cause of the oppressed. Racial ideology had led to African religious and political tutelage by Europeans, and from this they must be freed. A third source was historical: a romantic desire to affirm the past glories of ancient Egypt and Ethiopia, however mythical these may seem to be. The fourth was political: Sierra Leone physician Africanus Beale Horton, a key figure in the movement, declared that Ethiopianism was a response to the European nationalism that brought about the partition of Africa and through its domination restrained African initiative.

The core idea of Ethiopianism was the quest by blacks for identity and self-respect by having a place of their own in Africa. This would enable them to nurse Africa back to its former glory, as portrayed in the achievements of ancient Egypt and Ethiopia. Here was a conflation of myth and history; Ethiopia was both a place and an ideological symbol. The movement would re-create the golden age of African civilization, the splendor of the kingdoms of Meroe and Axum that had survived the seventh-century Muslim onslaught and retained the pristine traditions of early Christianity. This included the idea in the European imagination of the magical kingdom of Prester John that allured would-be crusaders. Ethiopia was an enchanted place, whose monarchs claimed to be the Lion of Judah, a descendent of the Queen of Sheba and King Solomon, and the Ark of the Covenant was supposedly hidden there. The Ethiopians maintained their independence into modern times, and their stunning defeat of the Italians at Aduwa in 1896 proved that whites were not invincible. Ethiopia was also a generic term for blacks, popularly seen as the descendents of Ham and Cush, and this idea inspired later black consciousness movements such as the Rastafarians in Jamaica.

---

[3]Adrian Hastings, *The Church in Africa, 1450-1950* (New York: Oxford University Press, 1996), pp. 478-79.

Beyond its myth and ideology, Ethiopianism was able to build upon confidence gained in the "Native Pastorate" experience. This effort by Bishop Crowther to place black pastors in Anglican mission churches was a direct outgrowth of Henry Venn's vision that missionary control over churches would disappear when the indigenous people assumed full responsibility for them. It held out the hope that Africans themselves would evangelize the continent, build an autonomous church devoid of denominationalism, and repudiate European cultural domination and control. Theologically this was grounded in Psalm 68:31, which assured the destiny of the black race. Although Ethiopianism was a coping mechanism that helped Africans endure ideological and material disadvantage, at times it led to active radicalism that sought to remove the source of the system of colonial control.

Adherents of Ethiopianism networked throughout the English-speaking colonies in West Africa and successfully enlisted various luminaries among the new educated elite. One was J. E. Casely Hayford, a lawyer and Methodist layperson who wrote *Ethiopia Unbound* (1911); another was the Gold Coast educator John Mensah Sarbah. In Nigeria, independent Baptist D. B. Vincent dropped his baptismal name for an African name (Mojola Agbebi), adopted African dress, founded a locally supported school and church, and promoted a nonmissionary version of African Christianity. James Johnson was known for his fervent evangelicalism and as an agitator both for African rights in education and ecclesial independence within the Anglican Church. West Indian–born Edward Wilmot Blyden relocated to Liberia and traveled widely throughout Africa and America promoting the Ethiopianist cause. His *The Return of the Exiles* (1891) encapsulated the heart of the Ethiopianist position. While acknowledging the sacrifices of the white missionaries, Blyden argued that the destiny of Christianity lay in the hands of Africans. He braided cultural, religious and political nationalism into a coherent response to the missionary structure and message.

MORE ADVANCED AFRICAN RESPONSES TO COLONIALISM

Contributing to tensions between Africans and Europeans was the widely held doctrine of social Darwinism, the application of Darwin's theory of evolution to society and social development that resulted in a pseudoscientific justification of racism. According to this worldview, African "natives" had lagged so far behind in the global struggle for survival that every aspect of their current existence, from agriculture to religion to sociopolitical organization, had to be remodeled if they hoped to have a place in the modern world. The Christian African response to this perverse conception of modernity took one of three forms: fully accepting the program of change the missionaries laid out for them; voicing dissent through Ethiopianism; or simply withdrawing from mission-founded churches and setting up new ones. The last approach challenged white church polity, liturgy and ethical standards. Neither rejecting Christianity nor fully disavowing denominational doctrines, its advocates simply founded new churches where they could express themselves. Innovations included refusing Western baptismal names, wearing African clothing, praying for chiefs instead of the British monarch and permitting those practicing polygamy to join the church.

1. *The white understanding of Ethiopianism.* This explains the divergent European responses to Ethiopianism. At first there was apprehension, but soon Europeans realized that some versions of it were actually conservative. The colonial authorities regarded these conservative expressions of Ethiopianism as useful for controlling the local populace. On the other hand, they considered varieties of Ethiopianism that were influenced by African Americans, such as the African Orthodox Church in Rhodesia, as dangerously subversive. The interest of Ethiopianism in education was welcomed, but its pushback against white power structures meant friction. When the movement challenged the ecclesiology and theology of the missionary church, it essentially became political activism in religious garb. The issues Ethiopianism raised—the tension between culture and gospel, affirmation of African self-identity and its contribution to world Christianity, the relationship with Western Christianity and Islam in a pluralistic environment—continue as concerns for the postcolonial African churches.

2. *African Americans and Ethiopianism in southern Africa.* In southern Africa, African Americans contributed to fostering the Ethiopian movement. In 1892 Mangena M. Mokone, an ordained Wesleyan Methodist minister, left his church because of its acceptance of racial segregation and founded the Ethiopian Church in Johannesburg. Four years later, through a niece who had studied in America, he contacted the (US) African Methodist Episcopal Church—which was involved in mission work in his area—and arranged to

merge their two churches. An associate of Mokone, James M. Dwane, was named general superintendent of the united church, but soon he broke away and took his group into the Anglican Church, while maintaining an identity there as the "Order of Ethiopia." Other Ethiopian secessions from existing churches in South Africa occurred in the 1880s and 1890s, the best known being Presbyterian P. J. Mzimba, who left the Free Church of Scotland work at Lovedale in 1890 and formed the African Presbyterian Church a few years later. As a historical sidelight, a member of this church, Mankayi Enoch Sonatonga, composed in 1897 the song "God Bless Africa" (*Nkosi Sikelel' i-Afrika*), the most popular patriotic song in Africa today. All of these men rejected the racism and European cultural domination that overshadowed the evangelical spirit in the missionary enterprise. They underscored the themes of a nondenominational African Christianity: self-expression and political and ecclesiastical freedom.

3. *African resistance: John Chilembwe.* Others were not so patient, as exemplified by the well-known story of John Chilembwe. Joseph Booth, an English/Australian Baptist missionary who had founded the Zambezi Industrial Mission in Nyasaland, nurtured Chilembwe. Recognizing the young man's talents, he treated him like a son and took him to America to be educated at a black college. Booth was also influential in introducing the "Watch Tower" movement (an offshoot of the American Jehovah's Witnesses) into southeastern Africa, but would eventually leave the group. Returning to Nyasaland in 1900 with African American Baptist backing and supervision, Chilembwe founded the Providence Industrial Mission at Chiradzu. Although it was a successful enterprise, he was in continual tension with the white landowner (David Livingstone's grandson) on whose property it was located.

On January 23, 1915, John Chilembwe launched the most significant uprising against colonial rule in Africa during World War I. It was the first armed resistance effort that challenged the white restoration of traditional authority structures and looked toward a future for Africans. It was a form of religious populism that reacted to the heavy losses suffered by blacks who were serving as transport workers in the conflict. Chilembwe doubted whether Africans would receive any recognition after the great struggle on behalf of "civilization and Christianity" had ended. He was killed, and his uprising quickly suppressed, and his apprehension proved to be correct. Africans gained little from the war; conversely, white settlers in Kenya and Rhodesia took advantage of British distraction in Europe and seized political power as well as more African land for themselves. The failure of Chilembwe's movement taught Africans the importance of nonviolent actions to counter the realities of European armed might.

4. *Diverse approaches in the white missionary community.* Varying African responses were paralleled by similar expressions of missionary Christianity. This diversity can be seen in the careers of two men, John Philip and Robert Moffat, both of whom worked with the London Missionary Society in South Africa. Philip combined evangelical Christianity with political and social activism by contending for the rights of black Africans in the Cape Colony in the 1820s. This differed from the evangelicalism represented by Moffat, an otherworldly personal piety that emphasized individual conversion and "civilizing" Africans while neglecting the importance of human equality. To be sure, Moffat achieved much in a half century—Bible translation, the Kuruman mission among the Bechuana, and promotion of agriculture as the basis for a better life for Africans living on the edge of the Kalahari Desert. At the same time, as he preached the gospel, he believed that African communal life needed reorganization. He envisioned the successful agricultural community, built by the labor of African people, as a Westernized entity where people who were disengaged from their cultural roots would become good Christians.

One strength of the missionary enterprise was its capacity for internal criticism. A fine example was J. H. Oldham, a central figure in coordinating the Protestant missionary movement's ecumenical dimensions in the early decades of the twentieth century. In 1924 he published *Christianity and the Race Problem*, a book that won him accolades as "the friend of Africa." Oldham argued that evangelicalism was like a variegated plant; no missionary represented its entire character. It could produce either apolitical quietism or energetic social activism. Further, he maintained that the Bible provided resources that could harmonize with African primal religiosity and an ideology that was liberation oriented. Africans could appropriate these materials in various ways, while missionaries could offer a vision, a sense of sacrifice and a range of social services to empower Africans as they adjusted to new situations.

Another aspect of evangelicalism that contributed to African Christian self-awareness was Bible translation. While translators provided the Scripture in a people's own language, they also preserved oral indigenous languages. Now in written form, these languages served as the bearer of an ethnic group's cultural memory. Further, translations meant that the power of the gospel was increasingly demonstrated by African agents who carried the burden of evangelization. In southern Africa, "Bible women" (a term used for lay women who taught the Bible and often evangelized) adeptly brought the message to villages in the Transvaal region. In the 1870s these Xhosa-speaking evangelists even worked in Nyasaland. Many migrant laborers in South Africa also found Christ and returned home to carry the Christian message to their countrymen.

5. *Into the twentieth century.* In June 1910, Euro-American Protestants of various stripes (plus a handful of Asian Christians) gathered in Edinburgh for the World Missionary Conference. Their intent was to foster a spirit of vibrant evangelicalism, mobilize global resources, and curb duplication of efforts, rivalries, and competition. After the conference, biennial meetings of Protestant churches began in southern Nigeria in 1911, while those in the northern part met annually, and similar gatherings occurred elsewhere in Africa. Many also took place in Asia. The conference created a Continuation Committee to carry forth the vision of missionary cooperation.

World War I threw the international missionary effort into turmoil. As the conflict dragged on, mission logistics were endangered—stations, transportation, human resources and unrest among Africans were major concerns. When the Allies captured the German colonies, they closed the mission stations and interned or repatriated the personnel. German missions in Allied possessions were restricted (South Africa) or transferred to other boards (Gold Coast, India). Throughout Africa mission staffs were stretched thin. At the same time, the war effort enlarged the space for African initiative, since they were usually loyal to the denominations of their missionary colleagues. Africans assumed that the high-flying Allied war aim of national self-determination would apply to them as well, but they were to be disappointed. In the peace settlement, Germany's colonies were turned over to the victorious Allies (Britain, France, Belgium, the Union of South Africa) as League of Nations "mandates." (The United Nations Trusteeship Council assumed these powers in 1946.) Theoretically the League's Mandates Commission could supervise the mandates, but the new masters usually did as they wished. By the late 1920s the British and South Africans allowed German missionary societies to return, but the French and Belgians never did.

Postwar mission strategy was oriented toward education; paradoxically, it would plant the seeds of the missions' demise. Many enterprises recorded noteworthy growth, and letters poured home from the fields pleading for funds, personnel and permission to expand into new territories in response to the volume of requests for schools. Often money was raised locally to cover a teacher's salary and build a schoolhouse. Most missions' strategy was to open a village school and church together. As the number of workers coming from the home base dwindled, indigenous people were employed to fill vacancies. Colonial government officials complained that many of these "teachers" were unqualified, and established inspectorates to oversee instructional quality and curricula. An incentive for improving schools was the prospect of receiving government educational grants in aid. The creation of mission-sponsored medical schools was a costly development, but in the long run it enormously benefited Africa.

By the 1940s African communities were building secondary schools and requested that missions supply them with teachers. The missions, however, had financially concentrated on primary education and were reluctant to invest scarce funds in more costly secondary schools. This factor, along with the fear of resurgent Islam (the bane of evangelicals) and Muslim influence in the higher schools, explains the missions' reluctance to enter secondary and tertiary education. Moreover, the Great Depression hit Africa quite hard, and World War II further weakened white rule. By the war's end, dwindling resources forced many missionary bodies to reevaluate their participation in the enterprise, but ingrained habits from so many years of control deterred them from immediately turning over their works to the indigenous people. The full decolonization of the churches still lay in the future.

AFRICAN INITIATED CHURCHES: FERVENT EVANGELICALISM

New religious developments occurred in Africa after World War I that continued into the era of independence. The old Ethiopianism faded as newer forms of self-expression came to the fore, such as "Zionism." In the African context, "Zionism" had nothing to do with the idea of a Jewish national homeland in Palestine, but rather appropriated and applied biblical language about "Zion" in such a way as to look forward to a new golden age in Africa. Another new expression was the Aladura (or "praying people") movement that originated in Nigeria around 1918. Although strongest among the Yoruba, Aladura gained strength among peoples in southern Nigeria in the 1950s. It challenged missionary Christianity and brought liturgical changes to many of the churches that had been originally European in character. A third expression was the Prophet Healing movement that created churches identifying themselves as prophetic or spiritual in nature. Scholars customarily lump these three forms into the category of "Independency" or African independent churches, today often referred to as "African initiated" or "African instituted" churches. Although the movements were quite diverse in their own ways, Independency followed a fairly regular pattern: a prophetic figure emerged who appropriated the Scriptures in a unique manner; the person then received some sort of divine revelations; finally, he or she gathered followers and formed a church, which either grew into a large movement or after a period of time fragmented. An example of this pattern was the early-twentieth-century Zulu prophet Isaiah Shembe. He reported that just as he arrived at a white farmer's home at dusk, he received a divine command to go pray alone. A voice then began giving him directions and soon more revelations followed. Finally, he responded by forming his own church.

1. African "Zionism." The Zionism that emerged in South Africa and spread to nearby areas has attracted much scholarly interest. A noteworthy example of Zionism was the Afrikaner (Dutch-speaking) Pieter L. Le Roux, who was strongly influenced by the noted white evangelical South African preacher Andrew Murray. Le Roux decided to become a Dutch Reformed Church missionary among the Zulu, and founded a chapel at Wakkerstroom in Mpumalanga Province. In 1903 he left his church for a group called the Christian Catholic Apostolic Church, a sect founded by the American John Alexander Dowie in 1896 and centered in Zion City, a utopian community near Chicago. Generally regarded as a forerunner of Pentecostalism, Dowie emphasized the gifts of the Holy Spirit and identified his movement with Jerusalem. Le Roux renamed the congregation he took with him as the Zionist Apostolic Church, an action he dubbed "crossing to Zion," and taught baptism by immersion, faith healing and speaking in tongues. Le Roux, however, continued his spiritual pilgrimage, left the Zionist church, and switched to a new body known as the Apostolic Faith Mission. This Pentecostal group was a product of the famous Azusa Street revival of 1906 in Los Angeles and was doing mission work in South Africa.

At first, many black Africans in the region did likewise. But when those who joined the white-led Apostolic Faith Mission experienced racial discrimination, they promptly founded new all-black churches, each of which held firmly to the Zionist and Apostolic terminologies. Le Roux's disciple Daniel Nkonyane replaced him as the leader of the Zionist Apostolic Church, and the black Africans promoted the tradition of Zion. By then the fast-growing Zionist tree was branching out and other popular figures spread the vision throughout South Africa.

How much African Zionism can be associated with protest and schism is controversial. The loss of tribal or communal land, political disenfranchisement, racial discrimination and economic deprivation that occurred under white settler rule certainly produced the kind of psychological pressures that such a form of religious expression could help alleviate. Zion was the dream for the recovery of lost land and a place where there would be no more tears. The home of the church's founder became a ritual Zion, a place of belonging. On the other hand, much like the mission churches, the Zionist churches were profoundly conservative. It was essentially a religious movement that kept out of politics. Rather than revolutionary protest, Zionists focused on experiential religion—revelations, dreams, visions, prophecy, oral expression and indigenous symbols and rituals. The liturgical side included traditional worship styles based on singing, dancing and folk music. Biblical symbols and themes played a central part in worship. Healing was a vital element of the ministry, both individually and in predictive prophecy, and it played a prominent role in medical diagnosis. An African sense of community pervaded the churches even though they were structured along traditional hierarchical lines.

Zionists often split over petty issues. A few observed in toto the dietary and other taboos of the Old Testament, avoided modern medicine, and permitted polygamy, while others were more selective in their behavior. But all employed prophecy in healing, dressed in colorful garments, displayed distinctive banners and enjoyed a lively liturgy. Some allowed a larger space to women and youths than others. Although the differences among the individual Zionist "utopias" were substantial, as a movement Zionism played a significant role in undermining missionary authority by its prophets' emphasis on the Holy Spirit's role in the Christian life. Even illiteracy was no hindrance to the moving of the Spirit, since it was manifested primarily in healing powers. The differences among the groups (and there were many) lay in their use of the Bible and the amount of traditional religion in their practices. This variety of practices led some observers to question whether Zionists were genuinely Christians.

2. *The Aladura or "praying people" movement.* A rather different category of Independency is the Aladura ("praying people") in West Africa. Their Ethiopianist tendencies as well as revivalistic qualities introduced Christian categories and symbols into African primal religion. Like Zionists, some Aladura groups traced their origins to "faith" and "charismatic" groups based in England or America. Others were forced out of mission churches when they manifested charismatic influences. In Nigeria, for instance, the "Cherubim and Seraphim" and the "Church of the Lord Aladura" arose during the influenza pandemic of 1918 when some Anglican Church prayer groups defied colonial government restrictions on holding public assemblies. These groups regarded as a prophecy a girl's dream that prayer could contain the disease. In fact, visions, dreams and healing were part of the spiritual arsenal in Aladura confrontation with the mission churches. When the "praying people" were ousted from the existing churches, they formed new ones. Joseph Oshitelu designed holy names and a script (sacred writing) for his newly founded "Church of the Lord." In 1928 a highway department worker Joseph Ayo Babalola heard a voice calling him to abandon his job and begin preaching. Babalola gathered followers among urban workers and a revival resulted. Eventually his people merged with the Christ Apostolic Church, originally a British charismatic body transplanted to Africa.

By the 1950s, some observers were questioning the orthodoxy of the Aladura groups. Olumba Olumba Obu, the leader of the "Brotherhood of Star and Cross," claimed to be a person of the Trinity. Its publications asserted that the organization was God's kingdom on earth and the leader was

King of Kings and Lord of Lords, immortal and omnipresent. If a bowing worshiper were to touch his forehead on the ground three times and call on the leader, he was assured that the person would actually appear. Some more orthodox Aladura became strong sabbath observers. Others were labeled in their beliefs as "Israelitist" because they accepted Jesus and the cross, or "Hebraist" because they adhered strictly to the Pentateuch and ignored the New Testament.

The "Army of the Cross of Christ Church" in modern-day Ghana combined both of these aspects. It originated in a Methodist prayer band founded by catechist Joseph William Egyanka Appiah in 1919. He created a "holy language" and "holy names," appointed himself as prophet and king, and dispensed holy names to family members and congregants. Interestingly, while in his Christology he was an Israelitist, in practice he acted as a Hebraist. He established a holy sanctuary housing an ark and engaged in animal sacrifices and other Old Testament rituals. He ran the group like he was an Akan tribal chief, and appointed his wife as the queen. This form of Independency had strayed quite far from the evangelicalism of most African initiated churches.

3. *Prophet healing churches in West Africa.* In the early twentieth century, West Africa was fertile ground for the "prophet healing movements," often called the "spiritual churches." William Wadé Harris and Garrick Braide were the most important leaders. Distinctive in appearance, prophets usually grew a beard and carried some kind of an emblem such as a cross, staff or a bowl with holy water. Being charismatic figures, prophets stringently opposed both traditional religion and nominal Christianity. They suggested that missionary Christianity had merely replaced an African culture with a Western one without addressing the issue of core allegiances. Africans were dialoguing with the missionary message on the periphery while preserving an interior where traditional allegiances held sway. Thus the prophets' message focused on the Africans' life, both individual and communal. Their praying and healing ministries were similar to the Zionists, but they had a forceful message of their own. They did not wish to found separate churches but desired to save people through the preached word and performance of miracles. These evangelists were known to pour holy water on traditional shrines that would burst into flames, astounding worshipers and onlookers

alike. They attacked the symbols and worldviews of traditional religions with the same vehemence as the missionaries, but backed up their words with signs and wonders. Wadé Harris itinerated on foot from his native Liberia into the Ivory Coast and Gold Coast between 1910 and 1914, preaching, performing miracles and ironically contributing to both Roman Catholic and Methodist membership growth.

Garrick Braide lived in the Niger Delta where he became a Christian and was appointed as a catechist by African Bishop James Johnson. Braide emerged as a popular preacher and faith healer by 1910, and was acclaimed by people as the Second Elijah because he won so many to his version of Christianity. Through his preaching against fetishes and idols and emphasis on spiritual healing, Braide won two-thirds of the region's Anglicans as his followers. In 1915 Bishop Johnson turned against him for alleged heresy and persuaded the British authorities to jail him on a trumped-up charge of sedition. He died in prison three years later. Braide's disciples created a new denomination, the Christ Army Church. The colonial regimes, both British and French, feared the power they had over the masses and harassed and imprisoned the prophets. Prophetism created an explosive religious atmosphere that aided the growth of the Aladura and other revivalist groups.

An American Pentecostal church, the Faith Tabernacle in Philadelphia, had considerable influence in Nigeria and the Gold Coast. The dominance of the US church rapidly waned when it became a hard-line faith-healing community and it would not send missionaries to the area. Since the presence of white personnel tended to be a legitimating symbol for African religious groups in this particular colonial setting, the local followers of Faith Tabernacle turned to the Bradford (UK) Apostolic Church for missionaries. Eventually this relationship soured over a question of faith healing, and in 1939 the Africans formed an indigenous Christ Apostolic Church modeled on the English church but with an Aladura orientation. In the Gold Coast a further schism produced the Church of Pentecost, today the largest Pentecostal church in Ghana. In Nigeria a breakaway church invited the Assemblies of God to begin work there in 1939. Thus, the emphasis on the power of prayer and healing did much to shape West African evangelicalism.

This prophetic form of spirituality thrived in other parts of Africa. The census of 1966 in Kenya identified over thirty Arathi (prophetic) groups.

These were strong biblicists who respected Kikuyu culture and were quite traditional as to education, clothing and medicine. Still, the politics of religious sectarianism lay just below the surface, and governmental suspicions were easily aroused. Such overreaction was excellently illustrated in the case of Simon Kimbangu in the Belgian Congo. (King Leopold's private colony had become so corrupt that the Belgian government assumed control of it in 1908.) Converted as a Baptist, Kimbangu worked as a catechist, received a divine call to preach and heal, and began his ministry in 1921. A few enthusiastic followers rapidly grew into a mass movement. The ever-suspicious Belgian authorities saw his healing and preaching ministry as subversive, since by diminishing the power of magic and witchcraft, it challenged the authority of local chiefs. Prodded by Catholic missionaries who feared the spiritual power of his message and its anti-European character, the regime had him tried for sedition and jailed for life. Kimbangu lived on for three decades in prison as a martyr (died 1951), while his followers went underground. The Kimbanguist church reemerged in the 1950s and today is one of Africa's largest independent Christian communities.

Clearly Independency is a major factor in the African religious landscape and is a complement to the mission churches. The debate among evangelical observers centers on whether independents are even Christian in the sense of holding to the faith once delivered to the saints. Others caution against lumping them all together culturally as an African contribution to Christianity or making the claim they are all Pentecostals.

4. *The East African revival.* Between 1930 and 1955, religious revivals swept East Africa. The Anglican Church in Uganda experienced a modest awakening in the 1920s that resulted in affirmation of holiness views. After 1930 a widespread revival movement surged from Rwanda through Uganda into other parts of East Africa whose hallmark was fervent evangelicalism. The principal source of the revival is generally believed to be the Church Missionary Society's Rwanda Mission, largely staffed by workers who had belonged to Cambridge's Christian Union. These individuals had experienced the Keswick holiness or "higher life" movement, which emphasized, as mentioned in an earlier chapter, a strong sense of sin, the cleansing power of the blood of Jesus, the filling of the Holy Spirit and the victorious Christian life. The spread of holiness teachings resulted in denunciations of "weak and

worldly" Christians who still practiced elements of traditional religion and the so-called modernists serving on the faculty of the theological college in Uganda. Scholars of the revival point out that it was primarily a lay charismatic movement that included a significant role for women.

On the whole, the forces of education and indigenous spiritual associations spurred the growth of African evangelicalism in the period up to the 1950s; this growth included some Independency movements as well as growth that remained and operated within the churches. The spiritual fervor of indigenous evangelicalism radiated across the continent and brought new life to the existing Protestant missionary structures. Simultaneously, Catholicism too was growing rapidly, thanks to its wide network of religious orders and charitable institutions.

DECOLONIZATION AND CHRISTIAN RESPONSES

1. What did decolonization involve? From the mid-1950s to 1975 the political landscape of Africa changed dramatically. In rapid succession, colonial possessions, beginning in North Africa and then spreading to Western and Eastern Africa, gained political independence. The issues of decolonization confronted evangelical and ecumenical Christianity alike. What were the nature, process and consequences of decolonization? Was it to be planned or compelled and pursued hastily? What changes were actually occurring? How would the expatriate missionaries who were uneasy about matters react? Certainly they were uneasy about the prospects. Further complicating matters was the surge in evangelical missionary recruits after World War II.

One concern was the resilience of primal (traditional) religion and the weakness of Christianity in the face of resurgent nationalism. Too many churches founded by whites suffered from disunity, dependency and poor utilization of human resources. After African independence was achieved, an unprophetic silence and passivity marked many of these churches. Could it be that the concentration on education had diminished the imperative to preach the Word of God? While the agendas of the colonial governments and missions were hardly identical, rulers were generally suspicious of—if not downright hostile toward—anything that detracted from purposeful modernization. Modernity was a key concern for missions as well. The regimes needed an educated colonial elite to assist them in governance, while missions saw education as crucial for successful evangelism. The new African nationalists saw both of these goals as unsatisfactory.

Already in the 1920s signs were evident that missionary authority could not be exercised in the same way as before. Influenced by antiforeign movements in Asia, many delegates at the International Missionary Council's Jerusalem Conference in 1928 pressed the case for fully indigenous non-Western churches and a reappraisal of attitudes toward other faiths. In Europe and America, fundamentalists and modernists (liberals) struggled over missionary policy. The Great Depression and World War II sapped Christian confidence, as recruits and funding fell significantly, and the ties among missionaries, colonial governments and indigenous Africans came under increasing strain. Although some mission agencies considered restructuring their efforts, most failed to grasp how much they needed to adapt to the changing times. The nationalist effort gained momentum, inspired by the wartime experiences and Indian independence in 1947, and the speed of decolonization overwhelmed the missions. Complicating matters was the enormous growth of North American evangelical missions after World War II, resulting in the creation of many new faith mission societies and a large influx of workers.

It has said been that the British stumbled out of their colonies, the French and Belgians abandoned theirs, and the Portuguese had theirs snatched away. The reasons for this rapid decolonization are clear. The nationalist elites, who resented their exclusion from power, ignited the process. Then, the geopolitical situation of the postwar era imbued this group with confidence, while the United States with its pro-democratic foreign policy put pressure on the colonial rulers. Added to this was the economic reality that Europe needed to rebuild and the resource base for imperial rule no longer existed. The British in particular realized that decolonization was in their own best interests. In other words, the liquidation of the empires was a response in crisis management. Missionary interests essentially played no part in the process.

Decolonization, however, did not mark as radical a change in socio-economic relationships as people had expected. Setting aside the excessive claims of radical ideologues that the independent nations were the victims of "neo-colonialism," what occurred was a move to "informal empire" where the former rulers retained sufficient economic and technological resources to exercise influence upon future development. Much more serious was that the transfer of power bequeathed an obsolete state apparatus. The new nations were burdened with artificial boundaries, incomprehensible constitutions and inexperienced rulers. They found themselves in an unfortunate state of dependency even as they sought to modernize and achieve economic development.

2. *Differing responses among Christians to the new situation.* The response of the expatriate missionaries to decolonization was ambiguous. They embraced modernity and sought to channel it in as positive a manner as they could. Their response to nationalist insurgency during the twilight of colonialism (1945–1960), however, differed in quality from the retooling strategies in the immediate aftermath (1960–1975). In the 1940s a new generation of African leaders educated in mission schools emerged who challenged both traditional rulers and moderates, and made their voices heard in the political parties springing up in colony after colony. Discouraged by the racism in the evangelical wing of the South African church, some of these Africans abandoned the ideal of racial cooperation.

Missionary responses to nationalism varied during the first postwar decade according to individual whims, denominational or institutional policies, and regional contexts. They found themselves powerless to halt the process and felt betrayed both by the governments and their own Christian followers. Some argued for a dichotomy between Christianity and politics. They used drama, public debates and lectures to warn Christians to eschew politics and seek first the kingdom of God. Generally, institutional attitudes varied; those at the home base expressed cautious sympathy for Africans, while those on the field were alarmed at the prospects of Marxism or a resurgence of paganism, angry about the ingratitude of the African elites, and resolved to contain the damage. All too often, these missionaries portrayed nationalism as irreligious and its adherents as too immature to lead nations with a democratic vision.

It must be noted that the regional differences were very important. Because the white community in West Africa was small, the indigenization policy in the mid-1950s was fairly well advanced. The churches related to the nationalists, installed indigenous people in clerical posts, and sought to adapt Christianity to African culture, believing that Africans needed to "baptize" elements of their culture. Since the clergy trained in the early 1950s were seen as the vanguard, the actual limitations of African Christian initiative in religion would only become evident later.

In other places, colonial regimes compromised with or directly incorporated churches into the state apparatus. Portuguese dictator Antonio Salazar's Concordat of 1940 recognized and funded the Catholic Church as the official instrument to promote his state's colonial aims in Mozambique and Angola. Accordingly, in both territories the leadership against colonial rule came from African Protestants. Likewise, the Belgians used Catholicism to legitimize their rule in the Congo. The Bishop of Katanga supported Belgian loyalists while the Kimbanguists were aligned with the nationalists. In Rwanda the Catholic Church's manipulation of religion for political ends was notorious. In independent Ethiopia, Emperor Haile Selassie co-opted the Abuna (head) of the Coptic Orthodox Church into the state structure by placing him on the Council of Regency. In the first elections in Uganda, Catholic Archbishop Joseph Kiwanuka jostled with Protestant Milton Obote, a long rivalry that divided the society.

Thus, the Christian response to the challenge of insurgent nationalism was to retool the churches with indigenous personnel and resources. This was the main thrust of the missionary policy of indigenization. Various measures were tried: more efficient utilization of human resources, promotion of church unity, funding policies to deter dependency by balancing aid and self-respect and nurturing stewardship, encouraging the involvement of more Christians in politics, promoting theological reflection from an African perspective, and frequently using the term *partnership* in social service matters. They hoped that these measures would remedy the negative effects of paternalistic control in the past, preserve the core of missionary structures and broaden African participation.

The more liberal ecumenical movement clarified its approach at the World Council of Churches (WCC) Assembly in Uppsala, Sweden, in 1968 in a manner comparable to that of many evangelicals. The delegates there and in Nairobi (1975) formulated a new understanding of mission, science and technology to enable facing the challenge of modernity, engaging in dialogue with other faiths, and fostering justice and racial reconciliation.

Similarly, the Second Vatican Council reoriented the Roman Catholic Church's policy in mission and social service. It emphasized unity and opened the way for Africans to play a greater role in leadership in the church, while a number of subsequent papal pronouncements spoke to all Africans irrespective of denomination. For example, in 1967 Pope Paul VI declared, "You must have an African Christianity. Indeed you possess human values and characteristic forms of culture which can rise up to perfection so as to find in Christianity, and for Christianity, a true superior fullness and prove to be capable of a richness of expression all of its own, and genuinely African."[4]

Another way ecumenism affected Africa was the involvement of its leaders in the global denominational fellowships, or as they are known today, world Christian communions. Black bishops from around Africa played a key role in the world Anglican community. Ishmael Noko of Zimbabwe served two terms as general secretary of the Lutheran World Federation, and Josiah Kibira of Tanzania, a seven-year term as president. Respected churchmen Lawi Imathis of Kenya and Sunday Mbang of Nigeria each served a term as president of the World Methodist Council. William Tolbert of Liberia was president of the Baptist World Alliance from 1965 to 1970, and the Baptist World Congress agreed to convene in Durban, South Africa, in 2015. The World Alliance of Reformed Churches (renamed Communion in 2010) was an essential player in the struggle for democracy in South Africa.[5]

The level of ministerial formation and quality of theological education provided by and for Africans gradually improved. Regional and continental associations encouraged theological reflection and revision of curricula in Bible schools. Many experimented with theological education by extension, while the Ecumenical Association of Third World Theologians linked people from the Southern Hemisphere who were interested in theological and social issues. Evangelicals made great strides in theological education through the seminaries and Bible schools they founded, and the Accrediting Council for Theological Education in Africa (ACTEA), created in 1975

---

[4]See the lengthy treatment of this theme in Paul VI's 1967 message to the hierarchy and all the people of Africa, contained in Joseph Gremillion, *The Gospel of Peace and Justice: Catholic Teaching Since Pope John* (Maryknoll, NY: Orbis, 1975), pp. 417-25.
[5]See Anthony Cross, ed., *Ecumenism and History* (Carlisle: Paternoster, 2002), pp. 106-19.

by the Association of Evangelicals of Africa, worked to improve educational quality at these schools. The Overseas Council in the United States and the Langham Partnership in Britain did much to assist the development of these schools through financial support and provision of library books. The Nigeria-based African Christian Textbooks (ACTS), launched in 1993 with the encouragement of ACTEA, strives to enhance the availability of quality academic literature in Africa, as does the Theological Book Network in the United States.

Church unity matters have held much interest for those Africans associated with the ecumenical movement, and two of the WCC's assemblies were held in Africa—Nairobi in 1975 and Harare in 1998—but church union talks as such (with one exception being the United Church of Zambia [1965]) never went anywhere. The failed effort in Nigeria (1965–1966) illustrates the problem. There, doctrinal differences, personality clashes and rivalries, longstanding denominational hostilities, competition for bishoprics, and ethnic differences torpedoed the negotiations. Many felt that unity, a popular trend at the time in Western mainline churches, was being imposed from the outside. African evangelicals, however, were willing to engage in cooperative efforts, as illustrated by the creation of the Association of Evangelicals in Africa in 1966, an affiliate of the World Evangelical Alliance.

3. Indigenization controversies. During the decade of 1965 to 1975, the indigenization of the Christian church became a matter of considerable debate. To be sure, control was increasingly being turned over to African leadership; even so, many saw its features as foreign imports—Gothic buildings, pietistic gospel songs and moralistic ethics not rooted in African traditions. Simultaneously, the mission churches had begun emphasizing the role of lay persons (both men and women) in ecclesiastical affairs and decision making, were incorporating African symbols, rituals and garb in their worship experiences, and also intentionally expressed an ebullient charismatic spirituality—all of which, of course, reflected the influences of the African initiated churches. Lay women's groups like the Mothers' Union in Anglican churches and Women's Guilds in Presbyterian churches fostered change, while Knighthood Orders (such as the Order of Saints Christopher and Mary in the Anglican Church of West Africa) were created to attract the political elite. Academics began publishing works on African theology and freely used such terms as *contextualization, traditionalization, incarnation* and *inculturation* to explain African Christianity. Theologians assured people that the spirituality of primal religion did not necessarily conflict with the canon of Scripture. Meanwhile, government takeovers of church schools and hospitals enabled church leaders to devote more time to evangelization.

In the early 1970s liberal theologians pushed the indigenization issue further by demanding a missionary "moratorium": a cessation of mission aid, both in personnel and money, for at least five years so the churches could learn how to stand on their own feet. This more strident approach reflected African impatience with the nature, pace and results of mission-initiated indigenization, and the suspicion that these efforts were simply cosmetic while the same old interests continued to hold the real power. Various ecumenical churchmen supported the idea, most notably Burgess Carr, secretary of the liberal ecumenical All Africa Council of Churches (founded in 1963). Although a vigorous debate occurred in ecumenical circles about the scheme's merit, evangelicals largely ignored it. The moratorium was eventually seen as impractical and was quietly dropped, although some maintained that the inaction proved that Africa's relationship to the West continued to be one of dependency and that the churches still needed to be decolonized.

The first twenty-five years of decolonization saw the dismantling of the empires of Britain, France, Belgium and Portugal. The new states, however, were marked by political instability, human rights abuses, environmental degradation and economic decline. Some were one-party states, others military dictatorships, and many were Marxist oriented. Few genuine democracies existed. The continent was fertile ground for Cold War meddling, and each side courted African rulers with money, weapons and political support. Communism itself did not take root, but leaders responded with home-grown political ideologies like African socialism, humanism and centralized democracy. Many of the new political entities deceptively expressed their goals by misusing Christian terminology: national redemption, economic salvation, political justification, national regeneration and the sanctity of the state. The actual impact of political pressure on the churches varied from country to country, but the power expressions of the new states imposed changes on the pattern of Christian presence in Africa.

The "Second" Decolonization, 1975–1995, and Church Involvement

1. *Southern Africa.* As political leaders aged, were ousted or died, a new generation was waiting in the wings to assume power. People were dissatisfied with the authoritarian regimes and desired democracy. Only South Africa had failed to come under black rule, and resistance there was crumbling. Contributing to this erosion was the WCC's Program to Combat Racism, founded 1968–1969. Among other things, it was channeling assistance to "freedom fighters." The white settlers in the British colony of Southern Rhodesia unilaterally declared independence in 1965 and a long civil war ensued. A negotiated settlement in 1979 ended the conflict and enabled the territory's transition to independence under the new name of Zimbabwe and with elections insuring black majority rule. South Africa held a UN mandate over the former German colony of Southwest Africa, but refused to grant independence although the other UN trust territories had gained theirs. A lengthy diplomatic struggle and guerrilla war ensued until it finally received independence as the Republic of Namibia in 1990.

South Africa had become increasingly isolated because of its official policy of *apartheid* ("separate development"). The atrocious racial legislation, enacted after 1948, aimed at completely separating the white, African and Indian populations from one another, an absurd idea since the industrial and mining economy, controlled by the white minority, could not function without nonwhite labor. As the country became an international pariah, leaders from the various Christian communities were involved in the long struggle to end the odious system.

The opponents of apartheid expressed a number of political theologies. They included the universalist vision of Albert Luthuli, Nelson Mandela and the African National Congress; the strong antiwhite position of Robert Sobukwe and the Pan Africanist Congress; the "black theology" of Steve Biko and the Black Consciousness Movement; and the nonviolent ideology of Desmond Tutu and the United Democratic Front. The positions of Luthuli and Tutu emerged from a prophetic/transcendent understanding of Christianity that saw apartheid as violating the central message of the Bible. Sobukwe and Biko considered Christianity a utilitarian instrument that harnessed ultimate concerns for immediate purposes. An important Christian statement was the Kairos Document of 1985–1986, a biblical and theological commentary on the deteriorating political situation that was widely discussed in South Africa and abroad.

Christian opponents of apartheid looked to two twentieth-century martyrs as role models—Dietrich Bonhoeffer and Martin Luther King Jr., both of whom had used the resources of their faith to stand up against evil and oppressive systems, and both of whom gave their lives at the age of thirty-nine. The role of individual Christian figures in the struggle against apartheid was extraordinary. To mention just a few, they included prominent academics—Ben Marais, John de Gruchy, Charles Villa-Vicenio and J. W. Hofmeyr—the Pentecostal (Apostolic Faith Mission) political figure Frank Chikane, Reformed Church pastor and activist Allan Boesak, and by far the most noteworthy, C. F. Beyers Naudé and Bishop Desmond Tutu. Naudé, a minister in the Dutch Reformed Church, helped found (1963) and directed the Christian Institute of Southern Africa, an organization that fostered racial reconciliation. He fearlessly opposed the cruelty and injustice of apartheid. Tutu, ordained in the Anglican Church, was named a bishop in 1976 and later Archbishop of Cape Town. Appointed the first black secretary of the ecumenical South African Council of Churches (SACC) in 1978, he used this base to advocate nonviolent resistance to the apartheid regime and an economic boycott of his country. The SACC revealed the usefulness of international ties with ecumenical bodies like the WCC as it worked to undermine apartheid.

The system finally collapsed under its own weight, and the first democratically elected South African government (1994) under Nelson Mandela created the Truth and Reconciliation Commission with Tutu as chair. It avoided the anticipated bloodbath of retribution by utilizing the cardinal Christian principles of confession and forgiveness to help heal the social wounds of apartheid. Its basis lay in the broader realm of Christian ethics, and commission members were drawn from various communities, including evangelical Christian ones.

Under majority rule and with its substantial industrial and mineral resources, South Africa was now the natural leader in the continent, but serious economic and social problems persisted that are likely to take decades to resolve. With the boycotts ended, international meetings once again could take place, including the most significant evangelical gathering ever held in Africa, the Third Lausanne Congress on World Evangelization. Some four thousand Christian leaders from around the world assembled in Cape Town in October 2010, with thousands more participating through six hundred global satellite links.

2. *Church-state concerns elsewhere.* During this period, people in Africa looked to the churches for leadership because so many other forms of civil society had lost legitimacy. Now the public realm was filled with new religious groups, together with the more secular ones, that advocated assistance to marginalized sectors of the community and confronted the horrific neglect of the physical environment. Poverty, pluralism and ecological degradation had become central realities of political life. Circumstances required Christians to adopt a new style of living and witnessing in a world they shared with Islam, secularism, renewed primal faiths and various cults. Ethnicity was another competitive force. Demagogic leaders gathered mass followings by claiming that other groups had appropriated natural resources for themselves and had deprived people of their just due. Such rivalry among the political and ethnic messiahs led to civil strife all over the continent.

Moreover, elections did not necessarily mean democracy. Many countries soon learned that it was one thing for a regime to transition to democracy and another to actually possess the structures of democratic governance. At the continental level, the Organization of African Unity, formed in 1963, vigorously supported national liberation movements. With that goal achieved, it restructured itself in 2002 as the African Union (now numbering fifty members), a managerial form of continental unity that hoped to enhance economic viability and resolve social problems.

For various reasons, many African states fell into extreme difficulties, of which the worst was the burden of debt. During the Cold War the Western and Soviet blocs provided economic and military help to their clients, but that ended after 1990. In some countries the economic situation became so bad that more money was spent on servicing the interest on the debt than providing necessary social services. At the same time, the International Monetary Fund (World Bank) assisted the lenders by imposing severe structural adjustment programs on the debtor countries. From 1992 church leaders were called upon to preside over various national conferences to design constitutions suitable for the new times. These Christians were not chosen because they fought against dictators or practiced justice in their own organizations; rather, they directed the only credible institutions available.

Evangelicals contributed to the process of democratization during this "second decolonization." In Malawi they played an important role in ousting the last of the old dictators, Hastings Banda, in 1994. In Cameroon, an individual churchman, Baptist Simon Bolivar Njami, was the catalyst for the democratic process. In Kenya, Anglican Bishop David Gitari and Presbyterian Timothy Njoya mobilized their followers to contend boldly for political reform in the later 1980s and 1990s. Due to violence, victory in Kenya and Malawi required a pluralistic, interfaith operation. Pentecostals were prominent in bringing about regime change in Guinea, Benin, Angola and Mozambique.

Noteworthy Contemporary Developments

1. The specter of war. Civil conflict was the dark cloud that hung over political developments in Africa in recent times. Innumerable wars have occurred from the time of independence, and they were due not so much to ethno-linguistic fragmentation as to the extreme levels of poverty, failed political institutions and economic dependence on natural resources. The horrific genocides in Rwanda and Burundi in the 1990s shocked the world, as did the lengthy, genocidal civil struggle in Sudan, from which emerged the newest African state, South Sudan, in 2011. Wars in such places as the Congo, Sierra Leone, Liberia, Ivory Coast, Angola and Nigeria caused catastrophic losses of life and destruction of property and resources. Particularly disheartening was that many of the participants were Christians, both as perpetrators and victims of the violence and mayhem. Efforts to resolve such struggles and bring peace to the continent were complicated by the rise of militant Islam in many places and the ensuing conflicts between Christians and Muslims.

2. The exponential growth of Pentecostalism. Pentecostalism evolved from its roots in both the Independency of the interwar years and in the missionary work from North America and Europe to a mature form of African Christian faith and spirituality. It was now a global, transnational faith, and it was sending African missionaries to other places in the world. The flow of charismatic/Pentecostal ideas and personnel was no longer one way; African Christian spirituality was now flowing to the rest of the world. The most distinguished figure in international Pentecostalism was the South African David J. Du Plessis, a recognized preacher in his homeland who, after World War II, moved in Western ecumenical, evangelical and Roman Catholic circles alike and was known as "Mr. Pentecost." German Pentecostal missionary and evangelist Reinhard Bonnke began holding meetings in Africa in 1975 and attracted massive crowds. At his spectacular "Fire Conventions," Pentecostal "signs and wonders" as well as thousands of healings and exorcisms occurred. He would set a large bonfire where converts could burn their magic amulets and charms.

The African roots of several groups and extensive cross-fertilization with similar movements in Latin America and Asia gave the lie to claims that Pentecostalism was simply an import from the West. It included a vast array of enterprises: interdenominational organizations (e.g., the Full Gospel Businessmen's Fellowship International) as well as evangelistic ministries that emphasized faith healing, the prosperity gospel ("health and wealth"), spiritual warfare and deliverance, Bible distribution, and work among women and children. The attraction of the "theology of prosperity" was quite great, as it gave hope to Africans whose lives were devastated by social and economic crises.

Since Africans recognized the role of the transcendental in the daily lives of individuals and communities, the struggle against demonic forces and spiritual evil easily occupied a central role in Pentecostal activism. One example was "Intercessors for Africa" (IFA), a group that regarded the causes for the failure of African states as fundamentally spiritual and utilized prayer to counter the evil forces behind the political agents. In the view of the IFA, prayer could combat both the political corruption and the civil wars that ravaged the continent. The bloodshed in conflicts polluted the land, corruption existed at all levels of the populace, and idolatry and life-denying customs had ruined the society—all of which led to social violence and poverty, because the land withheld its increase. Christians must redeem and sanctify the land, offer it to God, and receive it back under a covenant with him. Practical aspects of the IFA program were seminars for top government officials, encouraging the "brethren" to enter business and the professions and to run for political offices. These brethren would bring the reign of God into governance and educate congregations on rebuilding the lives of individual members so they could also enter into the struggle.

3. Economic development and the AIDS epidemic. Poverty, disease and unemployment are realities that plague African life. Economic development has seemed to elude most African communities, although NGOs (nongovernmental organizations) and the UN have contributed vast amounts of money to improve food production, provide better housing and sanitation, create microenterprises enabling simple people to earn a living through productive labor, and combat endemic diseases like malaria. African leaders have been enthusiastic supporters of the UN's Millennium Development Goals: to eradicate extreme poverty and hunger; achieve universal primary education; promote gender equality and empower women; reduce child mortality; promote maternal health; combat HIV/AIDS, malaria and other diseases; ensure environmental sustainability; and develop a global partnership in development. African leaders hold out great hope for Africa, but actually achieving these goals in the short term seems an unlikely prospect.

The most serious concern of all is the HIV/AIDS epidemic, which affects sub-Saharan Africa more than any other region of the world and has rolled back decades of development progress. Fighting HIV/AIDS requires massive international funding, creation of prevention and treatment programs, reducing stigma and discrimination, and empowering women in the male-dominated societies with knowledge of how to avoid HIV infection. The costs of medicines to treat it lie far beyond the means of the average African. Some politicians have been in denial, claiming that the AIDS campaign was a Western effort to characterize Africans as promiscuous and Africa as a continent of disease and hopelessness.

Combating AIDS is a difficult concern for a divided Christian community. Many conservative believers identify it with sexual promiscuity, polygamy and homosexual practices. For them it is the judgment of God, which leaves them unwilling even to face the problem. The practice of "safe sex" runs up against the strictures of various Christian bodies against "artificial" birth control. Many Christian politicians see homosexuality as an "evil" needing to be wiped out. Others, however, see the only valid Christian response to be that of unconditionally loving and caring for those infected. That includes providing medical care to the victims, educating people how to avoid infection, and supporting medical researchers working to find a cure.

4. *The African diaspora.* An important but little examined factor is the connection between churches in Africa and the African diaspora (those living outside the continent). Large African congregations exist in European cities and elsewhere that maintain spiritual and organizational ties with sister bodies in the homeland, as the seminal study *Christianity in Africa and the African Diaspora* (2008) excellently demonstrates. Also noteworthy is the role African bishops have played in the contemporary controversies within the Anglican Church. Many North American conservatives have sought and found support among African counterparts in their effort to keep Anglicanism moored to what both groups regard as its historic theological basis.

Conclusion

Africans absorbed the evangelical spirit early in their contact with Christianity. They responded from a charismatic worldview and saw much in common between their world and the soil on which the prophets and Jesus walked. They were fascinated with the stories of the Old Testament, since the individual and family life issues it dealt with were ones familiar to them. As translation brought them the Scriptures, they expressed their particular understanding of what the canon said. In the interaction with the missionaries who had their own ideas about Scripture, Africans created various modes of church polity—so many indeed that numerous groups in the evangelical family do not recognize their common heritage. Yet many Africans were fired with the same zeal to be grounded in the Word of God, the Word that they regarded as a true and reliable guide for daily living. They shared the passion to evangelize, telling others that each person must be born again. They confessed Christ as central in the pilgrimage of life and maintained this confession as the basis for transforming society. It should be no surprise that Christianity has grown and spread so rapidly in Africa, nor that some predict that within a couple of decades Africa will become numerically the most Christian of all the continents.

FURTHER READING

Adogame, Afe, Roswith Gerloff and Klaus Hock, eds. *Christianity in Africa and the African Diaspora: The Appropriation of a Scattered Heritage.* New York: Continuum, 2008.

Elphick, Richard, and Rodney Davenport. *Christianity in South Africa: A Political, Social, and Cultural History.* Berkeley: University of California Press, 1997.

Eshete, Tibebe. *The Evangelical Movement in Ethiopia: Resistance and Resilience.* Waco, TX: Baylor University Press, 2009.

Hanciles, Jehu. *Beyond Christendom: Globalization, African Migration, and the Transformation of the West.* Maryknoll, NY: Orbis, 2008.

Hastings, Adrian. *The Church in Africa, 1450–1950.* New York: Oxford University Press, 1994.

Hofmeyr, J. W., and Gerald J. Pillay, eds. *A History of Christianity in South Africa.* Pretoria: HAUM, 1994.

Ischei, Elizabeth. *A History of Christianity in Africa.* Grand Rapids: Eerdmans, 1995.

Kalu, Ogbu U., ed. *African Christianity: An African Story.* Pretoria: University of Pretoria, Department of Church History, 2005.

Korieh, Chima J., and G. Ugo Nwokeji, eds. *Religion, History, and Politics in Nigeria: Essays in Honor of Ogbu U. Kalu.* Washington, DC: University Press of America, 2005.

Sundkler, Bengt, and Christopher Steed. *A History of the Church in Africa.* Cambridge: Cambridge University Press, 2000.

6

LATIN AMERICA

C. René Padilla

EVANGELICALISM IN LATIN AMERICA has now become a significant topic of both scholarly and popular discussion, thanks to the rapid growth of the movement in recent decades. Estimates of how large a percentage of the population can be labeled *evangélicos* vary widely, depending on how one defines the term. Some use it as a generic label for all kinds of Protestantism or non-Roman Catholic expressions of Christianity. Others restrict it to evangelicalism as defined throughout the present book, including Pentecostalism in the definition. Still others place in the category those Roman Catholics who manifest a warm, personal faith in Jesus Christ. Thus there is a definitional uncertainty that commentators must deal with. Using the definition of evangelicalism that this book has been working with, it seems that there are about 87 million evangelicals (two-thirds of which—58 million—are Pentecostals or neo-Pentecostals) out of a total population of 580 million in Latin America; this works out to Latin American evangelicals constituting fifteen percent of the total population of Latin America.[1]

An equally knotty problem is that of what comprises Latin America. Contemporary geographers divide the Western Hemisphere (or the Americas) into three realms—North America (United States and Canada), Middle America (Mexico, Central America and the Caribbean) and South America.[2] The term *Latin America* itself comes from the two Romance (Latin-based)

---

[1] See M. Hutchinson and J. R. Wolffe, *A Short History of Global Evangelicalism* (Cambridge: Cambridge University Press, 2012), p. 240.

[2] For instance, John Wiley and Sons' widely used textbook *Geography: Realms, Regions, and Concepts*, edited by H. J. de Blij and Peter O. Muller, and currently in a 15th edition.

languages—Spanish and Portuguese—that are spoken by most inhabitants of the latter two realms. At the same, the historical process of European conquest produced extraordinary diversity within the hemisphere. In this chapter we are using the term *Latin America* to include Mexico, Central America and South America.

HISTORICAL BACKGROUND

While the Portuguese engaged in expansion along the African coast during the later fifteenth century, the Spanish reached the Caribbean in 1492 and soon established control over the larger islands. Thus, when Christopher Columbus returned home in 1493 with the news of his "discoveries," the Spanish-born Pope Alexander VI drew a line of demarcation through the Atlantic Ocean, to the west of which was Spain's, to the east, Portugal's. The two powers formalized this division in the Treaty of Tordesillas of 1494. For reasons historians have not clarified, the agreement placed the line farther west. This unwittingly ensured that Portugal would be able to claim Brazil when its seamen first landed there in 1500. In the years that followed, the two Iberian powers rapidly expanded their presence in the Western Hemisphere, establishing mines and plantations and setting up governmental structures. Because the treaty line never was surveyed, the Portuguese pushed far deeper into the interior of South America than they might have otherwise.

Both Spain and Portugal established complex administrative structures in their American empires. As a noteworthy emigration to the colonies occurred, the whites subsequently born there were known as *creoles* (*criollos*). Most of the power continued to be held by whites who came out from Spain and Portugal, and they treated the creoles as social inferiors. Considerable interbreeding occurred between whites and native Americans, universally mislabeled Indians, and that resulted in a large mixed, or *mestizo*, population. This group adopted the language and culture of their overlords, who nevertheless looked down upon them.

Another demographic element was African immigrants. In the Caribbean, the Spanish enslaved the native population, most of whom soon died off, and thus, for labor, turned to slaves imported from Africa. The first African slaves arrived in 1501, and were utilized mainly on the Caribbean plantations and the northern coast of South America. By midcentury the Portuguese in

Brazil were doing likewise, and Angola and Mozambique became major sources of African labor for their mines and plantations. Africans who bred with native Americans were called *zambos* and those who possessed some white ancestry were known as *mulattoes*.

In the American colonies, the key factor was the Roman Catholic Church. In 1493 the papacy granted the Spanish crown a "royal patronage" similar to that which it earlier gave to Portugal in the east (the *padroado* [1454]) and reaffirmed in 1551 as binding in Brazil. Modified and expanded over the next decades, the patronage gave the Spanish dominion over the "Indies," including exclusive authority to convert the indigenous people to Christianity and almost complete control of ecclesiastical affairs. Some seven archbishoprics and numerous bishoprics were established, as well as an array of church courts that had jurisdiction over the clergy and spiritual affairs. Even the Spanish Inquisition was introduced. The main religious orders—Franciscan, Dominican, Capuchin, Augustinian and Jesuit—carried on the work of conversion, instruction in European civilization, and preserving and extending Spanish control to outlying areas. Often accompanied by small groups of soldiers and civilian colonists, these orders established missions, instructed the native peoples in Christianity and developed agriculture, grazing and simple industry. These essentially self-supporting mission communities would become particularly significant in California and the northern Mexican frontier; the sad story of the fate of the protected villages (known as *reductions*) that the Jesuits established in Paraguay and the Parana River basin in the eighteenth century, is the theme of the popular movie *The Mission* (1986).

The native population became a largely servile people through the system of large Spanish land holdings, the *encomienda* system of tenant farming in which peasants worked for the landlords in perpetuity (peonage). These holdings gradually evolved into smaller, self-contained farming communities, the *hacienda*, where conditions were hardly much better. Some church figures, the best known being Bartolomé de las Casas (1474–1566), advocated for the natives against the excesses of Spanish rule. Meanwhile, the church itself became one of the largest landholders in Latin America.

Other European powers, mainly France, Holland and England, encroached upon the Iberian empires in the New World. Commerce and sugar production were the two main attractions. In the early seventeenth century, the Dutch gained temporary control over a large portion of northern Brazil but were ousted by 1654. The Caribbean was the most attractive area, and these three countries seized the smaller islands and parts of the coastal mainland. The English captured Jamaica and the French gained part of the large island of Hispaniola, later known as Haiti. The seemingly endless supply of slaves from Africa provided the labor for the sugar plantations—which in turn created the wealth that would help launch the Industrial Revolution. These European countries also sought to break the mercantilist trading monopoly that Spain had with its colonies.

The American and French Revolutions greatly impacted the Latin Americans. *Creoles* and *mestizos* desired greater participation in government and became increasingly resentful of Spanish economic policy. The successful struggle of the North Americans and French for political freedom, the revolutionary doctrines of liberalism and nationalism that were unleashed during this period, and Spanish inattention to the colonies because of incessant warfare and problems at home were all factors that led to insurrections and the quest for independence. Space limitations prevent a review of the complex story of the wars of independence; it must suffice to point out that a variety of new republics came to populate Spanish America during the nineteenth century, while Spain's last footholds in the Caribbean region, Cuba and Puerto Rico, were lost as a result of the Spanish-American War of 1898. Brazil separated from Portugal in 1822, becoming first an empire under a constitutional "emperor" and then a republic in 1889.

CHALLENGES TO THE ROMAN CATHOLIC RELIGIOUS MONOPOLY

Following independence, Catholicism remained the predominant, and, in most places, the legally established state religion, retaining significant financial support from the government. But secular liberalism, in the form of new ideas from Europe and indigenous anticlericalism, and Protestantism—both as the faith of new immigrants and the product of missionary work from without, especially Britain and North America—threatened Catholic hegemony. Church-state relations varied from country to country—from intimate and friendly ties in some countries, to holding the church at arm's length or demanding full toleration for other faiths in others, and even, in some, calls for the legal separation of church and state. Generalizing on these matters is quite difficult. Attempts by Protestant churches to establish a foothold in Latin America were fiercely resisted and deeply resented. Protestant Bible and missionary societies not only worked among the aboriginal peoples but also among Roman Catholic inhabitants, which led to considerable hard feelings. Allegations about the low morality of the Catholic clergy and the ignorance and superstition of the masses did much to rally support abroad for these missionary enterprises from Protestant countries. The most important denominational missions seeking to operate in the later nineteenth century were the Baptist, Methodist and Presbyterian works from the United States, but many other groups were involved as well, including the evangelical Anglican "South American Missionary Society" founded in England in 1844.

High-church Anglicans, however, sided with the Roman Catholic understanding and regarded Latin America as already "Christianized" and therefore not a potential site for missionary evangelism. As a result, the region was excluded from the agenda at the 1910 World Missionary Conference in Edinburgh. Those evangelicals unhappy with the action held a special mission conference in Panama six years later. The twentieth century saw an explosion of missionary endeavors there, which from the perspective of Roman Catholic leaders was an "invasion of sects" that threatened the (commonly assumed) "religious unity" of the countries of the region.

A growing number of social scientists agree that the growth of evangelicalism in Latin America is an unprecedented phenomenon with social consequences, and as such deserves careful analysis. Certainly, for an increasing number of astute politicians, this growth of evangelicalism constitutes a new popular force that can be used to serve their respective ideologies. Space limitations preclude a discussion of the manifold and sometimes contradictory attempts to explain evangelical expansion. Yet however one seeks to account for this development, the fact remains that Latin American evangelicalism is a growing force. It is changing not only the religious but also the sociopolitical landscape of Latin America.

No explanation of this phenomenon can be taken seriously if it fails to consider the explosive growth occurring within traditionally Roman Catholic societies where the "official" church has been losing—and continues to lose—

not only members but also sociopolitical influence. One can find evidence of this loss almost every day in the news media. Recently, for instance, a heated controversy arose in Peru between the Roman Catholic cardinal and one of President Alan Garcia's secretaries. As a way to reduce the number of unwanted pregnancies among teenage girls, the national health secretary decided to distribute contraceptives free of charge, thus bringing down the cardinal's wrath upon him. A Roman Catholic priest defended the action by retorting to the cardinal that Peru is not a theocracy but a democracy. Also, a member of the national congress took the opportunity to exhort the cardinal to spend his time making sure that the priests under his authority are not involved in sexual immorality, including pedophilia.

This sort of controversy would not have occurred a few decades ago, either in Peru or anywhere else in Latin America. It illustrates the deep crisis that Roman Catholicism is facing today. The church that the Spanish and Portuguese conquerors had brought was for five centuries regarded as unquestioned religious authority; in the past, few people would have ever dared to question the Roman Catholic clergy, and only relatively few would be willing to leave the church. Of course, not all Catholics who have left the Roman Church became evangelical Christians, but a large number of them have.

This chapter examines the main reasons for the present evangelical upsurge, arguing that such growth is the result of how the inherent characteristics of Latin American evangelicalism enable it to fill the gap that Roman Catholicism has left in the lives of people throughout the region. The first part examines the factors contributing to this "religious migration" away from Roman Catholicism in the last few decades. The second part seeks to understand why so many of these who leave opt for evangelical (mainly Pentecostal) Christianity. Finally, the negative aspects of current evangelical growth will be considered.

The Death of Colonial Christendom

At the time of the conquest of America the general assumption in the Iberian Peninsula was that the destinies of Spain and Portugal were inseparable from that of the Roman Catholic Church. Seen from the perspective of the medieval concept of Christendom as defined by Pablo Richard, it was "a specific historical model of insertion of the institutional church into social reality, a model that basically uses the political power (political society) and the hegemonic power (civil society) of the dominant classes."[3] These nations were regarded as God's chosen instruments to accomplish his purpose for the whole world. Accordingly, the conquest of the so-called New World was a "crusade" opening the way for the conversion of the heathen to Christ, a necessary step to fulfill the ideal of establishing a Christian kingdom under the auspices of the Roman Catholic sovereigns and the power of the pope. Consequently, the conquerors engaged in this religious-political project with a spirit that many critics saw as much more in harmony with Islam than Christianity.

The missionary strategy adopted by Catholics during the conquest was consistent with the ideological premises of Christendom, according to which both military conquest and evangelization worked together toward the formation of a Christian society under the tutelage of the church. As John A. Crow put it,

> While other countries were content to establish themselves under Protestant or mixed Catholic and Protestant regimes which would grow toward religious liberalism, the Iberian countries created the Church-State type of authoritarian absolutism in which government and religious doctrine became inseparable. Other countries made of religion a national expression, but Spain and Portugal maintained unbroken belief in the holy internationalism of the Catholic Church.[4]

This "authoritarian absolutism" was the most decisive factor in the history of Latin America, not only in regard to religion, but also to culture, politics, society and economics.

The form of Christianity established in Latin America at the end of the fifteenth century was deeply shaped by the "evangelization" carried out by the conquerors in association with the military. The church was conceived as essentially a top-down, hierarchical and sacramental institution, rather than a community of followers of Jesus Christ from below. Thus, it was crucial to subject all the social structures to the authority of the church, that is, the "Christianizing" of every human institution. Christianity functioned as a political religion used to legitimize the colonial establishment. As a result, what took place was in some ways less evangelization in the sense of

---

[3]Pablo Richard, *La iglesia latino-americana entre el terror y la esperanza* (San José, Costa Rica: Departamento Ecuménico de Investigaciones, 1980), pp. 96-97.
[4]John A. Crow, *The Epic of Latin America* (Berkeley: University of California Press, 1992), p. xvi.

spreading the gospel and more a transplanting of church structures closely associated with the sociopolitical structures. The result was that the main weakness of the colonial ecclesiastical model was its dependence on the secular order and the insufficient attention given to people at the grassroots. Rather than being a liberating community for the common people, the church was linked with the dominant system and often served as an agent of oppression. The assessment of Chilean Catholic theologian Pablo Richard is apt: "The church shaped by colonial Christendom was a church that bore the marks of dependence, slavery, and underdevelopment, and it shares in the responsibility for these three serious flaws in Latin American society."[5]

Given this situation, the attitude of Roman Catholics toward "heterodox" Christians becomes understandable. The defense of doctrinal orthodoxy was not merely a religious but also a social and political duty that could not be neglected without endangering the unity of the various "Christian nations" created by the conquest. To ensure that there was no such neglect, Roman Catholics made use of all and any means, including executions, to exclude Protestantism and eliminate heterodoxy. To be sure, some of the most moving pages in the history of contemporary Christianity are those related to the witness borne by Catholic martyrs such as Archbishop Oscar Romero of El Salvador. Still, the history of Christian martyrdom in Latin America will be incomplete if it does not include the Protestant martyrs who died at the hands of Roman Catholic zealots.

During the colonial times, the Roman Catholic Church also provided the justification for the authoritarian structures that subjected the population to powerful political elites. In the eighteenth century, as the winds of modernity began to blow, Latin American Christendom entered a period of crisis as a result of the revolutions and independence movements that detached the colonies from the Spanish and Portuguese crowns. With political freedom, the crisis was not resolved but only deepened. During the twentieth century, in the context of growing Latin American nationalism and economic development, the Roman Catholic Church redefined its relationship to the state in order to establish a "new Christendom," one more oriented to populist movements than to sociopolitical power structures.

---

[5]Pablo Richard, *Death of Christendoms, Birth of the Church: Historical Analysis and Theological Interpretation of the Church in Latin America* (Maryknoll, NY: Orbis, 1987), p. 27.

During the period from around 1930 to 1960, this attempt resulted in the strengthening of the presence and power of the church in civil society. It in turn provoked a new crisis: a clash between two models of Christendom, the colonial and the new populism.[6] By 1960, the Roman Catholic Church faced two alternatives: a revised model of Christendom, now beholden to the service of the capitalist economic system, or the dissolution of the old system in order to make way for a church that has broken from Christendom altogether. The contradiction between Christendom and church became so evident during the 1960s and 1970s that observers concluded that one would be able to survive only if the other disappeared.

Closely related to the crisis of Christendom was the impact of secularization on religious adherence. The changes that occurred in the last half of the twentieth century, particularly modern scientific and technological developments, as well as the mass media, have profoundly impacted personal and social life in Latin America. The Dutch theologian Arend T. van Leeuwen has proposed that the contemporary technological revolution is achieving what Christian missions were unable to: the unification of the world. This development started in the West and in modern times expanded to "all nations." It was one of the factors in the opening up of traditional societies to modern influences. The result has been the integration of these societies into a global village. For the first time in human history, declared van Leeuwen, *ontocratic* societies—ones that are "religious, closed, and traditional," in which it was very difficult for the values of other cultures and even the gospel to enter—were being replaced by *technocratic* societies, characterized by openness and change.[7]

Although his analysis actually was based on a study of the Asian situation, van Leeuwen's categories apply quite well to the "religious, closed, and traditional" societies of Latin America that have been shaped by Roman Catholicism since the colonial era. Today, even more than when van Leeuwen wrote these words, it is evident that Latin Americans have entered a period of history dominated by technocracy, the mass media and an openness to change in every dimension of life.

---

[6]Ibid., pp. 73-78.
[7]Arend T. van Leeuwen, *Christianity in World History: The Meaning of the Faith in East and West* (London: Edinburgh House Press, 1964), pp. 139-42.

It is not surprising that the transition to the technocratic period should have profound religious repercussions. In the West, the Industrial Revolution slowly displaced Christianity from its position of social dominance and put science and technology in its stead. This same process of secularization is presently taking place in Latin America, but with one great difference: secularization does not necessarily lead to atheism but it has led to a noticeable withdrawal of the faithful from the Roman Catholic Church, which is identified with the traditional authoritarian society of the past. This withdrawal cleared the way for a search for other religious alternatives that better respond to felt needs and are more consonant with the spirit of the day. It provides fertile soil for all kinds of religious movements, because fewer and fewer Latin Americans think that the religion inherited from their ancestors holds the title deed to their conscience. Latin America has become a shopping mall of religious options! As Peter Berger observed, secularization brings about a demonopolization of religious traditions and leads to pluralism. This leads in turn to a "market situation" in which "the religious tradition, which previously could be authoritatively imposed, now has to be *marketed*."[8] Christianity has no future in Latin America if Christians do not take seriously this aspect of today's religious context. The end of the Constantinian era, marked by "the death of Christendoms," is the starting point for understanding the growth of evangelicalism in Latin America and the role of evangelical churches at the beginning of the third millennium.

Is Latin America Turning Protestant?

This question posed by North American David Stoll in 1990[9] would have made no sense at all in 1900. By midcentury, however, things were changing, as the Argentinean Methodist scholar José Míguez Bonino points out:

> Pentecostalism multiplies, diversifies, and expands, and from the 1950s on it becomes the popular face of Protestant Latin America. Fourteen thousand five hundred in 1938, 1 million in 1950, 37 million in 1980.[10]

---

[8]Peter L. Berger, *The Social Reality of Religion* (Harmondsworth, UK: Penguin, 1973), pp. 139, 142.
[9]David Stoll, *Is Latin America Turning Protestant? The Politics of Evangelical Growth* (Berkeley: University of California Press, 1990).
[10]José Míguez Bonino, *Faces of Latin American Protestantism* (Grand Rapids: Eerdmans 1997), pp. 54-55.

As has been noted, scholars have recently (2012) estimated the number of Latin American Pentecostals/neo-Pentecostals at 58 million.

Protestant Christianity first arrived on the shores of South America in the sixteenth century. However, the two or three Protestant colonies established in Brazil and Venezuela during that century were isolated, ephemeral enterprises and in no way challenged the reality that the overwhelmingly predominant expression of Christianity in this part of the world was Roman Catholicism. From the Christendom perspective, the presence of the Roman Catholic Church in Latin America meant the whole continent was considered evangelized. As noted earlier, the 1910 missionary conference in Edinburgh did not invite the participation of any delegates from Latin America, and no reference to this region as "missionary territory" was allowed to appear in its official documents.

Just in the last few years was it possible for people to conceive of areas in the region as both Latin American and Protestant. In fact, until only recently in most countries no citizen could even be elected to public office unless he or she was a Roman Catholic. National identity was linked with Roman Catholic identity. On the other hand, by the late twentieth century the proportion of Protestant evangelicals had grown so rapidly that more and more of them were active in public life.

Several writers have explained this change from a sociological perspective. Emilio Willems proposed in *Followers of the New Faith* (1967) that Pentecostalism in Brazil and Chile expanded because it enabled its converts to cope with the problems of modernity that they faced as they migrated from the countryside to the cities. Christian Lalive d'Epinay, who studied Chilean Pentecostals in the 1960s, advanced the thesis in his classic *Haven of the Masses* (1969) that their numerical growth resulted from the effort to recreate in urban situations traditional rural society. They cast the pastor in the authoritarian role that the *patrón* (estate owner) played in the *hacienda*, the aforementioned large estates that the Spanish authorities originally granted to the military conquerors. Brazilian sociologist Paul Freston, perhaps the most prolific and insightful scholar of Pentecostalism in contemporary Latin America, reinforces this point in various works.[11]

---

[11]For a summary of Freston's take on the subject, see Paul Freston, "Contours of Latin American Pentecostalism," in *Christianity Reborn: The Global Expansion of Evangelicalism in the Twentieth*

Without minimizing the importance of sociological explanations, much more attention needs to be given to basic theological developments. Particularly important are the ecclesiological emphases that differentiate the Roman Catholic Church from the many and widely diverse non-Catholic churches. Understanding these differences is crucial for understanding the process of how religious barriers are breaking down and why people are attracted to alternate faiths.

These theological differences are rooted in history, and they must be understood in their historical context. The situation is analogous to the sixteenth-century Reformation in Europe. True, one requires a proper understanding of the socioeconomic and political circumstances in which the Reformation took place. On the other hand, it would be a gross oversimplification to claim that these circumstances are by themselves sufficient to explain the amazing changes that the Reformation brought about, not only in the church but also in society at large. It is essential to show how the Reformation was rooted in theological convictions and insights closely related to the rediscovery of the gospel as God's power for transforming human life. Among these rediscovered convictions was the notion of the nature of the church as a faith community and not just an institution.

As in the case of the sixteenth-century Reformation, Protestant growth in Latin America today is a concrete result of convictions and insights pointing to spiritual realities that escape the analysis of the social sciences. Three such convictions flowing out of the larger question of ecclesiology will be considered: the nature of the church, the indigenous character of the church and the priesthood of all believers.

THE NATURE OF THE CHURCH

One result of the way the Roman Catholic Church was planted in Latin America was the assumption that the region was undoubtedly a Christian continent. Consequently, any evangelistic effort carried out by Protestant churches would be considered proselytism—that is, the coercive attempt to

---

Century, ed. Donald M. Lewis (Grand Rapids: Eerdmans, 2004), pp. 221-72. Important books by Freston in English include *Evangelicals and Politics in Asia, Africa, and Latin America* (Cambridge: Cambridge University Press, 2001) and *Evangelical Christianity and Democracy in Latin America* (Oxford: Oxford University Press, 2008).

convert people to a different religion than what they currently practiced. This view, which has been taken for granted since colonial times, was the premise behind John Paul II's remarks in his opening address to the Fourth Latin American Bishops Conference held in Santo Domingo in October 1992. The pope challenged the bishops "to feed the flock" entrusted to them and to "defend it from rapacious wolves . . . the sects and 'pseudospiritual' movements . . . whose aggressiveness and expansion must be faced" as a threat to the cultural unity derived from the Roman Catholic faith in Latin America. He maintained that

> the gift of [Roman] Catholic faith has reached very deeply into its peoples, shaping the Christian soul of the continent during these five hundred years and inspiring many of its institutions. The Church in Latin America has indeed been able to make its way into the culture of the people and has known how to place the gospel message at the basis of its thinking, its fundamental principles of life, its criteria for judgment, and its norms for activity.[12]

Protestant ecclesiology sharply contrasts with the idea that Latin America is rooted in a hegemonic Roman Catholic culture. In a paper presented at the Second Consultation of the evangelical-oriented Latin American Theological Fraternity in Lima in 1972, Samuel Escobar argued that a common feature of Latin American Protestantism is its "Anabaptist" *talante* or style of doing things.[13] Besieged by Roman Catholic Constantinianism, the majority of evangelical churches, quite early in their history in this region, developed a great resemblance to those groups that in the sixteenth century participated in the so-called Radical Reformation in Europe. Instead of a politicized Christendom, they emphasized the spiritual nature of the kingdom of God. Rejecting an established "official church," they conceived of the church as an alternative community and advocated the absolute separation of church and state. Over against a religion of liturgical forms and rites, they underlined the importance of personal conversion and the experience of the Holy Spirit.[14]

[12]John Paul II, "Opening Address of the Holy Father," in *Santo Domingo and Beyond: Documents & Commentaries from the Historic Meeting of the Latin American Bishops Conference*, ed. Alfred T. Hennelly (Maryknoll, NY: Orbis, 1993), pp. 41-60.
[13]J. Samuel Escobar, "El reino de Dios, la escatología y la ética social y política en américa latina," in *El Reino de Dios y América Latina*, ed. C. René Padilla (El Paso, TX: Casa Bautista de Publicaciones, 1975), p. 131.
[14]Ibid., pp. 127-56.

No one who has at least a superficial understanding of the Latin American religious scene can minimize the difference that this Anabaptist *talante* has made for evangelical Protestant church growth. Shortly before the start of the evangelical explosion, William Stanley Rycroft, a respected Presbyterian missionary to Peru, wrote that

> Latin America needs all that Evangelical Christianity means and stands for: personal commitment to the Living God; strength of character and moral integrity in business, professional, social, and political relationships; the rehabilitation of multitudes of downtrodden men and women through the application of Christ's teachings, the principles of freedom and democracy, and the dedication of individuals and groups to a spiritual ideal in human life.[15]

One may not agree with Rycroft in placing "the principles of freedom and democracy" alongside "personal commitment to the Living God," and may even argue that his approach reflects a North American liberal Protestant cultural background. The fact remains, however, that what he emphasizes regarding human dignity and personal responsibility before God have been essential features of evangelical Christianity in Latin America from its very beginning. Evangelicals did not believe that Christianity could be established in a given city or in the countryside unless there was a *community of believers* personally committed to Jesus Christ and willing to suffer for his name's sake. That being the case, they made every possible effort to spread the good news, win people to Christ and encourage them to become a part of an evangelical church. This they did at the risk of their lives and even though they were criticized as intruders, invaders and proselytizers. One might suggest that there are parallels between these modern-day evangelical missionaries and the pre-Constantinian church, as church historian Justo González well put it:

> The largest part of the expansion of Christianity in the centuries that preceded Constantine took place not as a result of the work of people exclusively dedicated to that task but thanks to the constant testimony of hundreds and thousands of merchants, slaves, and Christians condemned to exile who went on witnessing to Jesus Christ wherever life took them, and in that way

---

[15]W. Stanley Rycroft, *On This Foundation: The Evangelical Witness in Latin America* (New York: Friendship Press, 1942), p. vii.

created new communities in places where the "professional" missionaries had not arrived as yet.[16]

Some Roman Catholic observers have acknowledged that one of the main factors explaining Protestant growth is the emphasis among evangelical Christians on personal conversion and active participation in the life of the church. José Pérez Guadalupe, for instance, rejects several of the usual answers given to the question "Why do Catholics leave [their church]?" as lacking in self-criticism. He insists that the basic reason why so many Roman Catholics are becoming Protestant is "a deep and intense religious experience that they never had in 'their' institutionalized Catholic Church." If one takes Pérez's argument seriously, it must be concluded that social and cultural changes are only the context—not the reason—for the remarkable religious transformation that the continent is presently undergoing. The real reason for the significant defections from the Roman Catholic Church is a religious experience that quite often is undeniably an encounter with Jesus Christ. Such an experience, according to this author, involves both an *internal process*, which is personal ("I have met God"), communal ("God is in this group") and doctrinal ("this group has God's revealed truth"), as well as an accompanying *external process*. The latter is also personal (a moral transformation of life), communal (a new sense of belonging to a living community) and doctrinal (a concern to live out the faith one believes in). A similar kind of conversion experience, says Pérez, is present in the Pentecostal-like "apostolic movements" within the Roman Catholic Church. Unfortunately, these are limited to "a small religious elite," inadequate in their follow-up and unrealistic regarding the theological knowledge their members are expected to possess.[17]

Some years earlier, Juan Luis Segundo claimed that, in view of the changes taking place in Latin America as a result of urbanization, modernization and secularization, the church can no longer depend on the various secular regimes to help it do its job as in the past. Nor can the church use violent and inhumane means to ensure the existence of a high percentage of members among the general population. The "machine to make Chris-

---

[16]Justo L. González, *Historia de las misiones* (Buenos Aires: Editorial la Aurora, 1970), p. 59.
[17]José Luis Pérez Guadalupe, *Por qué se van los católicos: El problema de la "migración religiosa" de los católicos a las llamadas "sectas"* (Lima: Conferencia Episcopal Peruana, Colección de Teología Pastoral, 1992), pp. 27-43.

tians"—Christendom—has broken down. The time is over when the church could hope to accomplish its noble, God-given mission through any means possible, including the Inquisition and Crusades. Speaking frankly, Segundo pointed out that the (absolute) end justifies (all) means, an idea attributed to Marxist morality, was the normal mode of conduct of the church and of individual Christians whenever they acted for the institution's benefit or defense. If the church today is to fulfill its mission in an open society whose population maintains only a vague attachment to Christianity, a new pastoral approach is required—one that nurtures freedom instead of exerting pressure, fashions a committed minority faithful to the gospel instead of protecting the "artificial consumerist majorities," and relies on the power of the gospel instead of alliances with the social system.[18]

Both Pérez and Segundo are Roman Catholics, but their analysis coincides with that of the respected evangelical José Míguez Bonino. In *Toward a Christian Political Ethics* (1983), he argued that the Protestant emphasis on personal conversion—"in keeping with the theology and practice of the Anglo-American 'spiritual awakenings'"—is very much in line with the transition that has taken place in Latin America since the end of the nineteenth century. The features of this transition are plainly reflected in the religious experience of Protestant converts.

One is *individualism*: people are invited to make a personal decision, even though that may imply breaking from friends and family. They are challenged to take in hand their own destiny. "Clearly we find ourselves here in the world of the 'free individual' of modern society." Another is *subjectivity*. In traditional Roman Catholicism, "religious categories are projected on a supernatural screen," and the supernatural may be affected—"either more or less magically as the case may be"—by religious actions or observances that are designed for it. Although the supernatural does not disappear in Protestantism, "its operation is perceived and portrayed . . . on the screen of subjectivity. . . . The cosmic struggle has been transported to the sphere of personal consciousness, but within the religious sphere." Finally, *the moral life*, including "the virtues of early capitalism—industry, honesty, moderation, frugality," come to the fore.[19]

---

[18]Juan Luis Segundo, *Liberación de la teología* (Buenos Aires: Carlos Lohlé, 1975), pp. 233-66.

[19]José Míguez Bonino, *Toward a Christian Political Ethics* (Minneapolis: Fortress, 1983), pp. 60-61.

To conclude, the concept of the church as a community of people who have voluntarily chosen to be Christians and to identify themselves with that community is gaining influence vis-à-vis that of the church as an institution heavily dependent upon the secular powers and resting on the assumption that Roman Catholic identity is one's cultural identity. The evangelical Protestant movement has grown as a committed minority, and, in the new post-Christendom era, is slowly occupying space that the medieval church imported from the Iberian Peninsula has for all practical purposes vacated. If Protestant growth demonstrates anything, it is that its ecclesiology, rooted in New Testament teaching, is more appropriate to an open, pluralist society than traditional Roman Catholic ecclesiology, shaped by Constantinianism. For the large majority of evangelicals, the proclamation of the gospel, personal commitment to Christ and active participation in Christian communion are essential elements of church membership. This contrasts with the older Catholic view that all of society has been incorporated into the church (and thus into Jesus Christ), and salvation is mediated through the church. The Constantinian ecclesiology is rapidly fading, along with the church-centered view of society. It is the view of many Latin American evangelicals that the day for the "Anabaptist" understanding of ecclesiology has arrived.

The Indigenous Nature of the Church

Closely associated with the "Anabaptist" approach to church membership is another distinctive of the evangelical movement: its indigenous nature. Evangelical churches, with very few exceptions, are deeply rooted in the Latin American context. Their indigenous character can be seen in their theology, leadership, liturgy and financial support.

Theology. In theological circles in Europe and North America it is usually (and wrongly) assumed that the only contemporary theology worth reading is produced in the West. Hardly any institutions of theological education in these areas of the world include courses on theology from the Two-Thirds World. Few publishing companies in the West are interested in producing books by non-Western authors. As a result, in the theological field, as in other realms of learning, people in the West are missing the opportunities presented by crosscultural interaction. As Lamin Sanneh put it,

We should grasp the ethical challenge implied in cross-cultural relationships and responsibility, approach human difference and diversity as a resource for truth-seeking, and accept the possibility of mutual correction and instruction as profoundly consistent with the enterprise of being human.[20]

Christians in the West are generally insufficiently aware of the works of theologians from Asia, Africa and Latin America, and the experience of interacting with these would greatly contribute to "building up the body of Christ, until all of us come to the unity of the faith and of the knowledge of the Son of God, to maturity, to the measure of the full stature of Christ" (Eph 4:12-13 NRSV).

A detailed survey of the theological works produced by Latin American evangelicals in recent years would exceed the limits of this chapter, but a few items deserve mention. What I affirmed in the first edition of *Mission Between the Times* (1985), that "the church in Latin America is a church without a theology," was even then a rhetorical exaggeration and soon proven to be inaccurate.[21] Already signs of change were evident, thanks to the contributions by members of the Latin American Theological Fraternity, founded in 1970. In 2010 Daniel Salinas competently analyzed the early stages of this development, and I filled in additional details in a second edition of *Mission Between the Times*, where I also showed the integral character of the Christian mission for Latin American theology.[22]

The period between the early 1970s and the late 1980s was the golden age of liberation theology in Latin America. Roman Catholic theologians Gustavo Gutiérrez, Juan Luis Segundo, Hugo Assmann, José Comblin, Leonardo Boff and many others distinguished themselves as theologians who sought to draw out the liberating implications of the gospel in a context of oppression. They often utilized Marxist categories to explain their ideas. Many of their works were published in English by Orbis Books of Maryknoll, New York, as well as other firms, thereby enabling their theology to make a significant impact far beyond Latin America. For a time, when people all over

---

[20]Lamin Sanneh, *Encountering the West: Christianity and the Global Cultural Crisis* (Maryknoll, NY: Orbis, 1993), p. 235.

[21]C. René Padilla, *Mission Between the Times: Essays on the Kingdom* (Grand Rapids: Eerdmans, 1985), p. 95.

[22]Daniel Salinas, *Latin American Evangelical Theology in the 1970s: The Golden Decade* (Leiden: Brill, 2009); Padilla, *Mission Between the Times*, 2nd ed. (Cumbria, UK: Langham Monographs, 2010).

the world spoke about liberation theology, they meant the Latin American variety of the term, although it soon became contextualized in other situations. Even Latin American evangelicals found liberation concepts attractive, to the dismay of their North American counterparts who feared the theology would undermine capitalism. Some said it was communist inspired.

The day of liberation theology, it would seem, is practically over. Several measures taken by the Congregation for the Doctrine of the Faith under Popes John Paul II and Benedict XVI questioning liberationist expressions, combined with open persecution by dictatorial governments and the fall of sympathetic socialist regimes in Europe in 1989, brought to an end what may well have been the most important theological movement in the history of the Roman Catholic Church in Latin America. This loss was definitely a strike against the indigenous character of the church in this region.

Leadership. Edward Cleary, a North American Catholic scholar with many years of experience in Latin America, concluded from his study of Pentecostalism that "on-the-job training produces pastors who live within the social sphere of their congregations, in contrast to the isolated training and unmarried lives of Catholic clergy. The result has been until recently a very large body of clergy, relatively close to the culture of the people served."[23] Beyond doubt, this "incarnational" approach to pastoral work is one of the most important keys to understanding the extraordinary growth among the Pentecostal variety of Protestantism in Latin America.

It is not uncommon to find that the pastors who are providing leadership to Pentecostal churches in the poorest areas of the cities are unpaid workers who live among the people and manage to support themselves by holding secular jobs—bivocational pastors, so to speak. The liberation theologians adopted the slogan "preferential option for the poor," while in fact these theologians were usually well-educated, middle-class people. Most Pentecostal pastors, however, do not *opt* for the poor: they *are* the poor, and they live among the poor. In general terms, Pentecostalism is a grassroots movement led by indigenous pastors whose main qualification may only be a high sense of God's call to service.

---

[23]Edward L. Cleary, "Latin American Pentecostalism," in *The Globalization of Pentecostalism: A Religion Made to Travel,* ed. Murray W. Dempster, Byron D. Klaus and Douglas Petersen (Oxford: Regnum, 1999), p. 139.

Why do more people seem to be called to the Protestant ministry than Catholic priestly vocations? Much of it has to do with training. Pentecostal preachers, for example, receive a simple education. They learn exactly what they will need in their ministry and nothing more. Their training is neither critical nor philosophical, and it is practical rather than intellectual. Such "training" has obvious shortcomings and runs the danger of reinforcing the anti-intellectualism often characteristic of popular religious movements, including evangelicalism. But on the plus side, Pentecostal churches, even those of foreign origin, are largely pastored by people who have solid local roots.

The contrast with the Roman Catholic Church can hardly be exaggerated. During the colonial period not much was done to develop an indigenous clergy, and the same was true in postcolonial times. It is so much the case that even today, after five hundred years of Roman Catholic presence, many foreign Catholic missionaries (mainly from the United States and Europe) are still necessary. Some have argued that this problem is due, in part, to the class discrimination that affects the selection of candidates for the Catholic clergy. José Comblin describes this discrimination:

> From the time of Constantine . . . the dominant social class has also provided the dominant class within the Church. A good indication of this is that the *Ratio Studiorum* [Study Guidelines] require that priests be trained within Western molds, and in accordance with upper-class standards. No one can become a priest without belonging culturally to the middle class. The poor occupy a subordinate position. They have been made to be receptors, not creators—molded by the Church, without being able to mold it.[24]

Liturgy. Puerto Rican Orlando Costas, an early observer of Pentecostalism in Latin America, described the typical worship service as "spontaneous, creative, and intensively participatory." He quoted Manoel de Melo, leader of the Pentecostal denomination Brazil for Christ, who said, "In the Pentecostal worship service people participate and express their agreements or disagreements through words and actions, giving glory to God. Furthermore, any lay person may preach the Word if he or she is trained to do

---

[24]José Comblin, "Brazil: Base Communities in the Northeast," in *New Face of the Church in Latin America: Between Tradition and Change,* ed. Guillermo Cook (Maryknoll, NY: Orbis, 1994), p. 223.

it."[25] For Costas, this worship service reflects an existential theology, one that emerged from a concrete historical situation and is articulated in indigenous cultural categories.

Costas contrasted the Pentecostal worship service with what he called the *repetitive worship service* characteristic of ethnic churches and those resulting from the work of foreign (mainly North American) missionaries. In subsequent years, however, the liturgy in many of those churches has changed to be much more spontaneous, creative and participatory, to such an extent that little difference exists between them and self-identified Pentecostal groups. Costas sees these as representing a psychosocial liberating experience—a genuine organizational and indigenous liturgical creation.[26]

On the basis of his deep knowledge of Pentecostal churches in Brazil and other Latin American countries, José Comblin compared the liturgy in these churches with that of his own Roman Catholic Church:

> Pentecostal religiosity is fairly simple, but nonetheless decisive. Their services are essentially expressions of praise and thanksgiving to God, in the Spirit and accompanied by manifestations of joy. These evidences of joyfulness and praise seem to compensate for the sadness of lives that are full of trials and tribulations. Some Catholics complain that after going through an entire week of tragedy, they have to sit and listen to a chorus of sad tales at mass on Sunday.[27]

Financial support. A common accusation leveled against evangelicals in Latin America is that they are heavily dependent on outside finances, whether from US supporting churches or CIA-funded front groups to counteract liberation-theology Marxism and keep the poor under oppression. This is not the place to discuss the weaknesses of such charges. Suffice it to say, the evidence does not support what essentially is an ideologically based accusation.

Informed Catholic observers, such as Edward Cleary, reject this charge made against Pentecostal churches:

> Latin American Pentecostals thrive in large part from their own resources. . . .
> The fundamental source of financial support for Pentecostal churches in Latin

---

[25]Orlando Costas, *The Church and Its Mission: A Shattering Critique from the Third World* (Wheaton, IL: Tyndale House, 1974), pp. 50-51.
[26]Ibid., p. 60.
[27]Comblin, "Brazil: Base Communities in the Northeast," p. 219.

America is the generosity of individual members. Church attendees give frequently, and they give from their substance, not their surplus. Contributing ten per cent of income is not uncommon, and is held up frequently as a goal.[28]

José Comblin completely agrees. Referring to the main Pentecostal denominations in Brazil, he writes, "All of these churches are led by Brazilians. They fit right into the cultural context of Brazil and even more so of the northeast. Not dependent upon foreign funding, they operate with the relatively high contributions they solicit from their members."[29] What Comblin states about Pentecostalism in Brazil can also be said about Protestantism in general all over Latin America: it operates on the basis of relatively high contributions by church members. No comment is needed as to the importance this factor has in relation to the indigenous nature of the church.

In contrast, in many countries the Roman Catholic Church continues to be heavily subsidized by the state. This is the case, for instance, in Argentina, where a 2010 document published by the School of Social Sciences of the University of Buenos Aires revealed that the annual subsidy the state provided to the Roman Catholic Church amounted to 625 million US dollars. Article 2 of the National Constitution states that Catholicism is the official religion of Argentina. Accordingly, the cardinal, archbishops, bishops and priests are supported with public funds, and Roman Catholic schools and universities receive subsidies. Roman Catholic seminarians receive government scholarships, and all Roman Catholic landed properties are tax exempt. And this is the homeland of Cardinal Jorge Bergoglio, who was elected as Pope Francis I in March 2013 and is seeking to bring about genuine change in the Church.

Article 14 of the Argentinean Constitution states there is religious freedom. This does not imply, however, that there are equal rights for all religious confessions: the Roman Catholic Church is regarded as a public institution and the only church. All other religious communities have the same legal standing as any nonreligious foundation or association in civil society, including a requirement that they be officially registered. The discriminatory nature of the law rooted in the obsolete concept of Christendom is quite obvious. Its most negative effect is the gap it creates between the

---

[28]Cleary, "Latin American Pentecostalism," p. 137.
[29]Comblin, "Brazil: Base Communities in the Northeast," p. 217.

powerful Church and those people searching for spiritual reality, especially at the grassroots level.

The Protestant evangelical churches that are growing most rapidly are precisely those characterized by indigenous theology, leadership, liturgy and finances. Many thousands of people leave the "official" Church because they feel attracted to faith communities that not only preach the gospel but also enable their followers to live the Christian life deeply rooted in their socio-economic and cultural context.

THE PRIESTHOOD OF ALL BELIEVERS

A third conviction flowing from the question of ecclesiology (the doctrine of the church) along with views regarding the nature and indigenous character of the church is the priesthood of all believers. This was one of the pillars of the sixteenth-century Protestant Reformation and is essential for understanding the development of non-Catholic churches in Latin America.

Beginning with the Second General Conference of Latin American Bishops (CELAM II) held in Medellín, Colombia, in 1968, the Roman Catholic hierarchy began taking steps to implement the *aggiornamento* (Italian for "updating") of the Church in their region. Their intention was to draw out the implications of Vatican II—the historic ecumenical council of the Roman Catholic church held between 1962 and 1965—for their own ministry at a time when it was patently evident that the poor—the majority of the population—were becoming increasingly alienated from their religious leaders. At CELAM II the "official" doctrine that legitimized an oppressive socioeconomic and political system inherited from colonial days was replaced, at least in theory, by a more prophetic teaching that took into account the plight of the masses. From then on, the church's "preferential option for the poor" became a *slogan* expressing a "progressive" view of the pastoral approach to be adopted. This would be quite a departure from the customary practice of giving preference to the rich and powerful.

Of particular importance was the positive appraisal the bishops gave to the so-called *comunidades eclesiales de base* (Base Ecclesial Communities). A major grassroots church reform effort, this movement occurred primarily in Brazil and attracted considerable attention abroad. An especially useful study is the one by Guillermo Cook, *The Expectation of the Poor* (1985). He described five attitudes that he found in the base communities: the centrality of the gospel, the option for the poor, liberation and conscientization (a peculiarly Brazilian concept that means the development of a critical awareness of one's social, economic and political situation through dialogue, which then seeks to identify sources of power and oppression), a missionary approach to changing ecclesiastical structures, and respect for others.[30] These communities originated in the 1950s, in part as a response to the challenge of Protestant growth to Roman Catholicism, and by the late 1960s they had become a sign of hope for the poor, of renewal for the church, and of radical change for society.

The next bishops' conference, CELAM III in Puebla, Mexico, in 1979, confirmed the preferential option for the poor, and in line with that option, described the base communities as "one of the causes of joy and hope in the Church" because "they have become centers of evangelization and moving forces for liberation and development," and because they "create more personal interrelations, acceptance of God's Word, reexamination of one's life, and reflection on reality in light of the Gospel."[31]

Controversies within the Roman Catholic Church during these years revealed the difficulty inherent in opting for the poor and simultaneously maintaining the traditional forms of control. At Puebla in 1979 the bishops warned that the grassroots communities might develop outside of episcopal control and become "sectarian." As the movement spread, the identity crisis grew more serious. In the late 1970s many hoped that through the base communities the whole church would be renewed in such a way that in it "the poor would not be the 'object' of the Church's preferential love, but the *evangelizing subject that builds up the Church.*"[32] During the following decade, however, this hope was thoroughly frustrated. Critics argued that the Vatican turned against the base communities in favor of the hierarchical-institutional church that was attempting to maintain its religious monopoly in Latin American society.

At the root of the problem were radically different ecclesiologies. In the base communities men and women from the margins of society were dis-

[30]Guillermo Cook, *The Expectation of the Poor: Latin American Basic Ecclesial Communities in Protestant Perspective* (Maryknoll, NY: Orbis, 1985), p. 131.

[31]John Eagleson and Philip Scharper, eds., *Puebla and Beyond: Documentation and Commentary* (Maryknoll, NY: Orbis, 1979), pp. 135-36, 211.

[32]Richard, *La iglesia latino-americana*, p. 71.

covering their own self-worth and taking to heart a view propounded by liberation theologians. In line with the ecclesiology of the Second Vatican Council they saw the church as the *community of the people of God* rather than as solely a hierarchical power structure. Accordingly, if the poor were going to participate in the decision-making processes that affected the life and mission of the church, the pyramidal church structure and the monopoly on the production and distribution of spiritual goods by the clergy had to be changed. Leonardo Boff, one of the most prolific liberation theologians, described the phenomenon as a "rebirth of the Church," an "ecclesiogenesis." It would not be an expansion of the existing institutional church but "the emergence of a new way of being the Church, based on the axle of the Word and the lay person."[33] He and many other like-minded theologians thought that the time had come for a new reformation whose consequences would be felt not only in the religious but also in the socioeconomic and political realms. They would have agreed with Guillermo Cook in describing these communities as "'schools for life' where the disenfranchised are learning to tackle problems through democratic community action" and perhaps the only hope for "radical social change and an effective evangelization of the masses."[34] What they failed to consider was how far those who identified the church with the ecclesiastical institution under the power structure of the Vatican would be willing to go to destroy the base community movement, regarded by them as an open revolt against the institutional Roman Catholic Church.

The Catholic Church's endeavor to discipline adherents of liberation theology and suppress the base communities is a long and very controversial chapter in Latin American ecclesiastical history. The Vatican's silencing of Leonardo Boff meant the preferential option for the poor concept would have to be shelved. The reaffirmation of clerical prerogatives and privileges killed any hope of introducing the priesthood of all believers into the church. Despite all the rhetoric of Vatican II regarding the place of the laity in the church, Rome was not about to restructure itself so as to enable all its members to exercise their ministries and have a share in the authority of the

---

[33]Leonardo Boff, *Eclesiogénese: Las comunidades de base reinventan la Iglesia* (Santander: Editorial Sal Terrae, 1984), p. 10.
[34]Cook, *The Expectation of the Poor,* pp. 41-42.

church. Boff had criticized the "essentially clerical" ecclesiology, according to which "without the clergy, ordained by the sacrament of ordination nothing decisive could take place in the community."[35] He offered a radically different ecclesiology, one founded on the assumption that the entire community is ministerial, not only a few of its members. Had he been successful, the Catholic Church would have been transformed from a power structure centered in Rome into a network of local communities centered in and committed to Jesus Christ. That would have been a veritable Copernican revolution in the church.

This background helps us to understand and better appreciate the ecclesiological significance of evangelical Protestant growth in Latin America. In the religious sphere, a substantial grassroots protest has been raised against the authoritarianism and clericalism of the Roman Catholic Church; positively put, this is a practical outworking of the priesthood of all believers. The Protestant/Anabaptist view of the church as the community of the people of God implies that every local church is a center for the spread of the gospel, and every member is expected to be an evangelist. Both the base communities and Pentecostalism rejected the authoritarian absolutism of the Roman Catholic Church. They are in general terms popular expressions of a search for freedom from religious structures that are closely related to the economically and politically powerful elite who have dominated these countries since colonial times.

The Vatican, in association with the conservative Roman Catholic clergy in the region, succeeded in stopping the advance of the base ecclesial communities but not in preventing the continued breakdown of Catholicism's religious monopoly in Latin America. This collapse was the result of a complex combination of factors, including the changes in society resulting from the erosion of authoritarian absolutism. Sadly, the official Church failed to see the great potential of the base communities for the evangelization of the continent and the transformation of the socioeconomic and political structures. By neutralizing them, it left the field open for the growth of churches with no links with Rome. It should not be surprising that the evangelical churches—shaped by their particular view of the nature of the

---

[35]Leonardo Boff, *Igreja: Carisma e poder: Ensaios de eclesiología militante* (Petropolis, Brazil: Vozes, 1981), p. 17.

church, by their indigenous character and by the priesthood of all believers—
have grown as they have.

PROBLEMS RELATED TO PROTESTANT GROWTH

The Protestant Reformation in sixteenth-century Europe had not only theological, but also socioeconomic and political ramifications, so it should not
be surprising if this is also the case in Latin America today. The ecclesiology
that views the church as a community of committed followers of Jesus Christ,
fosters an indigenous character and upholds the priesthood of all believers
is very likely to make a public impact on a continent where for centuries
"Christendom" utilized a version of Christianity to legitimize injustice and
the oppression of the poor.

In the past, Latin American evangelicals, like sixteenth-century Anabaptists, have generally seen themselves as a minority through which God is
going to fulfill his saving purpose at the end of history. This view provided
the incentive for sacrificial engagement in church activities and for moral
discipline, which distinguished them from "nominal" (that is, Roman
Catholic) Christians. Changes in this evangelical outlook began to take
place in the 1970s and have been described by Samuel Escobar as follows:

> It looks as if growth and our anxiety to have a new social role have trans-
> formed Evangelicals from a sacrificial and disciplined minority into a
> middle-class subculture in which ambition for power and social prestige
> have taken the place of discipleship. Eschatological hope and dynamics have
> been set aside.[36]

It would not be quite accurate to say that the growth of evangelical churches
has made no difference in the public sphere in Latin American countries.
The public influence of evangelicals varies from country to country, but in
none of them is it totally absent. Space does not allow a detailed discussion
of this topic. It will have to suffice to mention some of the most important
issues related to it.

First, there has been considerable growth of the social and political conscience of Latin American evangelicals since the 1970s. Much of this is due
to the influence of the Latin American Theological Fellowship, with its em-

---

[36]Escobar, "El Reino de Dios," pp. 127-56.

phasis on *integral mission*. From this perspective, the mission of the church is understood as active participation in God's mission on the part of all the people of God in the power of the Spirit, for the purpose of enabling people everywhere, as communities and as individuals, to experience *shalom* (literally, "peace")—the abundant life made available through Jesus Christ. An increasing number of churches all over this continent are becoming more and more engaged in integral mission in practical ways with the intent of transforming social reality from the bottom up. Many of them would undoubtedly be included by Donald E. Miller and Tetsunao Yamamori among the churches that they characterize as progressive Pentecostalism, which they describe as

> Christians who claim to be inspired by the Holy Spirit and the life of Jesus and seek to holistically address the spiritual, physical, and social needs of people in their community. Typically they are distinguished by their warm and expressive worship, their focus on lay-oriented ministry, their compassionate service to others, and their attention, both as individuals and as a worshipping community, to what they perceive to be the leading of the Holy Spirit.[37]

On the other hand, it must be acknowledged that these are not the fastest growing evangelical churches. As in other regions of the world, the churches in Latin America that register the highest rate of growth, both in number of attendees and membership, are quite often the so-called prosperity-gospel megachurches. They may not differ too much from other churches with regard to worship style, Christian experience, leadership and the presence of the church in society, but they attract people, many of them poor, by promising health and wealth in exchange for generous offerings.

An outstanding example of these megachurches is the *Igreja Universal do Reino de Deus* (the Universal Church of the Kingdom of God, or IURD, its acronym in Portuguese), whose amazing expansion not only in Brazil, where it began, but also in other countries has attracted considerable scholarly attention. The title of the carefully researched study of the church by Leonidas Silveira Campos reflects not only the content of the book but also the nature of the church that is its subject matter: *Theatre, Temple, and*

---

[37]Donald E. Miller and Tetsunao Yamamori, *Global Pentecostalism: The New Face of Christian Social Engagement* (Berkeley: University of California Press, 2007), pp. 2-3.

Market: Organization and Marketing of a Neopentecostal Enterprise.[38]
Campos demonstrated that the IURD has found the key to (numerical)
growth in the context of the present global system. That key consists in

- turning the worship services into theatrical shows;

- converting the temple (church building) into a place that radiates supernatural energy and provides protection and material prosperity through
  financial "sacrifice";

- adapting religion to the requirements of the marketing of "sacred goods"
  in a market where there are many other religious options;

- making professional use of the mass media for selling "spiritual mer-
  chandise" rather than "material goods";

- mastering a rhetorical discourse that communicates to people a sense of
  unity in a fragmented world.

The Universal Church of the Kingdom of God is a very striking religious
phenomenon, paradigmatic of the kind of evangelical popular religiosity[39]
which is rapidly spreading all over Latin America. The type of megachurch
that the IURD represents seems to have become the church model for many
pastors in this region, with the prosperity gospel as the order of the day.

Closely connected with the explosion of evangelical popular religiosity is
the emergence of Protestant political activism, especially in countries where
evangelical growth has been most significant. Such is the case, for instance,
in Brazil, where according to Paul Freston, "the rapid growth (a new church
per day) is largely among the poor (the needier the district, the more
churches per capita) and is popular (independent of the initiative of social
elites)."[40] Beginning in 1986, when thirty-three evangelicals were elected to

---

[38]Leonidas Silveira Campos, *Teatro, templo e mercado organizacao e marketing de um emprendi-
mento neopentecostal*, 2nd ed. (Petropolis, Brazil: Editora Vozes, Simposio Editora, 1999).
[39]The *popular* character of this evangelical religiosity should not be interpreted as meaning that
church membership in this movement is completely restricted to poor, uneducated people. As
Paul Freston has observed, "In contrast with the rather traditional ethic of the Assemblies [of
God], a long, disciplined haul to modest petty-bourgeois respectability, the Universal Church
offers a moralized version of the yuppie gambling ethic, an overnight flight to rapid enrichment."
"Brother Votes for Brother: The New Politics of Protestantism in Brazil," in *Rethinking Protestantism in Latin America*, ed. Virginia Garrard-Burnett and David Stoll (Philadelphia: Temple
University Press, 1993), p. 70.
[40]Freston, *Evangelicals and Politics*, p. 11.

the Constitutional Assembly in charge of drafting a new constitution for Brazil after twenty-one years of military governments, the presence of Protestant candidates for political positions became an expected trait of practically every local, regional or even national election. By no means does this happen in every Latin American country, for there are countries, like Argentina, where evangelicals are still a rather small minority. Even in these countries, however, well-known megachurch pastors dream of building a church on the assumption that this would garner them social and political influence in the corridors of power. One suspects that their unspoken aim is the replacement of the traditional Roman Catholic Christendom with an evangelical Protestant Christendom. They fail to see that, as Pablo Richard has rightly stated, "Evangelization is inherently incompatible with a Christendom model."[41] If it is true that the result of Roman Catholic Christendom is unevangelized Roman Catholics, it is also true that the result of Protestant Christendom will be unevangelized Protestants.

The Belgian-born Roman Catholic liberation theologian José Comblin, who has been living in Brazil for many years, recently declared, "The Roman Catholic Church has abandoned the popular classes. . . . The future of Latin America is to be an evangelical Protestant continent, except for the high class." Comblin is probably right—the evidence presented in this chapter points in that direction. Explosive church growth, however, could easily become a red herring for evangelicals in Latin America unless they face with all seriousness the challenge posed by numerical growth. A lesson that the evangelical movement should learn from the historical experience of the Roman Catholic Church in Latin America is that numerical growth can be very adverse to the kingdom of God if it is not placed, in both theory and practice, in the context of a biblical understanding of God's mission. The church is called to share in the mission to make disciples of Jesus Christ who then learn to obey all that he taught his own disciples. Discipleship as a disciplined and all-embracing process of transformation in the direction of the kingdom of God—the kingdom of the fullness of life made available for all humankind though Jesus Christ in the power of the Spirit—is at the very center of God's purpose for humankind. It is in this process that

---

[41]Richard, *Death of Christendoms*, p. 114.

churches and individual Christians are called to participate in Latin America and around the world.

FURTHER READING

Costas, Orlando E. *Liberating News! A Theology of Contextual Evangelization.* Grand Rapids: Eerdmans, 1989.

Dussel, Enrique, ed. *The Church in Latin America, 1492-1992.* Maryknoll, NY: Orbis, 1992.

Dussel, Enrique. *A History of the Church in Latin America: From Colonialism to Liberation.* Grand Rapids: Eerdmans, 1981.

Escobar, Samuel. *The New Global Mission: The Gospel from Everywhere to Everyone.* Downers Grove, IL: InterVarsity Press, 2003.

Freston, Paul. "Contours of Latin American Pentecostalism." In *Christianity Reborn: The Global Expansion of Evangelicalism in the Twentieth Century,* edited by Donald M. Lewis, pp. 221-72. Grand Rapids: Eerdmans, 2004.

———, ed. *Evangelical Christianity and Democracy in Latin America.* New York: Oxford University Press, 2008.

Martin, David. *Tongues of Fire: The Explosion of Protestantism in Latin America.* Oxford: Blackwell, 1990.

Míguez Bonino, José. *Faces of Latin American Protestantism.* Grand Rapids: Eerdmans, 1997.

Padilla, C. René. *Mission Between the Times: Essays on the Kingdom.* Carlisle, UK: Langham Monographs, 2010.

Salinas, Daniel. *Latin American Evangelical Theology in the 1970s: The Golden Decade.* Leiden: Brill, 2009.

Sánchez Walsh, Arlene M. *Latino Pentecostal Identity: Evangelical Faith, Self, and Society.* New York: Columbia University Press, 2003.

ASIA

Scott W. Sunquist

PROTESTANTISM IN ASIA BEGAN WITH the evangelical awakenings in Europe and North America, which means that the true roots of Asian Protestantism are found in evangelicalism. The "mainstream" expressions of state-church Protestantism (Calvinism in Scotland and Holland, Anglicanism in England, the Lutherans in the German lands) and various Anabaptist groups can trace their roots to the first half of the sixteenth century, but a significant Protestant presence in Asia did not arise until the advent of German Pietism in the last decades of the seventeenth century and the awakenings in North America and Britain in the eighteenth century. Thus, the earliest forms of Protestant Christian witness in Asia were evangelical, and this stream has been the dominant one up to the present time. This marks a great contrast with Protestant Christianity's beginnings in North America and the Caribbean, where the Anglican, Lutheran and Reformed churches of Christendom generally came before the advent of evangelicalism. Thus, it would be accurate to say that evangelicalism is normative Protestant Christianity in Asia, both because of its genesis and its recent developments.

This chapter will first look at early evangelical missionary movements in Asia, movements that began in the first decades of the eighteenth century in India and in the first decades of the nineteenth century in China. These early movements set patterns and established values that have continued to characterize Asian evangelicalism. Next, we will note the development of indigenous leadership and indigenous movements, discussing how evangelicalism, as a global movement, has had to be redefined in the light of evangelical movements in the non-Western world. The next sections will look at themes that have developed in and through evangelical Christianity in Asia: revivals and political resistance, Pentecostalism, the place of women, persecution and martyrdom, and interreligious relationships. In our final section we will look at what these characteristic developments of evangelicalism in Asia tell us about the possible future of this expression of Christianity for Asian cultures. As we will see, Christianity has developed more slowly in Asia than on any other continent, and yet its influence upon governments, religions and cultures has been historically significant.

EVANGELICAL BEGINNINGS IN ASIA

Although Protestant presence in Asia began with the British East India Company (founded in 1600), the Dutch United East India Company (1610) and the Danish East India Company (1616), these early companies had little missionary interest. The door was open to Asia for Protestant missions in the first decades of the seventeenth century, but without the evangelical impulse there was no concerted Protestant missionary activity until a century later. The Dutch established their center in Batavia (Jakarta) in the East Indies, the British in India and the Danish on a small strip of land on the southeast coast of India centered on the village of Tranquebar ("song of the waves"). Since evangelical missions could not start on lands owned or controlled by Roman Catholic nations (Spain, France and Portugal), it was not until the twentieth century that evangelical missionaries began to work in places like Indochina and the Philippines. Other Asian countries resisted all foreign intervention until late in the colonial period: China was "forced open" during the "Opium Wars" between Britain and China (1839–1842 and 1856–1860);[1] Japan was confronted by Admiral Perry's steamships in Edo Bay (1853); and the first resident Protestant missionary did not arrive in Korea—the "Hermit Kingdom"—until 1884. Thus, evangelical Christianity came very late to most regions of Asia.

Evangelical missions in Asia began with the international and ecumenical initiative called the Danish-Halle mission to Tranquebar.[2] King Friedrich

---

[1]For a brief overview, see G. Thompson Brown, *Earthen Vessels and Transcendent Power: American Presbyterians in China, 1837–1952* (Maryknoll, NY: Orbis, 1997), pp. 25-27.
[2]See Dennis Hudson, *Protestant Origins in India: Tamil Evangelical Christians, 1706–1835* (Grand Rapids: Eerdmans, 2000).

IV of Denmark controlled a small colony on the southeastern coast of India called Tranquebar. It was reported that Catholic kings were propagating the Roman Catholic faith in their colonial lands, and so, in consultation with his court preacher, the Pietist Franz Julius Lütkens (who in turn consulted with August Hermann Francke in Halle), King Friedrich became the first Protestant ruler to send out missionaries in the same manner as the Catholic kings of Portugal, France and Spain. The good court preacher, Lütkens, chose missionaries wisely. The first evangelical missionaries were the German duo of twenty-four-year-old Bartholomäus Ziegenbalg (1682–1719) and twenty-nine-year-old Heinrich Plütschau (1677–1752). On these young German shoulders were carried the first evangelical missions in Asia. Without any formal training in missions, these young men established trends that would mark most evangelical missions.

The evangelical anthropology of these missionaries taught them that all people were made in the image of God and therefore all Indians had some knowledge of God, even though that knowledge was imperfect and distorted. It was their responsibility to present the gospel to those in South India in a way they could understand most clearly. Thus, Ziegenbalg and Plütschau studied local languages (especially Tamil) and local religions. In Ziegenbalg's earliest letters he was involved in religious dialogue with his language teacher, who taught him much about the four types of practices in local religious piety (disciplined behavior, liturgical ceremony, unified consciousness and esoteric knowledge). One of the first and the most outstanding works that Ziegenbalg produced was titled *Genealogy of the Malabar Gods*. However, the Pietists in Germany were more concerned that their German missionary translate the German Bible for the Indians than that they receive the Indian gods in German, and the volume was not published for over 150 years.

Other trends in evangelical missionary work that the early Germans established included Bible translation (1715 for the New Testament and 1727 for the whole Bible), schools for both boys and girls (focusing on literacy and basic biblical knowledge), establishing local churches and training local leadership for the new churches. This early work was ecumenical and international. Through the "Halle Reports," sent out from Germany, Protestant leaders in England, Scotland, the Netherlands and even North America

could keep up with this early Protestant work in Asia. Anglicans from the
Society for Promoting Christian Knowledge (SPCK) donated a printing
press that would revolutionize literature production in India. The first ordained Protestant from India (1733) was a Velalan convert from Shaivism
named Arumugam Pillai, to whom Ziegenbalg gave the name Aaron. With
a strong foundation built on translations and writings in Tamil, the Evangelical (Lutheran) Church that developed under the Danish-Halle missionaries sprang out of Tamil life and with Tamil sensitivities. In the nineteenth century, the famous Tamil poet convert Vedanayakam Sastri
produced a wealth of Tamil poetry and epic songs that expressed the
gospel in ways friendly to the Tamil ear. Evangelicalism began to develop
as a Tamil religion.

   In this early period of Protestant missions in Asia, it was the colonial
powers that were the major hurdle in evangelical missionary work. Revivals
had awakened Protestants from their missionary slumber, but the political
powers of these same "revived" nations now emerged as an impediment to
mission. Even the Danish authorities in Tranquebar made missionary work
difficult for Lutheran missionaries. In Dutch lands, the Dutch United East
India Company (*Vereenigde Oost-Indische Compagnie* or VOC) made missionary work all but impossible in the East Indies. When the VOC went
bankrupt in 1799, things began to change. In 1806 freedom of religion was
proclaimed, and only from that point did evangelical missions (along with
Catholic) begin to extend their work in the East Indies. Ceylon (now Sri
Lanka) followed a similar pattern, although freedom of religion came much
later and after much more persecution of the Roman Catholics by the Dutch
Reformed rulers.

BEGINNINGS OF ENGLISH-SPEAKING EVANGELICALS

The English-speaking evangelical presence in Asia began with the great pioneer missionary William Carey (1761–1834).[3] Carey, a self-taught and self-
made man, was not only a pioneer Protestant missionary to Asia, but was
also one of the early advocates for the English-speaking Protestant world to

---

[3]There were a few evangelical chaplains, such as David Brown (1763–1812), who worked on British lands overseas, but their work, though well-meaning, did not have a major impact. One of
the most influential was Henry Martyn, whom we will briefly look at later.

take initiative in missions. A strange hyper-Calvinism seemed to have hamstrung Protestant missions as a convenient excuse since the late Reformation period.[4] It is reported that Carey was told by a Baptist preacher in 1786: "Young man, sit down. . . . When God pleases to convert the heathen, He'll do it without consulting you or me." Carey, however, was convinced from Scripture of the call to carry the gospel, and was convinced of his own need to go after reading some of the reports from the explorer Captain James Cook. Carey made a reasoned defense of the church's missionary responsibility in a small 1792 publication with a large title: *An Enquiry into the Obligation of Christians to Use Means for the Conversion of Heathens, in which the Religious State of the Different Nations of the World, the Success of Former Undertakings, and the Practicability of Further Undertakings are Considered.* The title said it all. Christians were responsible to actually do something ("use means") to bring about the conversion of the heathen.

Carey and two close associates—the schoolteacher Joshua Marshman (1768–1837) and the printer and preacher William Ward (1769–1823)—made up the famous Serampore Trio. Guided by their own missionary covenant, the three founded a college (1819), translated the Bible into numerous languages, began to develop horticulture as part of missionary work, and took on social reform (such as education for women and working to end the practice of *sati*, the burning of widows on a deceased husband's pyre)—all while founding the Baptist Church in India. Four issues here are of special note. First, Carey believed that missionary work, like all Christian work, should be self-supporting; thus he and others in the mission carried on work as teachers and printers. Second, Carey's top priority was planting churches of Indian converts and led by Indian preachers. Despite all of the education, horticulture and translation work, the Trio never wavered from this sense of purpose. Third, Carey and Marshman's translation of the Bible was remarkably extensive, if not remarkably accurate. They completed six translations of the Bible and another twenty-three complete translations of the New Testament. Carey had no university education, nor did he have mentors in the translation work to guide him. He learned as he went along, revising the important Bengali New Testament eight times. The Bible, rather than the

---

[4]This topic is dealt with in greater detail in Dale T. Irvin and Scott W. Sunquist, *History of the World Christian Movement,* vol. 2 (Maryknoll, NY: Orbis, 2012), chap. 23.

foreign missionaries, would be the foundation for their churches.[5] Fourth, we should note the broad understanding of mission that these pioneers held and how similar their priorities were to the early German Pietists. Carey developed new plants in India, both for income and to help enhance the Indian diet, and he founded the Agri-Horticultural Society of India for ongoing research. Although the Serampore Trio believed that Hinduism was a false and "heathen" religion, they worked on a translation of the famous Hindu epic poem, the *Ramayana*, into English, and Ward wrote a book on the manners and customs of Hindus. The college provided a broad education, and was called the "College for the Instruction of Asiatic, Christian and other Youth in Eastern Literature and European Science."

As Carey illustrates, one major theme in evangelical missions in Asia was Bible translation. From the time of Martin Luther, evangelical faith has been built upon biblical knowledge available for all people. Luther's Bible was a central plank in his platform of reform, and evangelical missionaries stood firmly on this plank in their missionary work. The first goal for evangelical missionaries was not to plant a church or start a school, but to learn the local language and to translate the Bible. In fact, most of the early missionaries in Asia ended up being Bible translators, even if they did not leave for the mission fields with that goal in mind. An important byproduct of Bible translation was the conversion of local assistants, primarily due to the fact that Bible translation brought the missionary and the missionized in close relationship. Most of these translation assistants became the earliest converts, evangelists and, at times, the first Asian Christian writers. By 1900 the New Testament or the whole Bible had been translated into at least sixty-three languages of Asia.[6] This phenomenal translation project—a project almost solely of evangelical missionaries and Asian scholars—marked evangelical Christianity in Asia more than anything else. With ever-increasing numbers, Asian Christians were hearing God's word in their own language, carried by their own idioms, and they were thus able to pioneer Asian reflections on Christianity without Western dependency.

---

[5]Carey's translation work is all the more incredible when one notes that by 1920 the New Testament was completed in only nineteen Indian languages.

[6]"Bible Translation," in *A Dictionary of Asian Christianity*, ed. Scott W. Sunquist (Grand Rapids: Eerdmans, 2001), pp. 81-83.

BEGINNINGS IN CHINA, EAST ASIA AND THE MIDDLE EAST

India, with its ecumenical and international beginnings in Tranquebar, was only slowly followed by other evangelical missions working in China, Burma (now Myanmar), Malaya, the East Indies and the Middle East. China would quickly become the main preoccupation among European and North American evangelicals, with China's pioneer missionary hero being Robert Morrison (1782–1834) of the London Missionary Society (LMS). Prevented from traveling to China by the British East India Company, this pioneer Scotsman traveled to New York to get to China in 1807. Morrison's strength of character and evangelical convictions helped him to carve out the earliest evangelical mission in China, at a time when the penalty for advocating Christianity in China was death by strangulation.[7] Compromises had to be made to attain the goal of evangelizing the Chinese. Morrison's first years were spent in seclusion and disguise while studying Chinese with the help of Roman Catholic priests. Later he was able to stay in south China by taking up employment with the very company that blocked his entrance just two years earlier. Walking the very thin and dangerous line between obeying the law and obeying his Lord, Morrison, working in the employ of the East India Company, chose to devote his time to translation of the Bible, a less public and thus less dangerous ministry. By 1822 Morrison had translated a Chinese grammar (1815), the Bible (1819), and produced a Chinese-English dictionary (1822). Evangelical commitment to the Bible and to vernacular translation kept the conversion rate low (only 10 converts in 25 years!), but Morrison and others were committed to building strong indigenous congregations that could only come as a product of Chinese Bible readers.

Public missionary work was very hazardous at this time in China. Morrison and later colleagues William Milne and Dr. Walter Henry Medhurst from the LMS made the difficult decision in 1815 to surround China with a "wall of light," by working with the Chinese diaspora (Nanyang Chinese). To this end, the LMS's "Ultra Ganges Mission" set up their base in Malacca (Melaka) on the west coast of Malaya, evangelizing and educating Chinese to go to China as missionaries. The strategy had little success until China was forced "open" at the end of Western guns during the Opium Wars, after which missionaries

---

[7]See Samuel H. Moffett, *A History of Christianity in China*, vol. 2 (Maryknoll, NY: Orbis, 2005), chap. 13, on early Protestant work in China.

began to abandon their work in the East Indies and Malaya and to flood into China. Under the first treaty (Treaty of Nanking, 1842) missionaries were restricted to five treaty ports: Guangzhou (Canton), Xiamen (Amoy), Fuzhou (Foochow), Ningbo (Ningpo) and Shanghai. But at the end of the second Opium War (1860), missionaries were allowed to reside inland. The great compromise, however, was that the same treaty that protected missionary presence also protected the trade in opium. Most evangelical missionaries spoke against the use of opium and the opium trade, but for the Chinese, Christian identity was foreign identity, and foreign identity included forcing opium on China.

One major transition in evangelical work during this period was developing modern medical missionary work as a viable way of opening a "mission field." It was said that Peter Parker (1804–1888) was the medical doctor who "opened China to the gospel at the point of a lancet." Parker, an ordained Presbyterian minister who had also studied medicine, pioneered missionary medical work. Parker quickly saw the great need for medical work in China, so he put out a call for more medical missionaries and, more importantly, began to train Chinese in modern Western medicine. Parker's record mirrors many of the ambiguities of early evangelical missionary work in China. He was concerned to proclaim the evangelical message to Chinese, and yet he spent most of his time in medical, educational and even political work. He established the first medical training center, undertook the first major surgery in China, was the first ophthalmologist in China and established the first Medical Missionary Society in China. However, because of his knowledge of Chinese and Chinese culture he was later recruited and then enlisted as the US Commissioner to China. In this capacity he acted more as an expansive Western imperialist to the degree that he even supported military intervention to expand Western trading and residential rights in China. He helped to write, translate and negotiate the Treaty of Tientsin in 1858, which opened up China to Western traders and missionaries. As Parker's story illustrates, evangelical missions were sometimes caught in reprehensible methods while clinging to admirable goals.

China became the greatest and most sought after of all mission fields after the 1850s. Two major developments occurred in evangelical work in China after the middle of the century. First was the pioneering work of James Hudson Taylor (1832–1905). Taylor, the son of a pharmacist and Methodist lay minister, had a transformative spiritual experience when he was seventeen, which propelled him toward missionary work in China. Although he started with the Chinese Evangelization Society at the age of twenty-four, he soon left to begin his own work, which would be marked by pioneering work inland, trusting God through prayer for financial support, and working as closely as possible in the local cultural contexts. In 1865 he founded the China Inland Mission (CIM), which was undergirded by evangelical piety and strong evangelistic passion. The CIM promoted a type of piety and approach to mission that spread, in part, through Taylor's extensive travels and prodigious recruiting. By the end of the nineteenth century, one-third of all Western missionaries in China were affiliated with the CIM. After the communist victory in China in 1949, CIM missionaries relocated to work among Chinese in East and Southeast Asia. Thus the "faith mission" and contextual approach of Taylor's CIM continued throughout East Asia under the banner of the Overseas Missionary Fellowship (now OMF International). Its penetrating influence came not only directly through their missionaries and Asian Christian leaders, but also through its model and example for other Protestants working in East Asia.

A second major development that contributed to the progress of evangelical Christianity in Asia came from John L. Nevius (1829–1893) of the American Presbyterian Mission. Nevius worked in Shandong Province in eastern China, where he noted that sending young converts off to Bible schools far away from their home villages weakened church leadership. His ministry of church planting and leadership development led him to the conclusion that each Christian should be a witness in his or her own community, with their own friends and family, with training of leaders being done on a short-term basis in a central location. These ideas were published in a series of articles in the *Chinese Recorder* in 1885. In 1890 Nevius spoke about his method to American missionaries working in Korea, whereupon Presbyterian missionary Horace Underwood described the basic lessons from Nevius in the following way: "Let each man 'abide in the calling wherein he was found'; teaching that each was to be an individual worker for Christ, and to live Christ in his own neighborhood, supporting himself by his trade."[8] Presbyterians in Korea followed this model closely.

---

[8]Allen D. Clark, *A History of the Church in Korea* (Seoul: The Christian Literature Society of Korea, 1971), pp. 114-15.

Connected with this idea of Christians remaining in their own contexts was the idea that local Christian converts then become fully accountable for their churches. Each church must be self-supporting, self-propagating and self-governing from the beginning. This "three-self" principle had been proposed earlier by the two leading missionary strategists of the nineteenth century: Rufus Anderson of the American Board of Commissioners for Foreign Missions (ABCFM) and Henry Venn of the Church Missionary Society (CMS). However, Nevius clearly connected the "three-self" model to the idea of local leaders not being removed to a far-off seminary or university for training. When Nevius's ideas were applied, local Christian communities tended to be more evangelical: they were dependent from the beginning on their own study of the Bible, prayer and evangelism. Evangelicalism, as we have seen, is marked by biblicism, crucicentrism, activism and conversionism, thus taking the Great Commission as a primary task for the church. These ideas of Nevius may seem obvious to some, but even today it is difficult for a "missionary" to let go of a new Christian community, especially when that community is poor, persecuted and naive about the Christian faith. However, when the young church has this localized identity and independence from the start, it does not have to work at being contextualized or indigenized, and it never has the chance of being a "foreign religion." The local church also naturally expresses its biblical faith, as local leaders apply Scripture to local contexts. This was the experience throughout Asia as evangelical Christianity moved from shoreline ports and trading centers to highlands and outlying islands.

India and China were among the earliest and largest fields of evangelical missionary outreach, but evangelical missionaries were not just driven to the "nations" in the sense of political states, but rather to every language and ethnic entity. Evangelical missions began work among the ethnic Burmese in Burma in 1807, and by the 1820s they were working among the Karen, but it was not until 1899 that work began among the ethnic Chinese. In Thailand missionary work began among the ethnic Thai (1833) and later among the Thai-Lao and even the Chinese. The same concern for indigenous churches with indigenous languages and leadership drove evangelical missionaries to move further and further inland as they translated and established schools. The last South and East Asian countries to receive evangelical missionaries were Japan (1859), Korea (1884), the Philippines (1899) and Nepal (1952).

In western Asia evangelical Christianity encountered a very different context, but was guided by the same principles mentioned above. The earliest Protestants to reach out in regions of the Ottoman Empire were Congregationalists, Wesleyan Methodists and Episcopalians. Episcopalians and Anglicans, though inspired by evangelical revivals in Europe and Asia, struggled with how to undertake missions among the Orthodox. High-church Anglicans resisted any Anglican witness to Orthodox churches, even if these churches seemed listless to evangelicals. In true evangelical fashion, the main strategy for the early missionaries in western Asia was twofold: to work with the Orthodox churches to try to bring about revival, and missionary concern for Muslims through biblical literacy and preaching. The strategy had little success, but over the years many Orthodox churches received a new impetus for their ongoing witness.

The earliest forms of evangelicalism throughout Asia carried this same basic DNA, which combined elements of the Protestant movement in the sixteenth century with others from the evangelical revivals in the eighteenth century. In each place the translation of Scripture was a priority, and from this followed the need for schools to teach biblical literacy and basic theological concepts. Indigenous Christian leadership soon followed. One of the most dramatic results of this translation priority was the early contextualization of evangelical Christianity in Asia, which produced a great diversity that remained centered around evangelical piety and theology. Other results from these primary evangelical concerns in mission will be seen in the following sections.

INDIGENOUS MOVEMENTS AND INDIGENOUS LEADERS

The Protestant principle of access to the Bible and the evangelical concern for conversion combined early on to create indigenous leadership as well as indigenous movements in Asia. For example, one of the first Burmese women to convert, Ma Min Lay, learned to read the Bible from Ann Judson and then started the first school in the country for women in 1820. Thus, in the first generation indigenous leaders were beginning to assert themselves. However, this was not always the case among Protestants in general. Some high-church Anglicans and other nonevangelical missionaries relied on a well-trained church hierarchy, and as a result indigenous leadership was longer in coming. However, evangelical piety and missiology resisted more extreme forms of colonial missionary control. A few examples will help us to understand how Asian forms of evangelical Christianity became the main expression of Christian faith in most of Asia.

The first example comes from the same province in China, Shandong, where John L. Nevius had worked. A residential seminary had been founded in the last decades of the nineteenth century in Shandong, but by the end of the second decade of the twentieth century much of the theological education reflected modern American trends, many of which had no place in China. This was a time of antiforeignism in China, and unsurprisingly, this mood extended to the seminaries when a group of Chinese Christians took theological education in their own hands and established the North China Theological Seminary in December 1919. The seminary was started in reaction to the Western university model of theological education that was developing in China. The Chinese were clear about what they wanted in theological education: more Bible, less criticism of the Bible, more spirituality and Chinese control of the seminary.[9] It was this strong indigenous identity of the Chinese church in this particular area that gave them the confidence to say no to liberal education— explicitly rejecting Union Theological Seminary in New York—and to seek their own evangelical teachers and teaching. The new seminary insisted that all teaching be in Chinese.

Many other independent Christian movements in China rejected the liberalizing and secularizing tendencies of Western missionaries that came about in the first decades of the twentieth century. Until the last decade of the nineteenth century, Western missions had expressed a broadly evangelical approach and held on to evangelical goals. Churches developed evangelistic ministries in Asia in the pattern taught from the West. Eventually, however, Western theological "modernism" was exported to Asia, creating a rift between indigenous Asian evangelical churches and some of the newer missionaries who no longer endorsed conversion, but rather emphasized

---

[9]John J. Heeren, *On the Shantung Front: A History of the Shantung Mission of the Presbyterian Church in the USA, 1861–1940 in its Historical, Political and Economic Setting* (New York: Board of Foreign Missions of the Presbyterian Church in the U.S.A., 1940), pp. 161-62.

educational theory and sociology over established evangelical patterns of preaching and care for the poor. Thus, Asian resistance to modern theological movements became the catalyst for Asian church independence and indigenous movements.

These indigenous movements of Christian renewal were further promoted by revivals and mass movements in the early twentieth century, all of which furthered Chinese resistance to Western imperialism and ideologies. Nee To-sheng, known to the West as Watchman Nee, is another example of this resistance that helped to shape Chinese evangelicalism. Raised to respect the Confucian classics, Nee attended an Anglican high school, but it was the revivalist approach of Methodism that touched his heart in 1920. He studied for a year in Shanghai at the Bible school of Dora Yu, one of the most important Chinese evangelists of the early twentieth century, who led Watchman Nee to faith, discipled him and gave him spiritual nurture and confidence that was Chinese from first to last. Nee was then influenced by literature from the Keswick movement and from the Welsh Revival (1904–1905), as well as a broad range of Protestant literature including Martin Luther, George Müller, Jonathan Edwards, John Wesley, D. L. Moody, Charles Finney and Charles Spurgeon. The motto for his great evangelistic ministry would be "I want nothing for myself; I want everything for the Lord." Other Chinese evangelists, church planters and missionaries—such as John Sung (Song Shangjie) and Wang Mingdao—followed in this same evangelical stream: deeply engaged in biblical texts, passionate for evangelism, and resistant to Western imperialism, denominations and theology. Their evangelical faith was expressed only in the Chinese language, and it was strong enough to endure great suffering. Resistance to the West was an essential ingredient in indigenous evangelical movements in all of Asia.

Another way this evangelical indigenization accelerated the growth of Christianity in Asia was through mass movements. Evangelical development in Asia was more democratic than either Roman Catholic or later mainline Protestant missions. For example, the work of many evangelical missions was more extensive, going beyond major cities and reaching out into villages and, therefore, to the poor. In South Asia, the outreach to Dalits and tribal groups sometimes turned into mass movements of conversion. Andrew Gordon, an American Presbyterian missionary working in the Punjab from the 1850s, came to the conclusion that trying to reach Punjabis through modern education and science was effective only for a few of the high-caste Urdu speakers. Thus, Gordon reasoned that direct preaching in the local languages would bring about conversion and then education would come later. Conversions did come, and mass movements began when local evangelists were trained, such as those among the Megs and Chuhras in the 1870s and 1880s. These South Indian Christian communities experienced very rapid growth—100 percent or more a year at times. Such dynamic, local expansion made it unlikely that these communities would reflect Western structures or theology.

Indigenous leadership also arose in resistance to Western ideas and Western control of churches. One important example from India—both because he reveals a pattern and because he became a pattern for others—is Sadhu Sundar Singh (1889–ca. 1929). Raised by a devout Hindu mother and a Sikh father, Sundar Singh attended Christian schools but ridiculed Christians until, in 1904, he had a vision of Jesus Christ who asked him, "Why do you persecute me? See I have died on the cross for you and for the whole world." Upon his conversion after this vision, Sundar Singh was persecuted by his own family, and so he escaped and became a wandering pilgrim, studying the Bible as his own sacred book. He attempted to fit into Western Christian norms by studying at St. John's Seminary in Lahore, but it was too confining for him. Instead, Sundar Singh became an Indian Holy Man, called a Sadhu, wandering in bare feet throughout India and even into the mountains of Tibet as a witness to Jesus Christ. His rejection of Western theology for Indian spirituality was his strength and the secret to his very important and influential ministry. Other indigenous Asian evangelical leaders began to arise in the twentieth century, and in each case resistance to Western models, structures and theology was a major push factor in their development.

When Asian Christian leaders began to lead churches, they often also developed their own institutions. Educational institutions, such as the North China Seminary mentioned above, were only one form of indigenous initiative and resistance to the West, among many others. In 1903, in response to the great transformation that the gospel had brought to their lives, and in the context of a series of revivals in Tirunelveli, YMCA Indian Secretary V. S. Azariah gathered together eight Anglican clergy and twenty-two laymen in

Tamil Nadu to form the Indian Missionary Society (IMS). Through the international associations available in his work with the YMCA, Azariah had gained a larger vision to bring the benefits of the gospel to the oppressed in India. From its inception in 1903 the IMS was a completely indigenous movement; all of the missionaries were Indian, their mission field was India, and their support came from Indian Christians. Much of the support came from local sextons or church workers who collected handfuls of rice. Later, Azariah would become the first Indian Anglican bishop.

After Indian independence, another significant Indian missionary society was formed: the Friends Missionary Prayer Band (1959). This indigenous missionary society also reflected basic evangelical themes in Indian dress (or more accurately, expressed Indian evangelicalism). It focused on a fourfold objective: (1) proclaiming the gospel in the mother tongue of the people,[10] (2) planting indigenous congregations among these peoples, (3) producing local leaders and (4) providing holistic development.

Indigenous leadership development in Asia began much earlier in evangelical contexts than it did in Roman Catholic missions or in the nonevangelical Protestant missions. In Korea the first resident missionaries arrived in 1884, and by 1907 the first indigenous presbytery was established by the Presbyterian Church, of which the majority of the leaders were Korean. There was no looking back. The Korean church has always been very evangelical, with an emphasis upon Bible knowledge and Christian witness, and its indigenous leadership came very early. Evangelical leadership in Asia, as in the West, often received revivals as an expected outcome of faithful preaching.

EVANGELICAL REVIVALS AND POLITICAL RESISTANCE

As we have noted above, one of the main catalysts for Protestant mission and for indigenization was the occurrence of revivals. Revivals reinforced the

---

[10]"[For] those Indians who can understand major languages such as Hindi or Telugu, no new translation of the Bible is needed. But tribal people who do not understand these languages should have the Bible in their own mother tongue because they can hear Jesus Christ and his apostles speak their language and better understand the content of the Bible. Full New Testament is already available in *Vasavi, Malto* and *Chodri*. The New Testament is being translated into *Varli, Pawri, Kurux, Hariyanvi*, and *Khandeshi*." Daniel Jeyaraj, "Christian Message in Life and Action: Two Case Studies from India," unpublished paper presented at Pittsburgh Theological Seminary, December 11, 2009.

evangelical character of the Asian churches, strengthened indigenous cultural themes and at the same time empowered Asians to lead. The empowerment directed by the Holy Spirit acted as a more direct route for Asian leaders to be discipled than empowerment by Western leaders or long-term training dominated by Western forms and structures. However, revivals also often had a political characteristic to them and expressed themselves as a type of resistance to other authorities. One good example of this was the Korean revival beginning in 1907. This revival seems to have been directly related to reports of other revivals, including the Welsh Revival (1904–1905), the revival in Northeast India, the revival in the Mukti Mission in India and the Shandong Revival.[11] All of these revivals had the effect of deepening the identity of Christian communities in the local contexts, strengthening the communities and empowering them for crosscultural witness.

The Korean revival, though not unique, did have expressions that were unique to Korea. First, when the revival began, missionaries were more observers than leaders. The revival started in Pyongyang and touched church leaders, women's groups and even children in school. Second, the revival initiated Korean unity and cooperation for evangelistic outreach. By 1909 the bold Korean Christian initiative—the Million Souls movement—was announced, in which Koreans were to begin to pray and work for one million individuals to convert to Christianity. Third, Korean leaders emerged and were elevated by the rising tide of revival waters. Kil Sun Joo, the nearly blind preacher of the revival, became a nationally known evangelist and church planter. Kim Ik Du became a great evangelist with a gift of healing, and eventually died as a Christian martyr under the communists.

Finally, the Korean revival, coming at a time of increased oppression from the Japanese Empire, expressed identity with Jesus Christ as uniquely being Korean, standing against Japanese hegemony. Korean Christianity, from this revival, identified Korean Christians as real Koreans in opposition to foreign domination. Evangelical Christianity was being shaped by

---

[11]For the relationship between the Korea and Shandong revivals, see Lian Xi, *Redeemed by Fire: The Rise of Popular Christianity in the Modern World* (New Haven: Yale University Press, 2010), pp. 87-89. J. Edwin Orr, Baptist historian of church revivals, identified the period from 1900 to 1910 as a period of global "Fifth General Awakening." See Orr's *Evangelical Awakenings in Eastern Asia* (Minneapolis: Bethany Fellowship, 1975).

indigenous leaders who were responding to social, religious and political contexts that were their own.

Other revivals or periods of rapid growth were even more directly related to political events. Christianity in Singapore, especially after independence from Great Britain, has been strongly evangelical both in its traditional Western denominations and through newer evangelical churches. When the Singaporean government made the decision to redistribute the population of Singapore in order to ensure a mixing of races and religions, this had a positive, almost revivalistic, impact upon Christianity. In the anxiety caused by the disruption to families, many people lost their religious moorings that attached them to a local temple or mosque. The "new towns" and housing estates grew rapidly in the 1970s, and this accompanied a period in which Christianity in Singapore grew from about 6.5 percent in 1970 to about 13 percent in 2000.[12] Technically speaking, many would not call this a revival or awakening, but after 180 years of Christian witness, this sudden growth had many of the marks of a true revival.

Similarly, social policies in neighboring Indonesia (in resistance to the communist insurgency threat) also helped create an environment for very rapid church growth. In 1965 the Indonesian government faced a coup d'état. The response was to weed out the communists who at the time were the largest political party in the country. Since communists were understood to be atheists, all Indonesians were required to identify their religion and carry with them religious identity cards, with the five recognized religions being Islam, Protestantism, Catholicism, Buddhism and Hinduism. Those who had no religion before or who had attended Christian schools often chose Christianity. The result was a large influx of new Christians into the churches, such that where Christians were strongly supportive of conversion, the preaching and teaching stimulated rapid growth. Evangelical presence in Indonesia grew from 1.5 percent in the mid-1960s to over 5 percent by 2000.[13] Political disruption, forced migration, and communism or threats of communism have all tended to promote evangelical revival in Asia.

---

[12] According to *Operation World*, ed. Jason Mandryk (Milton Keynes, UK: Authentic Publications, 2010), pp. 743-46, evangelical Christianity in Singapore during these thirty years grew from 1.8% to 7.8%.

[13] Ibid., pp. 446-53.

Pentecostalism in Asian Evangelicalism

Because historians are now clear about the origins and precursors of modern Pentecostalism, it is not historically accurate to divide Pentecostalism in Asia from evangelicalism. Asian Pentecostalism originated in Asia and was soon linked with similar movements from the West. Pentecostalism in Asia created its own unique forms, structures and institutions and soon became a new stream of Asian evangelicalism.[14] Since Pentecostal-like movements occurred in Asia in the late nineteenth century, much like they did in the West, it is not helpful to talk about Asia borrowing from the West or to see a one-way, direct influence. It is more accurate to talk about the global cross-fertilization that occurred during the rise of Pentecostalism. For example, in both Asia and the West there was a very close relationship between the holiness movements and Pentecostalism. In 1901 a holiness movement began in Japan, initiated by one of the most famous Japanese evangelists, Nakada Juji, in partnership with Charles and Lettie Cowman[15] and Ernest and Julie Kilbourn. This movement, which emphasized indigenous leadership training, self-support, the imminent return of Christ (in premillennialism) and holiness as a second experience of the Holy Spirit[16] was both a precursor of Pentecostalism and, more specifically, of the Oriental Missionary Society, an Asian-initiated missionary movement. Without tracing the lines of all the various movements, some general themes can be highlighted for a better understanding of Asian Pentecostalism as an Asian evangelical movement.

First, evangelicalism in Asia in the nineteenth century often looked more like the book of Acts than Calvin's *Institutes of the Christian Religion* or the Anglican *Book of Common Prayer*. By this we mean that European and North American evangelical missionaries encountered spirits, demons, dreams and visions throughout Asia—even though most did not have a theology that included such occurrences. For some of these missionaries, experiences of the Holy Spirit were part of their heritage, and thus they saw these more direct spiritual encounters as simply a new dimension of the Spirit coming with power. John L. Nevius, the aforementioned Princeton-

---

[14]Michael Bergunder, in his important study of Pentecostalism in South India (*The South Indian Pentecostal Movement in the Twentieth Century* [Grand Rapids: Eerdmans, 2008]), discusses the historiography of Pentecostal origins in his introduction (pp. 1-19).

[15]Lettie Cowman was the author of the enduring devotional classic *Streams in the Desert* (1925).

[16]Or as a series of subsequent experiences.

educated missionary to Shandong Province, China, heard and observed so much about the spirit world that he wrote a book called *Demon Possession and Allied Themes*. Although not a Pentecostal, Nevius dealt with Pentecostal themes, including healings, casting out demons and other "supernatural" expressions of the Spirit of God. As with the development of Christianity in Africa, many Asian societies were culturally and spiritually closer to the world of the Bible than the world of the North Atlantic missionaries. Thus, the spiritual experiences during worship or prayer meetings of revivals resembled indigenous spirituality much more than Western theology. When the Great Revival in Korea broke out, it was among Presbyterians and Methodists for the most part, but the experiences were nothing that Calvin or the Protestant Reformers would have regarded as helpful (although they would have been more familiar to Wesley). Missionaries described it as being disorderly, filled with impassioned cries of repentance, and later marked by miraculous healings. Even though classic Pentecostalism (with attendant speaking in tongues) did not arrive in Korea until 1930, many of the connections with worldwide revival and Pentecostalism were already present. Asian cultures were ripe for Pentecostal Christianity even without Pentecostal leadership.

A second characteristic we might call the Indian connection. Most of the features of classic Pentecostalism were first seen in India, beginning with an unlikely pioneer: Pandita Ramabai, a Brahmin widow, Christian convert and founder of a home for orphan girls. Ramabai teamed with an American, Minnie Abrams, beginning in 1897; in 1905 a revival broke out among the girls at Ramabai's Mukti Mission and spread throughout the Maharashtra state. Girls were overwhelmed by their sin, cried out to God for forgiveness and were overcome with weeping followed by great joy. Two manifestations of this revival—speaking in tongues and evangelistic outreach—were recorded by Minnie Abrams. While Pandita Ramabai would eventually step back from the Pentecostal movement, this revival marked the birth of Pentecostalism in South Asia, and soon missionaries from the Azusa Street Revival in Los Angeles were working alongside Indians in Pentecostal missionary outreach in India. Soon Indian Pentecostals were initiating missionary work elsewhere in Asia: to Ceylon (Sri Lanka), as well as to Southeast and Northeast Asia. Indian Pentecostalism was also a catalyst to indigenization and ministry to the poor. Ramabai channeled the spiritual power and awakening of the revival at Mukti into famine relief efforts and other ministry to the poor. The Pentecostal experience, as an empowering event, also enabled indigenous Christians to resist foreign leadership or domination. Having experienced the power and grace of God, they were free to engage in ministry without dependence upon foreign missionaries. In this way, Pentecostalism spread by indigenous leaders (including many "Bible women") and advanced church independence and indigenization.

A third characteristic of Asian Pentecostalism was its immediate missionary outreach. In this regard, global Pentecostalism is homogenous; Pentecostalism everywhere breaks out of old patterns and focuses its energy on both personal transformation and missionary outreach. In other words, empowerment leads to mission. The origin of the contemporary missionary movement from China, known as the "Back to Jerusalem Movement," can be found in earlier revivals (Pentecostal, holiness and evangelical) in Shandong and other provinces in China.[17] Likewise, revivals (both charismatic and Pentecostal) that began in 1907 in Korea would inspire Korean missions overseas, and other island revivals such as those in Nias (1916–1922) and Timor (1965) led to island-wide missionary outreach. Pentecostalism in Asia continues to inspire and empower believers for crosscultural outreach in Asia, and although not as dominant as in Africa or Latin America, it remains a vital dimension of Christian growth in Asia.

According to the Pew Forum on Religion and Public Life, Pentecostals went from 1 percent of the population of Asia in 1970 to over 4 percent in 2006, which amounts to 160 million individuals.[18] Pentecostalism is still a young movement in Asia and is still more movement than institution, which means that it is not as organized and unified as older movements are. In one state of India, Tamil Nadu, there are presently over thirty-three Pentecostal bodies, and twenty-seven of these are indigenous or founded by local leaders. In many countries in Asia it is difficult to distinguish Pentecostal churches from non-Pentecostal by their worship, missionary work or organization. Many churches in Asia have been influenced by the Pentecostal immediacy

---

[17]Its earliest history is most likely found in a vision that came out of the early Jesus Family community in Shandong in the 1920s.

[18]Quoted in David H. Lumsdaine, ed., *Evangelical Christianity and Democracy in Asia* (Oxford: Oxford University Press, 2009), p. xi: www.pewforum.org/2006/10/05/overview-pentecostalism-in-asia.

and intimacy of the Holy Spirit. Pentecostalism continues to grow both as a distinct movement and as a spiritual dimension within Asian evangelicalism.

WOMEN AS SUBJECTS IN ASIAN EVANGELICALISM

Pentecostalism, as we have seen, has been a movement for the empowerment of women in Asia. The case can be argued that evangelical missions have done more for women's liberation and advancement than any other single force or cultural movement in Asia. Islamic regions in Asia have provided no education for young girls or women, and in most Muslim regions of India traditionally women were also kept at home living in *zenanas* (parts of houses where women were to reside). In South Asia, for over a millennium before the arrival of Protestant missionaries, there had been *devadasis*, or temple prostitutes, who were dedicated to a particular god in a local temple. These *devadasis* started out as young girls and were taught ritual dance as part of their role in the Hindu temple. In China, meanwhile, the feet of upper-class women were bound from a young age to keep them small and beautiful ("little flowers") and to prevent women from traveling away from home. Each of these structural elements in Asia—keeping women ignorant, temple prostitution and foot binding—are evidence of how women were treated as inferior to men in most of Asia.

In a number of ways, the evangelical mission to Asia pushed back against these denigrating practices and norms. Although evangelicals have not always held to complete gender equality in every area, evangelical Christianity had always treated girls as equal to boys in basic knowledge of literacy and study of the Bible. For example, the first law regarding education in the Puritan Colony of Massachusetts required every town to have compulsory education for both boys (up to twenty-one) and for girls (up to eighteen). The law was called "The Old Deluder Satan Act," since the reason for education was to fight against Satan who could less easily delude a person who could read the Bible (1647). Equal treatment of women began with literacy for girls, so they could read the Bible, and this evangelical conviction was carried to Asia.

Further, evangelical Christianity had a democratizing and a gender equalizing effect. The early exposure of evangelical Christianity in Asia was through married couples and families serving in their homes, a factor in the success of evangelicalism that cannot be underestimated. The contrast with the earlier Roman Catholic priests, monks and friars is immediately evident. Protestant converts came to understand marriage as the norm for Christian leaders, which in turn made pastoral and missionary recruitment far easier: the modeling of Christian family life created a home environment in which the full range of Christian ministry was available not just to celibate unmarried people. This was an enormous boon for the indigenization of evangelicalism in Asian societies. By the middle of the nineteenth century single women were often serving in Asia, but not only to reach women in the *zenanas*; others were "Bible women," traveling through villages and distributing and teaching the Bible. Thus, for many Indians, Indonesians, Chinese and Thai, their first exposure to Christian teaching was from Bible women. Asian women learned from what they saw and heard. They received a message that was every bit as important for them as it was for the men in the villages.

Evangelical Christianity raised the status of women in all Asian cultures. One of the examples already mentioned was Ma Min Lay, the early convert among the Burmese. Other Asian converts recognized, through Christian teaching, the need for social reform—especially regarding the treatment of women. The Hindu convert Krishnan Mohan Banerjea (1813–1885) wrote an influential essay in support of women's education titled "Native Female Education" (1841). Such a conviction challenged Indian cultural norms for decades. According to C. B. Firth, "In those days of child marriage, female infanticide, the burning of widows, and, in the North, the Purdah system, there was little thought of the emancipation of women. . . . The idea was prevalent that education was not for respectable women. When, therefore, the Calcutta students, in 1831 debated the subject of female education they were handling a new and revolutionary idea."[19]

As in the early church, the gospel proclamation in Asia meant liberation for women.[20] Women were often attracted to Christianity both because it was often proclaimed by women, and because of the dignity with which women were treated in the faith. Many examples of the changed status of

---

[19]Cyril Bruce Firth, *An Introduction to Indian Church History* (Serampore, India: The Senate of Serampore College, 1968), pp. 186-87.

[20]See Rodney Stark, *The Rise of Christianity: A Sociologist Reconsiders History* (Princeton: Princeton University Press, 1996), chap. 5, "The Role of Women in Christian Growth."

women could be offered. We have already mentioned one of them, Pandita Ramabai (1858–1922). Ramabai was raised by an enlightened Hindu father who taught her to read Vedic texts in Sanskrit. She married only briefly, and, when her husband died, she traveled to England where she became a Christian. With a new view of humanity, sin, salvation and responsibility before God, she became a poet, writer, social reformer and advocate for the most needy girls and women in India. In 1881 Ramabai founded the Arya Mahila Sabha, which was the first feminist organization in India. Her Mukti ("liberation") mission, rescuing widows and young female brides, is still in existence today.

There are many other examples of how evangelical Christianity has liberated Asian women, such as the ending of *sati* in India and the elimination of foot binding in China. One less obvious example is the strong leadership of women in churches in Asia today. China, a traditional Confucian society with two generations of communist rule, holds one of the fastest growing churches today, and much of the leadership is female. In fact, even where traditional patterns of gender roles continue in the church, women are educated and are actively involved as evangelists and missionaries. Asian societies have been transformed in large part by the pioneering work of Asian Christian women reached through evangelical witness.

Persecution, Martyrdom and Political Influence

Persecution has been more a part of Christianity in Asia than on any other continent. From the Mediterranean to the Pacific, Christian communities have lived almost exclusively as minority communities among major religions (which are often supported by governments).[21] When Christian witness challenges long-held traditions, such as the role or place of women, tensions often escalate into violence. Conversion, one of the core emphases of evangelicalism, becomes a flashpoint for tensions and subsequent persecution. These persecutions are sometimes popular and at other times political. Whether government sanctioned or not, we can identify four major types of persecution of evangelicals in Asia in the past three centuries. The first, as was detailed earlier, was persecution (or at least strong resistance)

---

[21]The one exception is the Philippines. But even in this predominately Christian country, persecution continues in the southern island of Mindanao, which is predominately Muslim.

from colonial multinational companies and colonial governments. It may seem odd, but Western colonial administrators and business leaders have often resisted missionary work—especially among Muslim communities—primarily because of economic and trade concerns. However, during the first half of the twentieth century, it was not a European but an Asian colonial government that caused much persecution and suffering: Japan. Empires—whether Western or Asian—often resisted evangelical witness, especially to the poor and uneducated.

The second type of persecution has come from the newly independent Asian governments, whose independence often accompanied an affirmation of their traditional religious heritage. Thus, Pakistan's Islamic identity and Burma's Buddhist identity both conflict with Christian freedom and evangelical witness. The decolonization of Asian nations (all Asian nations except Thailand, Bhutan, Nepal, Afghanistan and Saudi Arabia had been colonized) not only restricted international connections with indigenous Christian groups, but also stoked the flames of religious revivals among national religions. Such movements as *Hindutva* in India promote "Indianness" as "Hinduness" and portray Christian conversion as opposed to Indian identity.

Third, Christian persecution has been fiercest among newer secular ideologies. The rapid growth of communism in East Asia brought about the largest and most extensive Asian persecution since the early persecutions in Persia. Christians were one of many groups that were persecuted under the Cultural Revolution in China (1966–1976); but in proportion to their numbers, their suffering was great. With the rise of communism in Vietnam and the country's reunification, there was an exodus of many Christian leaders from the young Protestant church. Many other Vietnamese Christians were imprisoned. But as is often the case, the persecutions in these communist countries have had the remarkable effect of increasing the rate of growth of Christianity.

Finally, modern persecution of evangelicals has been both through governments and popular uprisings. Anticonversion laws (often called "freedom of religion laws") have been proposed and passed in at least five states in India. The enforcement is uneven and imprecise, but the message is clear: we want to keep Hindus as Hindus. It was estimated that there were only 700 Christians in Cambodia and Laos after missionary work from 1923 to 1970. In 1965, Prince Sihanouk expelled all missionaries from Cambodia as CIA agents. When missionaries returned in 1970 Christianity began to grow, but the rise of the Khmer Rouge in the mid-1970s meant the collapse of the church in Cambodia. This was a largely secular, communist vision of remaking all of society as an egalitarian, strict and austere state. All religion was outlawed, and the Christian population quickly dropped from 10,000 to about 400. Since then, most of the rapid growth (from the time missionaries were allowed back in the country in 1970) has been evangelical growth.

Popular persecution is also common and is often encouraged by the state. One example is the Boxer Rebellion (1900) in China. "The Society of Righteous Harmony Fists," as the insurgency was known, was a nationalistic and religious uprising against both colonial powers and Christianity. The decline of the Qing Empire and the failure of the reform movement in the 1890s led Empress Qixi to encourage rebellion against foreign powers. The Boxers were willing and able to respond. Violence was greatest in certain regions of the east, but even Muslims from western China were encouraged to join the Boxers in their revolt against foreigners and foreign religion. Many more Chinese Christians (over 32,000, including 30,000 Chinese Catholics and several hundred Orthodox Christians) were killed than missionaries (136 Protestant adults, 53 of their children, and 47 Roman Catholic priests and nuns). The loss of mission property and lives led to an Eight-Nation Alliance to put down the rebellions. The Boxers had many slogans, but one of the most popular expressed a primary concern: "Defend Chinese Religion and Get Rid of Foreign Religion."

Persecution of evangelicals continues to be a major theme in Asia, both because of evangelical commitment to conversion and because of their emphasis on the Bible. Biblical preaching and small groups studying the Bible often leads evangelicals to patterns of ministry among the most needy, which has the potential to lead to direct social engagement. While this social engagement—on behalf of the poor, the oppressed, for women and children—does not always translate into political engagement, at times it does. We seldom see public protest and other types of direct confrontation between evangelicals and governments in Asia, but Christian resistance to injustices and oppressions remains evident.

The Boxer Rebellion in 1900 was only the beginning of a century of persecution of Christians in Asia, and this persecution persists in places today. The communist advance in China, Vietnam and Laos—along with the revived Muslim nations of Iran (with the Iranian Revolution of 1979), Afghanistan, Malaysia and Pakistan—have together contributed to increased suffering for Christians in Asia. One of the main causes of persecution has been the perception of a loss of social order or social harmony when many people convert to Christianity. Today, mass movements (or even the perception of these) among Dalits (traditionally known as "Untouchables") in India continue to evoke persecution. Christian converts are rewarded for conversion back to Hinduism (though many were never Hindus to begin with), and, when these Christians do not convert, Christian leaders and buildings are often targeted. In East Malaysia, tribal people are "encouraged" to convert to Islam by being offered free (or reduced tuition) education, access to the university or new housing. Christians are excluded from basic social services in many countries of Asia as a form of passive persecution. In west Asia, Islamic laws often prescribe death to the person who leaves Islam, although this is seldom carried out. Thus, it is still true that in most countries of Asia, evangelical witness continues in creative and careful ways in the context of persecution.

Persecution is not the only political story of evangelicalism in Asia. One of the most observable byproducts of evangelicalism in Asia is the development of democratic movements, which counters the inaccurate but common assumption that evangelicalism is "other-worldly." Evangelicals (especially of the Pentecostal variety) tend to be activist in their piety—meeting to study the Bible, pray and develop social networks—and in their social networks they commonly begin to engage society. Informal associations of evangelicals are often the seedbed of democracy. Thus, with the spread of evangelicalism has come less hierarchical associations and greater participation in social collectives.

In addition, evangelicalism has had a more direct impact upon politics in Asia through the participation of evangelicals in the democratic process (where this is viable). More than any other continent, Asia has been dominated by non-Christian religious states that have often excluded and persecuted Christians. However, this is slowly changing. As Timothy Samuel Shah has noted,

Evangelicals participated in national and regional politics with important consequences for democracy and civil society in several parts of Asia, including the Philippines, Korea, Indonesia, and Northeast India. In the Philippines, Korea, and Northeast India, evangelical politics has proven especially significant largely because evangelicals have been more numerous than in almost all other parts of Asia.[22]

Christian participation in China today reveals another way evangelical life contributes to political engagement. Evangelical witness in the face of the communist "liberation" laid a foundation for Christian life that included participation in the social witness in each local community. When persecution increased, especially under the Cultural Revolution, Christian communities organized locally and through networks. Christians are negotiating their place in the social and political matrix of modern China, and, in doing so, are promoting public discussion and debate—the foundations of democracy. As evangelical Christianity grows and matures, its place in society will continue to be a major theme, whether in persecution or in participation.

EVANGELICALS, ASIAN RELIGIONS AND SUB-CHRISTIAN CULTS

Of all the continents, Christian history is unique in Asia because of the distinct religious encounters that have occurred there. Only in Asia did Christianity encounter major multicultural and even continent-wide religions—in all other continents almost all of the religions that Christianity encountered were limited to a particular culture or ethnic group. Larger intercultural religions like Buddhism, Islam and Hinduism are more established and thus have been more resistant to Christian witness, with the result that the interreligious encounter is more drawn out and complex. The earliest evangelical missionaries encountered these major faiths in India. Searching for ways to relate the gospel, they studied native texts and experimented with innovative patterns of Christian witness. Adoniram Judson, the pioneer missionary in Burma (Myanmar), studied the ancient Pali Buddhist texts and set up a *zayat* (rest house) alongside a road where he would sit and engage Buddhists in discussions about religion. His approach was

---

[22]Timothy Samuel Shah, preface to Lumsdaine, *Evangelical Christianity and Democracy in Asia*, p. xiii.

positive, dialogical and attentive. Not all evangelicals were so quick to listen, however. Especially later in the nineteenth century, at the height of colonialism in Asia, many missionaries became more critical and judgmental, especially of Hindu temples and gods.

By the twentieth century, evangelicals were encountering many of the religious and cultural issues in their witness that the Roman Catholics had encountered centuries earlier. Asian religions were often totalistic, directing every area of life and even death. How, for example, could a Chinese young man become a Christian and abandon his responsibility to carry on sacrifices for the ancestors? How could a good Hindu girl become a Christian and refuse to participate with family worship at a local temple? Could a Muslim girl profess faith in Christ and still live with her family? Would they accept her, and if so, how must she dress? These webs of cultural meaning hampered evangelical witness, particularly among the Buddhists, Hindus, Sikhs and Muslims in Asia. Where there were conversions, they were predominantly among mountain people, tribals in the highlands of Thailand and Vietnam, or Dalits who were excluded from Hindu temples.

When evangelicals developed new forms for witness—distributing Christian tracts, the Young Men's Christian Associations (YMCAs), Sunday schools—Buddhists and Hindus responded both by rejecting and imitating evangelical missions. Hinduism, for example, was transformed by its encounter with evangelical missions. Hinduism began to be defined in Western fashion as a religion, but the various responses to Christianity and Western education show that Indians were appropriating Christian teaching on their own terms. Hindu social reform movements began with India's encounter with missionaries. In addition, many Hindus began to study the life of Jesus and found him very attractive. Ram Mohan Roy (1772–1833) argued for monotheism behind the many gods and avatars of Hinduism and, like Mahatma Gandhi many years later, he studied and followed many of the ethical precepts of Jesus. By the end of the nineteenth century, Buddhism was responding to Christian missions by starting a Young Men's Buddhist Association (1899) and Buddhist Sunday school classes for both boys and girls.

As Asians appropriated some of the teachings and structures of evangelical witness, evangelicals searched for contextually appropriate ways to relate in Asian religious cultures. In India, a Christian ashram movement began in the late nineteenth century—a Hindu religious model of retreat and religious reflection that was now focused upon the teachings of Jesus. One of the pioneers in this type of Indian Christian witness was the Methodist missionary E. Stanley Jones (1884–1973). Whereas much evangelical witness began with teachings, Jones would often start with listening to the spiritual experience of the Hindu or Buddhist, and then encourage the Christian to explain their experience of God through Jesus Christ.[23] His "round table" discussions attracted many religious leaders because of the nonthreatening environment, and thus provided a context where more people could hear the Christian witness. In Korea, it was a Korean convert who adapted an indigenous religious practice, where the religious would go to a mountain temple and pray to the spirits before daybreak, and used it for Christian worship. As part of the 1907 Great Korean Revival, the Rev. Kil Sun Ju initiated "Daybreak Prayer Meetings," which continue to be a mark of Korean Christianity today.

Asian evangelicals continue to struggle with witness to the great blocks of religious adherents in Asia. Secularization has had both a negative and positive impact upon Christian witness in this "continent of world religions." In Singapore the Christian population is about 15 percent, the same percentage as of "free thinkers" (no religion). In China, a half century of secular communism has left many people questioning life without religion. Yet in both of these countries Christianity is growing. However, in Japan, Thailand and Taiwan, where secularization is also having a great impact, Christianity is not growing rapidly. While evangelical Christianity is growing in most countries of Asia, there is also a revival of certain forms of Buddhism, and there are vigorous movements within Islam.

Not all encounters with religions in Asia have been a straightforward meeting of Christians with Hindus or Buddhists. Evangelicalism, with its more diffuse authority structure and greater propensity to contextualize, has unwittingly spawned many syncretistic sub-Christian cults that mix essential elements from various religions. In Asia, it must also be recognized that evangelical witness has at times led to the formation of quasi-Christian—

---

[23]E. Stanley Jones, *Christ at the Round Table* (New York: Abingdon, 1928).

and usually strongly millenarian—sects. In each case a charismatic leader has risen to give a definitive interpretation of Scripture and of the times. The most obvious example is the Unification Church of Moon Sun Myung.[24] At the age of fifteen, Moon, while praying at daybreak, claimed to see a vision of Jesus who spoke to him and asked him to complete his work in bringing unity and peace to the church in the world. Raised a Presbyterian, Moon began his own church in North Korea and eventually moved his ministry to South Korea after the war, and eventually to the United States. Unlike evangelicals, who are devoted to Scripture, Moon developed a new scripture for his followers called the *Book of Divine Principles*. We are not interested here in the myriad of unusual teachings, ministries and businesses of the Unification Church; however, it should be noted that Moon himself came out of the very evangelical Presbyterian church of North Korea, like many other indigenous movements of the colonial era, before recentering his church on his own teachings and personal kingdom.

An earlier and far more lethal sect that came out of evangelical missions was the Taiping Tianguo (Heavenly Kingdom of Eternal Peace and Prosperity) of Hong Xiuquan (1814–1864). After failing his civil service exams many times, Hong turned to Chinese Christian literature produced by one of the first Protestant Chinese evangelists, Lian Fa (Leong Kung Fa). After reading Lian's "Good Words for Exhorting the Age" and portions of the Bible, Hong had a series of visions and he began to construct his own religion. "He believed he had received a divine mandate to lead the people."[25] From the Bible he picked up the need to destroy idols and to be fully devoted to God, and from Chinese culture he retained morning prayers, burning paper containing confessed sins, the lunar New Year celebrations and other practices. Most significantly, Hong elevated himself to the status of the brother of Jesus, and one who was called to cleanse China of demons. Resembling Old Testament law more than New Testament grace, his teachings were spread through an earthly kingdom, and soon his army numbered in the hundreds of thousands. By the time Hong's kingdom was crushed, the Taiping Rebellion had lasted fifteen years and had resulted—directly and

---

[24]The full name of the church is the Holy Spirit Association for the Unification of World Christianity.
[25]Patricia Siew and China Group, "Hong Xiuquan," in *A Dictionary of Asian Christianity*, ed. Scott W. Sunquist (Grand Rapids: Eerdmans, 2001).

indirectly—in the death of about twenty million people.[26] Having spent some time studying the Bible with a Baptist missionary and being devoted to the Bible himself, Hong had many evangelical advantages. However, missionaries would not baptize him because his motives were unclear. It was immediately after he turned his back on evangelical teaching that he began to shape his own earthly kingdom using Christian resources.

These stories are not isolated examples, as instances of eccentric cults spinning off evangelical structures can be found in most Asian countries. Two other brief examples will help illustrate the trend. Indian Pentecostalism, as we noted, is easily traced back to the earliest years of the twentieth century, but indigenous Pentecostal evangelists came much later. One of the earliest and most controversial was Paulasser Lawrie (AKA Shree Lahari Krishna, 1921–1989). Lawrie came from an Anglican and Salvation Army background in South India and Ceylon, and until later in life he endeavored to remain a Church of South India communicant while preaching Pentecostal sermons and being engaged in a ministry of healing. As Lawrie's reputation developed, he traveled and gathered an American following, and eventually he claimed that he himself was Jesus Christ. Strongly eschatological in the mid-1970s, Lawrie eventually said that he himself would fulfill other religions as well. By the time he finished his ministry he was revealing other formerly hidden (gnostic) teachings, and claimed to be an avatar who would return again after his own death.

Another millenarian group is the Dongfang Shandian (Eastern Lightning Sect) of eastern China. This sect is also an eccentric Christian group, which began around 1989. According to their teachings the Messiah has returned as a Chinese woman to release people from evil, and they hold to an additional sacred book called *Lightening from the Orient*. The Chinese government considers this fairly large group an illegal cult because of its strong millennial hopes and longings. What do these and many other quasi-Christian sects tell us about evangelicalism in Asia? We must be careful not to make quick conclusions, nor assume that the causes are all found in the genetic make-up of evangelicalism (as Roman Catholicism in Vietnam and the Philippines and throughout Latin America has also

---

[26]For a full discussion of the Hong's theology and the rebellion, see Jonathan Spence, *God's Chinese Son: The Taiping Heavenly Kingdom of Hong Xiuquan* (New York: W. W. Norton, 1996).

engendered numerous syncretistic movements). And yet the combination of democratizing social movements (and the free-market structures), the priority to contextualize (or translate) the message, and interaction with many Asian religions does continue to produce new evangelical spin-off movements in Asia.

Evangelical Future

It has been said that Asia is the one continent where Christianity has failed to win allegiance of great populations of people. On one level this is true. In countries like Japan, Taiwan and even the subcontinent of India, Sri Lanka, Pakistan and Bangladesh, the Christian population remains under 5 percent. In western Asia the Christian population remains even smaller, with Christianity never having recovered from the Arab Muslim invasions of the seventh and eighth centuries. The two countries that stand out—neither having a large evangelical population—are located at the far eastern and far western ends of Asia: Lebanon (over 70 percent Christian in 1900 and about 40 percent Christian today) and the Philippines (over 92 percent Christian). It is true that evangelical Christianity has not broken through the large block of Muslim communities that spread across western and southern Asia, and it has barely started to reach the largely Buddhist and Hindu regions. The exceptions to this generalization are that Christianity has spread rapidly among Koreans, Chinese and Southeastern Buddhist regions where communist rule (or the communist threat) has caused a great disruption in societies. Thus, in China, Vietnam, Cambodia, Malaysia, Singapore and Indonesia, the Chinese are coming to faith, and this is happening mostly through Asian evangelical outreach.

Although statistics do not tell us everything, they do tell us something. In 1900 the Protestant population in Asia was mostly evangelical, but it was less than 1 percent of the population of the continent. Roman Catholics constituted about 1 percent of the Asian population. In 2005 about 3 percent of Asians were Roman Catholic and 6 percent were Protestant. In countries like Nepal, Vietnam and Korea, where there were very few Christians at all, there are now vibrant evangelizing communities. The growth is uneven, but the witness to unreached areas is overwhelmingly Asian and evangelical (including Pentecostal) today.

Certainly, "evangelical" looks and sounds very different in Asia than in North America or Europe. In countries like Vietnam, Malaysia, China, Singapore or Korea, where most of the Christians are recent converts, the evangelical aroma is very strong. There is great zeal for evangelism, discipleship of young converts and an activism that most Western Christians find more in their history than in their churches today. Conversion is a central element in defining evangelicals, and, since the overall growth of Christianity in Asia has been from conversion in the past two generations, conversion is thus seen as part of the normal Christian life. In countries like China, Vietnam, Cambodia, Nepal, Malaysia, Indonesia, Singapore and Korea, where Christianity has experienced its greatest growth ever since the 1960s, most of the Protestants would be described by outsiders as evangelical, even if it is not their own self-designation. What Western Christians would call "mainline" churches (Methodist, Presbyterian, Lutheran and Anglican) are growing, confident and very evangelical in much of Asia. Thus, identifying evangelicals in Asia involves more than counting self-identified evangelicals in evangelical churches. Still, the Asia Evangelical Alliance modestly claims that nearly half of the 300 million Christians in Asia (140 million) are evangelical.[27] The number is probably much higher. A recent (2012) scholarly estimate of evangelicals in Asia (including both evangelicals and Pentecostals/neo-Pentecostals, puts the figure at 201 million.[28]

Many of the themes we have looked at above will continue to be key themes for evangelicals in Asia. Their encounter with major religions will be an issue, as will their concern for the poor, women's issues, and translation of texts and worship patterns. However, some more recent issues are becoming more important. In East Asia there is a growing minority of very wealthy Christians who are using their financial resources for evangelistic outreach. The great disparity of rich and poor in Asia creates a context similar to that of evangelical missions in the late nineteenth and early twentieth centuries. Rich Taiwanese or Chinese engaged in mission to Vietnam or Indonesia or Nepal may have trouble adapting to the different economic

---

[27]David Barrett's *The World Christian Encyclopedia*, 2nd ed. (New York: Oxford University Press, 2001) estimates 312,849,430 Christians in mid-2000, and of these about 166 million are evangelical or Pentecostal.

[28]Mark Hutchinson and John Wolffe, *A Short History of Global Evangelicalism* (Cambridge: Cambridge University Press, 2012), p. 240.

standards. Some groups of well-connected Asians raise money from wealthy Asians and Westerners to support Asian pastors and missionaries. Financial issues are beginning to be a problem again, but now from newer money sources. Another will be militant Islam—not a new issue for Christians in Asia, as it dates back thirteen hundred years; however, the new dispersed and popular forms of violence creates a new missional context that is less clearly defined.

Another ongoing issue at the heart of modern evangelicalism is that of unity. Evangelicalism in the modern world has promoted more new churches and has been less of an agent for renewal in existing churches. For example, Pentecostals in India have a difficult time working together, and other evangelicals will not always work with Pentecostals. Even though restrictions and persecution in countries such as Vietnam, Laos, Malaysia, China and Myanmar force Christians to work together, Christian unity continues to be a major problem among evangelicals. Evangelicals from outside of these countries often promote their own kingdoms at the expense of the unified body of Christ. In China, where sporadic, localized persecutions continue, Christians often resist cooperating in areas like pastoral formation, worship and mission. Evangelical divisions, unfortunately, are often related to economics. Will there be missionary fidelity in unity when many countries are becoming wealthy? We might also ask, will evangelicalism continue to care for the poor and the outcasts as evangelicals become wealthier in East Asia? It may be that the unity and wealth issues are even more closely related. As the church in Asia holds together, the witness of the poor Dalit Christians in India and outcast Christians in Pakistan and Bangladesh will help to re-center the wealthier Asian Christians back at the foot of the cross. Evangelical witness will continue to thrive as the suffering servant makes his home in the suffering church of Asia.

FURTHER READING

Anderson, Allan. *Spreading Fires: The Missionary Nature of Early Pentecostalism.* Maryknoll, NY: Orbis, 2007.

Barrett, David, George T. Kurian and Todd Johnson. *World Christian Encyclopedia.* 2nd ed. New York: Oxford University Press, 2001.

Bays, Daniel H. *A New History of Christianity in China.* Oxford: Wiley-Blackwell, 2012.

Bergunder, Michael. *The South Indian Pentecostal Movement in the Twentieth Century.* Grand Rapids: Eerdmans, 2008.

Brown, G. Thompson. *Earthen Vessels and Transcendent Power: American Presbyterians in China, 1837–1952.* Maryknoll, NY: Orbis, 1997.

Clark, Allen D. *A History of the Church in Korea.* Seoul: The Christian Literature Society of Korea, 1986.

Freston, Paul. *Evangelicals and Politics in Asia, Africa and Latin America.* Cambridge: Cambridge University Press, 2001.

Harrison, Brian. *Waiting for China: The Anglo-Chinese College at Malacca, 1818–1843, and Early Nineteenth-Century Missions.* Hong Kong: Hong Kong University Press, 1979.

Hattaway, Paul. *China's Christian Martyrs.* Oxford: Monarch Books, 2007.

Hudson, D. Dennis. *Protestant Origins in India: Tamil Evangelical Christians, 1706–1835.* Grand Rapids: Eerdmans, 2000.

Irvin, Dale T., and Scott W. Sunquist. *History of the World Christian Movement, Vol. 2: Modern Christianity from 1454 to 1800.* Maryknoll, NY: Orbis, 2012.

Lindell, Jonathan. *Nepal and the Gospel of God.* Kathmandu, Nepal: United Mission to Nepal, 1979.

Lumsdaine, David H., ed. *Evangelical Christianity and Democracy in Asia.* Oxford: Oxford University Press, 2009.

Martin, David. *Pentecostalism: The World Their Parish.* Malden, MA: Blackwell, 2002.

Moffett, Samuel H. *A History of Christianity in Asia,* Vol. 2: 1500-1900 Maryknoll, NY: Orbis, 2005.

Mullins, Mark R. "The Empire Strikes Back: Korean Pentecostal Mission to Japan." In *Charismatic Christianity as a Global Culture,* edited by Karla Poewe, pp. 87-102. Columbia: University of South Carolina Press, 1994.

Sunquist, Scott W., ed. *A Dictionary of Asian Christianity.* Grand Rapids: Eerdmans, 2001.

World Christian Database. Center for the Study of Global Christianity, Gordon-Conwell Theological Seminary. Copyright 2004 Breuer & Co. www.worldchristiandatabase.org.

Xi, Lian. *Redeemed by Fire: The Rise of Popular Christianity in Modern China.* New Haven: Yale University Press, 2010.

8

AUSTRALASIA AND
THE PACIFIC ISLANDS

Stuart Piggin and Peter Lineham

EVANGELICAL CHRISTIANITY'S MOST OBVIOUS CONTRIBUTION to glo-balization is its missionary outreach to the whole globe, dating mainly from the end of the eighteenth century. Australasia was one object of this mis-sionary zeal. The area includes the European colonies in Australia and New Zealand and more broadly Oceania, which includes Polynesia (the islands of the Southeast Pacific peopled by one ethnic group with similar languages), Melanesia (the islands on the east from Fiji to Papua New Guinea, with is-landers with darker skins and many languages) and Micronesia, the smaller islands spread north of Melanesia. Being most distant from Europe, the mission to Australasia called forth a powerful demonstration of the evan-gelical conviction that the kingdom of God must be brought near to all the peoples of the earth. Globalization, understood as the shaping of local soci-eties by distant forces, then, is dramatically illustrated by the evangelization of Oceania. The evangelical vision of "the world for Christ" overwhelmed the apathy induced by what has been called "the tyranny of distance."

Evangelicalism was also involved with another globalizing mission—that of capitalism. Capitalists sought to create in Australia and New Zealand major agricultural economies that had a competitive advantage over more traditional suppliers of European markets. The close connection between mission and capitalism is demonstrated by the fact that many of the political and commercial leaders in nineteenth-century Australia and New Zealand were evangelicals.

In more recent decades, evangelical communities have been sufficiently strong in Oceania to contribute to significant social transformation in the arenas of Aboriginal rights and aid to developing countries. The strength of this contribution reflects the strong legacy of social engagement from the early years of the movement and its maintenance of uncompromising supernaturalism in the face of theological liberalism at the beginning of the twentieth century. These issues will be addressed in this chapter.

Beginnings, 1730–1850

1. The origins of evangelical interest in the Pacific. Evangelicals understood that the Bible taught that the gospel had to be taken to the entire world. Biblical prophecy had influenced their high expectations for the evangelization of the globe, expectations that would give birth to the modern Protestant missionary movement at the end of the eighteenth century. Australasia was part of these expectations from the beginning. In June 1723, the nineteen-year-old Jonathan Edwards—who would go on to become the famed philosopher-theologian of the Great Awakening—speculated that come the millennium, divine and human learning would cover the earth and that wonderful new discoveries for the blessing of the globe would come from as yet undiscovered lands in the South Seas, then labeled Terra Australis Incognita.[1] In the following year, when meditating on Isaiah 42:4 ("and the isles shall wait for his law" [KJV]) Edwards wrote of the certainty of the "gospelising" of "America, Terra Australis Incognita [the hypothesized great southern continent], Hollandia Nova [the coasts discovered by Abel Tasman in 1644], and all those yet undiscovered tracts of land."[2]

The understanding that Christ must have the world—including the then uncharted and unnamed Australasia and the Pacific islands—was to become a fundamental hope of the evangelical movement. Evangelicals demonstrated their confidence that the gospel had the power to transform the souls of people from non-Western countries in the evangelical revivals that erupted in Europe, Britain and America in the 1730s. Practically, the revivals

---

[1] John E. Smith, ed., *The Works of Jonathan Edwards, Vol. 2: Religious Affections* (New Haven: Yale University Press, 2009), 13.212-13.
[2] Jonathan Edwards, *Apocalyptic Writings* [1724], ed. Stephen J. Stein (New Haven: Yale University Press, 1977), p. 143.

resulted in the mass conversion of Native Americans and black slaves in America and of the last still largely unreached European groups in Estonia and Livonia. It was believed that the evangelical message had been purposed by God for the renovation of the whole world—even Oceania, which had captured the attention of the British by the explorations of the celebrated Captain James Cook from 1769 to 1779. Cook's voyages were a key moment in the commencement of globalization. In the wake of Cook, evangelicals determined to reach out to the native peoples of the Pacific.

2. *The beginnings of evangelical missions to the South Seas: New South Wales, Tahiti and Tonga.* When in 1786 the British government resolved to create a convict colony in New South Wales (NSW), the coast of which had been charted by Cook in 1770, the evangelicals saw an opportunity to make known the gospel. At the forefront of this initiative was the newly converted William Wilberforce, who would go on to organize the successful campaign to abolish the slave trade. Wilberforce prevailed upon his friend William Pitt, the prime minister of Britain, to send an evangelical chaplain with the first fleet of soldiers, settlers and convicts to NSW. The young evangelical minister chosen for the chaplaincy of the infant colony was Richard Johnson. John Newton, excited by the prospect of the creation of a base for missionary expansion in the Pacific, bestowed on Johnson the title "Patriarch of the Southern Hemisphere."[3]

Six years later, in 1792, William Carey and the Northampton Particular Baptists established the Baptist Missionary Society. In his *Enquiry into the Obligations of Christians to Use Means for the Conversion of the Heathens*, Carey, an avid reader of Cook's journals, included a gazetteer, an elaborate table of the population of every known country in the world and the known religious allegiance of all the world's peoples. He gave the number of inhabitants of New Holland—as Australia was then known to the English—as 12 million, and labeled them all pagans (though he conceded that "1 or 2 ministers are there").[4] His geographical and demographic enterprise was typical of the evangelical conviction that the gospel was for the world and all its peoples.

---

[3]Newton to Johnson, December 1792, *Historical Records of New South Wales*, I, II, p. 474 footnote; N. Macintosh, *Richard Johnson, Chaplain to the Colony of New South Wales: His Life and Times, 1755-1827* (Sydney: Library of Australian History, 1978), pp. 14-15.
[4]William Carey, *Enquiry into the Obligations of Christians to Use Means for the Conversion of the Heathens* (1792; facsimile, London: Carey Kingsgate Press, 1961), p. 51.

In 1795 the London Missionary Society (LMS) was formed. One of its directors, Thomas Haweis, an Anglican minister in connection with the Countess of Huntingdon, was convinced that God was calling the society to send artisans (skilled craftsmen) as missionaries to reach the peoples of the South Seas. Alerted by Captain William Bligh of the *Bounty* to the evangelistic opportunities, he believed the islanders were ready to be converted.

In August 1796 the *Duff* set sail for Tahiti, the goal of Captain Cook's first voyage. On board were thirty-four artisans, including five women and three children. Some of the missionaries were taken to Tonga, while others attempted unsuccessfully to plant an outstation in the Marquesan Islands. From the beginning, the Tongan mission was unrealistic and far too extended over vast distances, and it would fail at the cost of three lives. In Tahiti tensions over a demand to supply guns led eleven of the missionaries to flee to Sydney, NSW, where they arrived on May 14, 1798.[5]

Outstanding among the missionaries who had remained in Tahiti was a Birmingham bricklayer, Henry Nott. Nott developed a friendly working relationship with King Pomare II, who saw political advantage in the missionaries' presence and thus presented himself for instruction in the faith. In NSW, chaplain Samuel Marsden encouraged perseverance with the Tahiti Mission, and was appointed by LMS as its trusted agent in the South Seas. In October 1812 Pomare forsook the worship of Oro and turned to Christ, but the wary missionaries would not baptize Pomare until 1819. Because the form of the new faith was evangelical, it was determined to avoid creating "nominal" Christians or forcing baptisms.[6] Nevertheless, Pomare's conversion was followed by his military conquest of the whole of the Society Island group of which Tahiti is part, a conquest that lead to the establishment and growth of churches and the mass Christianization of the population. This was celebrated as a great vindication of the evangelical cause and a reward for the suffering of the missionaries. LMS missionary William Henry hailed this conversion as "one of the greatest miracles of grace ever exhibited

---

[5]Niel Gunson, *Messengers of Grace: Evangelical Missionaries in the South Seas, 1797–1860* (Melbourne: Oxford University Press, 1978).

[6]A. T. Yarwood, *Samuel Marsden: The Great Survivor* (Melbourne: Melbourne University Press, 1977), p. 127; S. M. Johnstone, *A History of the Church Missionary Society in Australia and Tasmania* (Sydney: CMS, 1925), p. 97.

on the stage of this world."[7] The missionaries swiftly adjusted to the role of lawgivers, courtiers and facilitators of trade. They also translated the Bible and created strong Congregational churches.

Among the missionaries who had arrived in NSW from Tahiti in 1798 was Rowland Hassall, whose son, Thomas, became the founder of Sunday schools in NSW. The first of Rowland's children to be born in Australia was Mary Cover Hassall, who married Methodist minister Walter Lawry. Together they served in Tonga from 1822 with the Wesleyan Methodist Missionary Society (WMMS). Walter found the mission very challenging. It was no easier for him than working among convicts. Indeed, a convict by the name of Morgan had escaped to Tonga from Sydney and infected the Tongans with a virulent distaste for Christianity. "To this day," complained Lawry, "they remember Morgan's lies and believe them, consequently they detest our acts of religious worship more than anything we do or say."[8] If Walter made heavy weather of it, Mary seemed to adjust to it readily. She befriended the mothers and thereby learned their customs and their speech. When she and Walter left Tonga in 1824, they were stunned by the emotion engendered by their departure. Amidst a chorus of much sniffling, one eloquent Tongan said,

> We thank you for coming among us. Before you came, it was dark night in Tonga; now it begins to be light. Your friends in the foreign lands have sent for you. Go, and tell them that Tonga is a foolish land. Let them send us many teachers. Our hearts are sore, we are pained in our bellies, because you are going away from us.[9]

Methodism would reap a harvest in Tonga that would be celebrated throughout the evangelical world. Thomas Haweis, who had persuaded LMS to commit to missionary work in the South Seas, had already seen sufficient missionary success to exclaim on his deathbed in 1820, "Wonderful things the Lord is doing upon earth!"

3. *The beginnings of evangelical missions to New Zealand.* In Australia, Samuel Marsden felt largely unrewarded in his mission to convicts and ab-

---

[7]Henry to LMS Directors, 17 June 1813, *Evangelical Magazine* 22, 1814, p. 158.
[8]S. G. Claughton, "Lawry, Walter," *Australian Dictionary of Biography,* vol. 2 (Melbourne: Melbourne University Press, 1967).
[9]M. Reeson, *Currency Lass: The Moving Story of a Young Woman in the Convict Town of Sydney and the South Seas* (Sutherland, Australia: Albatross, 1988), p. 206.

original people, but his labors among the Polynesian peoples of the South Seas bore gratifying fruit. He had a passion for souls and a vision, acquired from his mentor, Charles Simeon of Cambridge, of a Christianized South Seas. In 1800 he accepted the position of agent for LMS missionaries in the South Seas. It was to New Zealand, however, that he was chiefly drawn. He first met Maoris (the Polynesian people in New Zealand) when, in 1803, some visited him in Parramatta, near Sydney.

In England in 1807, Marsden pleaded for a mission to the Maoris before the Anglican Church Missionary Society Committee (CMS). Marsden had made strong contacts with Ruatara, a Maori chief who was visiting England, and had concluded that the mission's first responsibility was to "civilize" the "natives" and only then evangelize them. After a long delay caused by tensions between Maori people and European traders in the heavily populated northern part of New Zealand, plans for the mission were launched in 1814, with two artisans (William Hall and John King) and a schoolmaster (William Kendall) appointed as missionaries. Marsden parted with £1,400 of his own money to purchase the ship *Active* for the mission.

Marsden himself first set foot on the mainland of New Zealand at still unspoiled Matauri Bay in the beautiful Bay of Islands on December 20, 1814. Unlike the first Sunday at Sydney Cove, when no church service had been held, elaborate preparations had been made for the solemn ceremony to be held on the following Sunday—Christmas Day. Marsden rejoiced to see the British flag flying over the bay, and interpreted it as signifying "the dawn of civilisation, liberty, and religion in that dark and benighted land."[10] He preached on a text from Luke (2:10): "Behold I bring you glad tidings of great joy." The sermon was translated, or at least its drift explained, by his Maori friend, Ruatara.

Unfortunately Ruatara died only a week later, and Hall, King, Kendall and their families found themselves at odds with one another, and were slow to gain acceptance from local Maori communities. Kendall, the one missionary interested enough to investigate Maori spirituality, was distracted by a Maori woman with whom he lived in preference to his wife. With tensions among the missionaries, attempts to find additional missionaries only caused further rifts in the missionary team.

---

[10]Samuel Marsden, *Missionary Register*, November 1816, pp. 470-71.

In spite of the risks involved and his propensity to suffer excruciatingly from sea sickness, Marsden made seven voyages to his New Zealand mission over the course of his life. He made his last journey when over seventy years of age, lame and almost blind. In New Zealand, by contrast with his reputation in Australia, Marsden was revered as an apostle, and among the evangelicals his counsel was always sought and his advice usually respected.

Marsden encouraged a third evangelical missionary society, the Wesleyan Methodist Missionary Society, to enter the South Seas. Samuel Leigh, the founder of the first Wesleyan circuit in Australia, was a friend of Marsden, and he visited New Zealand in 1819 at Marsden's suggestion and persuaded the London secretaries of the WMMS to appoint him "General Superintendent of Missions to New Zealand and the Friendly Islands." Leigh's work in New Zealand lasted only from 1822 to 1823. The Wesleyan mission was based at Whangaroa, north of the CMS base, but local warfare forced them to seek refuge at the CMS station in the Bay of Islands in 1827.

The breakthrough in Maori evangelization came through the appointment by the CMS of a former naval officer, Henry Williams, and his wife, Marianne, who had deep evangelical Anglican and Dissenting roots in England. Williams, who was strongly committed to evangelism, rejected both Marsden's "civilizing" strategy and particularly the trade in arms that helped to ensure the mission's acceptability with the warring tribes. Instead, his missionary team established themselves as educators and peacemakers, the education task greatly assisted by Henry Williams's brother, William, and his wife, Jane. The New Testament translation was completed and published in 1837, and a missionary ship extended the mission beyond its confinement to the tribes of the Bay of Islands. The first baptism took place in 1825, and widespread conversions were reported through the next ten years. Converts were carefully catechized in evangelical theology. This successful CMS mission was complemented by a revived Wesleyan Mission, and the two works agreed upon clearly defined spheres of influence and thus limited competition between them. The arrival of Catholic missionaries in 1837, however, changed the balance, and the stability of the mission was further upset in 1841 with the appointment by the British government of a high-church bishop, George Augustus Selwyn.

4. The evangelical domination of Polynesia. Meanwhile, the LMS mission in the Pacific Islands faced major challenges as well. The Tahiti Mission depended on the sponsorship of the Pomare dynasty, and thus ran into troubled waters when Queen Pomare IV showed little interest in Christianity. Further, the mission found itself competing with French Catholic missionaries. The LMS's hold on power was undercut when the French and British governments struggled with each other for influence, and the French established a protectorate over the island group in 1838 to uphold Catholic interests. As the LMS missionaries were drawn into opposition politics, it became expedient to hand the mission over to the Paris Evangelical Missionary Society, which took place after 1863. That Society slowly imparted to the evangelicalism of Tahiti a less expansionist and evangelistic flavor, manifesting instead the habit of resistance exhibited by French Huguenots over many centuries.

A new team of LMS missionaries arrived in 1817 and imparted a new quality to the Pacific work that was to have enormous implications. Among the missionaries was the remarkable John Williams, who was a superb publicist for evangelical causes and quite unwilling to confine himself to one island group. Williams recruited a group of "native missionaries," indigenous agents of the mission, and launched a ship in 1823 from which he explored the southern Cook Islands, leaving on Aitutaki two Tahitian teachers. By the late 1820s the Cook Islands were Christianized, and Raratonga became a crucial base for the adventurous missionary vision of John Williams. In 1830 the LMS placed native teachers in Samoa, and a new work developed from there that was largely commenced by converts from other parts of Polynesia, although European missionaries were sent in 1836.

When the Wesleyans conducted work in the South Pacific, one arm was New Zealand, but the other was "the Friendly Islands," including Tonga, where the LMS had failed during the first missionary wave. Thomas Lawry's brief stay was the first attempt to reach Tonga, but a visit by a group of Tahitian converts and then the appointment of John Thomas to Tonga in 1826 made the critical difference. The conversion of an able man, Peter Vi, who became an ardent witness to his people, and the subsequent conversion of three key chiefs, Tupou, Tuafa-ahau and Finau, created a mass Christian movement. In 1834 a wave of Methodist-style revival struck the islands, ce-

menting evangelical Christianity into the fabric of the society. Another Protestant kingdom emerged, and one far from generous to Catholic rivals.

In Fiji, Wesleyans again were the principal missionary body, and Tongan
Wesleyans intervened in support of them in 1855. The first Western missionary was sent in 1825 from the LMS. Wesleyan missionaries arrived in
1835, and they united with the Tongan visitors to spread the faith. A huge
revival movement spread in the 1840s. Tongans also spread Wesleyan Christianity to parts of Melanesia to the east of Fiji.

Overall the Christianity adopted in these islands was sharply differen-
tiated into LMS, Wesleyan and Catholic forms. There was huge tension with
the growing Catholic mission, with its emphasis on sacraments, priesthood
and ceremony; but there was also a sharp difference between the more
fervent Wesleyan style of worship and the grave and sober LMS form.
Overall, Protestant forms became strongly institutionalized, at the expense
of the warm-hearted evangelicalism of the early founders.

5. *The development of a Melanesian church.* In the far more disparate communities of Melanesia, where language differences made large-scale evangelism difficult, Christian missionary work tended to be much more diffuse
and the evangelical impact weaker. The Anglicans of New Zealand sponsored the high-church Melanesian Mission, and Catholics were also active
in the region. Missionaries were relatively late arriving in some of the islands,
preceded by traders and those in search of laborers—kanaks—for
Queensland plantations. John Williams, the first of the LMS contingent to
venture into the area, was killed on the beach at Erronanga in the New Heb-
rides (Vanuatu) by islanders suspicious of the sandalwood traders. Cook
Islanders and Samoan indigenous missionaries sought to establish a
beachhead on the island, but it was a Presbyterian missionary from Scotland,
John Geddie, from a strongly evangelical separatist Presbyterian church,
who founded the church after his arrival in 1848 with the assistance of native
preachers from LMS. A later missionary, John Paton, exploited political
factors in support of the mission.

LMS native missionaries were very active in the Melanesian island of
New Caledonia from 1841 to 1845, but Catholic missions later established
dominance in that island group, and the Protestant work was handed over
to the Paris Mission when New Caledonia came under French control. In

the Loyalty Islands, evangelical missionaries of the LMS battled for influence against Catholic interests, with each side invoking imperial authorities for support. The largest evangelical mission in the Solomons was the South Seas Evangelical Mission, originating in Australia and New Zealand. Founded in 1904, it originally ministered to Pacific laborers and was first known as the Queensland Kanak Mission. Its interdenominational character meant that it drew much of its support from the smaller churches, particularly the Brethren.

On the largest of all the Pacific Islands, New Guinea, it was not until the 1870s that evangelism commenced. The LMS workers, William Lawes and James Chalmers, depended heavily on the pioneering work of Ruatoka from the Cook Islands in their work in the Papua region on the southern coast. At the eastern end and surrounding islands, Wesleyans established a presence led by the Australian George Brown.

Colonial Constructions

Apart from chaplains, clergy and missionaries, the rapidly globalizing evangelical movement was given much support by men of influence, including high officials in the Colonial Office such as James Stephen (1789–1859), the governors of new settlements and colonies, merchants, and sheep and cattle farmers. The majority of such men in high places, of course, were not committed evangelical Christians, but a surprisingly large number of them were. There is room here for only a few examples.

1. Evangelical colonial governors: Arthur, La Trobe and Hobson. Among Australian colonial governors, the strictest was George Arthur (1784–1854), and the most lenient, Charles Joseph La Trobe (1801–1875), but both shaped decisively the communities they governed and both owed much of their creative genius to their evangelical faith. In 1824 Sir George Arthur arrived in Van Diemen's Land, as Tasmania was known until 1851, which was then an island jail for Britain's convicts. A devout Calvinist, Arthur relished the opportunity that virtual sovereignty gave him in Van Diemen's Land to create a pure Christian community in the tradition of John Calvin's Geneva by converting the convict settlers of the island.

Arthur developed a system of incentives and punishments for the convict population through seven grades of treatment, which ranged from ticket of leave at the lenient end of the spectrum to hard labor in chains in a place of secondary punishment at the other. The system was designed to allow convicts to be certain that they would free themselves from servitude through compliance, and surrender any liberty through resistance. His was to be a self-regulating machine that eliminated the element of luck whereby a convict's fate depended on the master whom he served or the warden under whom he was incarcerated. The colony he inherited in 1824 had a population of 12,000, its exports earned £45,317, and it had four churches. When he departed in 1836, the population was 40,000, the exports were worth £540,221, and there were eighteen churches.[11]

Charles La Trobe was the superintendent of the settlement of Port Phillip, later the Colony of Victoria, from 1839, and lieutenant governor from 1851 to 1854. He was a man of deep evangelical convictions. Both his father and grandfather were Moravian clergymen who had known John Newton and William Wilberforce. He was perhaps one whom the settlers needed rather than wanted. He sought to moderate the aspirations and prejudices of settlers and miners and to implement the policies of the Colonial Office, which, then controlled by evangelicals, was (at least in intent) protective of the indigenous people.

La Trobe insisted on the provision of parkland in the plan of Melbourne and gave every encouragement at considerable personal expense to the development of churches and of charitable, cultural and educational institutions. Timid La Trobe may have been, but his evangelical commitment helped him to remain faithful to his religious and cultural convictions, which he expressed in his first speech in Melbourne:

> It is not by individual aggrandisement, by the possession of numerous flocks or herds, or by costly acres, that the people shall secure for the country enduring prosperity and happiness, but by the acquisition of maintenance of sound religious and moral institutions without which no country can become truly great.[12]

New Zealand did not have quite the same legacy of evangelical governors. Captain Hobson, who became the first governor after annexation of the land

---

[11]Robert Hughes, *The Fatal Shore* (New York: Alfred A. Knopf, 1987), p. 394.

[12]Jill Eastwood, "La Trobe, Charles Joseph," *Australian Dictionary of Biography,* vol. 2 (Melbourne: Melbourne University Press, 1967), online: http://adb.anu.edu.au/biography/la-trobe -charles-joseph-2334.

in 1840 by the British government, had evangelical sympathies. Henry Williams of CMS had been delighted at his arrival in New Zealand early in 1840, and used his influence to persuade the Maori to meet Hobson and himself translated Hobson's treaty of annexation into the Maori language and urged the chiefs to sign. Other missionaries helped to collect other signatures until Hobson pronounced himself satisfied that the annexation was by native consent, and the Treaty of Waitangi was signed. But there was little time for Hobson's evangelical sympathies to influence the shaping of the country before he suffered a stroke in 1841. His successor, Fitzroy, was suggested by the CMS. Unfortunately this link was disliked by the growing number of British settlers, and he also compromised the Treaty of Waitangi's protection of Maori rights out of concern for the Crown's financial plight. Complaints from the settlers led in 1845 to his recall and replacement by George Grey, a devout Anglican but not an evangelical. Thus the evangelical impact in New Zealand waned after 1840.

2. *Evangelical settlements in Australia and New Zealand.* Of all the Australian settlements, South Australia owed most to evangelical influence. "Paradise of Dissent" is Pike's accurate description.[13] The founders and first settlers of South Australia were passionate about religious and civil liberties. Among the many settlers who left the evangelical liberal stamp on South Australia, George Fife Angas (1789–1880) stands out as the most influential.

From England, Angas had arranged for the colony to be supplied with the agents of evangelical Christian civilization: ministers for the nonconformist chapels, teachers for the schools and missionaries to the aborigines. His success in persuading men of character and ability to migrate may have been his most significant contribution to the colony. It has been estimated that in the first five years of the colony, at least a third of the names that appear in the emigrants' registers were selected by Angas or his protégés.[14] He financed the immigration of confessionalist Lutheran settlers under Pastor Kavel, settling them on his own land in Klemzig and Angaston, and rejoicing that consequently there could be bestowed on South Australia "the honourable epithet of Pilgrim land."[15]

---

[13]Douglas Pike, *Paradise of Dissent* (Melbourne: Melbourne University Press, 1967).
[14]Ibid., p. 137.
[15]Ibid., p. 131.

The more obvious evangelical presence in New Zealand came in some of the planned settlements, most particularly that of Otago in 1848. While the first European settlements in Wellington, Nelson and New Plymouth had been secular in outlook, and the later and much larger Canterbury settlement of 1851 had high-church roots, Otago was established by those who had seceded under the leadership of Thomas Chalmers from the Scottish establishment in 1843 and formed the Free Church. Theirs was a strongly evangelical vision, and Captain Cargill, who led the small group of five hundred settlers, was imbued with it to the hilt. This was a highly conservative Scottish vision of a Christian society, emphasizing the positive virtues of education, but also the need to avoid compromises over issues like the sabbath, the use of the organ in worship or the use of other than the metrical Psalter. Nevertheless, the roots were laid for a profoundly Protestant culture, and in later years the liberal view of education and ideas struggled with a revivalistic vision in the hinterland of Otago.

Other smaller evangelical communities settled in New Zealand in the secondary waves of settlement in the nineteenth century. For example, a small group of Scottish Highlanders under the Rev. Norman Macleod came via Nova Scotia and South Australia, and they left a distinctive mark in Northland. Not until the waves of Pacific Islanders came to New Zealand from the 1960s, however, was the evangelical community replenished with additional believers from outside.

3. *Establishing evangelical denominations.* The growth of an evangelical Protestant community rested largely on two factors: settlers (especially from Scotland) who shared an evangelical theology, and evangelistic movements within Australia and New Zealand. The appointment of evangelical bishops to Australian dioceses (Charles Perry to Melbourne in 1847, Frederic Barker to Sydney in 1855, Mesac Thomas to Goulburn in 1863 and Samuel Edward Marsden to Bathurst in 1869) gave a strong initial evangelical presence in Australian Anglicanism, maintained and, indeed, strengthened in Sydney, if eventually lost elsewhere. In New Zealand the general tone of the dominant (but not majority) Anglican Church was affected by its first bishop, George Augustus Selwyn. The evangelicals were minorities except in the small Nelson Diocese, where a New Zealand Church Missionary Association was founded in 1894, and in the Waiapu Diocese in the center of the North

Island. Here the mission to the Maori retained an evangelical flavor, and a former CMS missionary in India, Edward C. Stuart, served as bishop from 1877 to 1894, after which he returned to missionary work in Persia. In the twentieth century, Waiapu became more mainstream, whereas Nelson established a close link with the stridently low-church, evangelical Sydney Diocese, from which three of its bishops—W. G. Hilliard in 1934, P. W. Stephenson in 1940 and F. O. Hulme Moir in 1953—were drawn. Elsewhere, the Anglican Church was unsympathetic to the evangelical cause.

Presbyterians and Methodists in the nineteenth century were very different from the Anglicans. The lay colonists tended to be theologically conservative and defenders of Reformation traditions. As theological colleges became more influential, the evangelicals were largely relegated to backwoods appointments, and the lay preachers, who had been prominent in the church extension work of the nineteenth century, lost status. Throughout Australia and New Zealand, a major impact was also made by visiting evangelists seeking to encourage revival. The names are simply too numerous to mention, but the evangelical groups in most denominations were encouraged by visitors, while many overseas missionaries were recruited, and social movements—temperance, women's franchise, campaigns against prostitution and gambling—were inspired. Two American visitors to Australia and New Zealand, Reuben Torrey in 1902 and J. Wilbur Chapman in 1912–1913, demonstrated the populism of evangelicalism. In the early twentieth century, the larger Protestant denominations drifted toward more inclusive and liberal positions. Presbyterians retained a more conservative position through their continued emphasis on confessionalism, while Baptists were even more conservative still and suspicious of theological trends.

In the late nineteenth century, the evangelical configuration of both Australia and New Zealand was transformed by the rapid growth of a number of new revivalistic denominations. These had originated in Britain and the United States and came to the colonies primarily through evangelism rather than immigration. The Campbellite Churches of Christ was one such group, whose evangelists made an impact beginning in the 1850s, spreading out from Nelson in the South Island and sponsoring preaching in many places. The Plymouth Brethren made a deep impression—far more extensively than in Britain—in Tasmania and in the country districts of New Zealand, where small farmers responded positively to a church built on lay endeavor that also discounted theological education and rejected ordination. As dairying became crucial to the New Zealand economy, the Brethren became very strong and their evangelism created a conservative core to the Protestantism of the country. Then in the 1880s, the Salvation Army sent missionaries to Australia and New Zealand and caused quite a sensation through their outreach to the working-class urban communities. These three denominations gave a somewhat sectarian flavor to the evangelicalism of the community, but they provided an evangelistic spirit from which other evangelicals drew encouragement.

The Defensive Years

In the first half of the twentieth century, evangelicalism in Oceania, along with evangelicalism in most parts of the world, passed through a very defensive phase in reaction to biblical criticism, theological liberalism, the theory of evolution and the social gospel.

By the end of the nineteenth century, modernist theological ideas were rapidly spreading into theological education. There was concern among lay people that these ideas would threaten the values of evangelicalism if they continued unchecked. Fundamentalism came quickly to Australia: there was a conference on "Fundamentalism" in Sydney as early as 1921 and another in Melbourne in 1922. The Australian Bible League was formed in 1921 to defend the Scriptures; the Bible Union of Australia, with C. H. Nash as president, was formed in 1923. The chief institutionalizations of fundamentalism in Australia were the Bible college and convention movements, although it is important to remember that both predated fundamentalism and existed primarily for positive reasons of aiding evangelism and missionary work rather than as a defensive response to theological liberalism. Under the influence of fundamentalism, evangelicalism became narrower and more defensive. Energy went into defending the Bible, and preachers focused on individual evangelization rather than on the reformation of society. Part of this focus was due to the widespread belief that both Australia and New Zealand were already "Christian" countries based on Christian values. This was exacerbated, however, as the social gospel became identified with liberalism, and thus fundamentalism served to dull the evangelical commitment to social reform. Evangelicals began to be suspicious of social reform, and this attitude continued until the 1970s.

Australasian fundamentalism never put down the deep roots that it did in America. Certain doctrines such as premillennialism, which identified American fundamentalism, while readily found in Australia, never dominated there. Premillennialism was more common in New Zealand, however, even among Anglican evangelicals. Originally an incentive to evangelism, premillennialism became an esoteric and divisive issue as it developed into dispensationalism influenced by the Scofield Bible version, seen by many in nonmainstream conservative evangelical denominations as authoritative. In Australasia, a gap developed between liberal and conservative evangelicals. The many Bible colleges, most of which were launched to train lay people for evangelism and mission, became bastions of conservative evangelicalism, while some of the mainline theological colleges tended to cultivate more liberal forms of Protestantism.

It was a sharp debate. The Rev. E. H. Sugden, warden of the Methodist Queen's College in Melbourne and editor of the *Methodist Spectator*, and Principal W. T. Whitley of Baptist College Melbourne were both known and criticized for their support of higher criticism and the theory of evolution. The Methodist Conference of New Zealand debated hotly but did not censure the liberal views of the Bible of C. H. Garland, its theological college's principal. The Presbyterian Church in New Zealand was unwilling to suppress John Gibson Smith's liberal views of the atonement in 1907.

In the 1920s the rising tide of modernism was represented by the giant figures of Harry Emerson Fosdick of New York and H. D. A. Major, a former New Zealand priest who moved to England.[16] In New Zealand, Major's return home in 1929 touched off a "Great Bible Demonstration" from many churches. But liberalism was not easily defeated. Within the NSW Presbyterian Church, modernism was represented chiefly by Samuel Angus, professor of New Testament at St. Andrew's College, University of Sydney. He taught in the United Faculty, where Presbyterian, Methodist and Congregationalist clergy were trained. Angus affirmed both a "Christianity bigger than the Bible" and a religion "of Jesus" as distinct from the orthodox re-

---

[16]H. D. A. Major published *English Modernism* in 1927.

ligion "about Jesus," a distinction beloved of Angus's liberal mentor, the German scholar Adolf von Harnack (1851–1930).

In Sydney, clerical Presbyterianism, Methodism and Congregationalism surrendered to the forces of modernism led by Angus. But the Sydney Anglicans, deftly marshaled by the conservative evangelical triumvirate of D. J. Knox, R. B. Robinson and H. S. Begbie, responded to Angus by deposing the liberal evangelicals in their own church. In 1928 they took over the Anglican Church League and in 1933 succeeded in having Howard Mowll elected to Sydney as archbishop. Meanwhile, the Baptist ministry was preserved in its biblical conservatism by G. H. Morling, founding principal of the Baptist Theological College and a close personal friend of Archbishop Mowll.

In New Zealand, it was the Baptists who began the fight against modernism in the person of J. W. Kemp. Formerly a pastor of prominent Scottish and New York churches, he accepted a call to the Tabernacle in Auckland in 1920. He immediately introduced the strategy of the urban fundamentalist chapels of America: strongly apologetic Bible teaching, support for the new interdenominational missions, the establishment of a holiday spiritual convention and what he called the Bible Training Institute (BTI). Kemp was a brilliant evangelist. His best-known convert was E. M. Blaiklock, who became a professor of classics and an influential Bible commentator and apologist. Kemp was also effective in reshaping the tone of the Baptist community. With a strongly dispensational theology and an evangelistic passion, he made these various institutions beacons of conservative Protestantism with influence that extended far beyond the Baptist denomination. As conservatives rallied around Kemp, the Bible Training Institute became an increasingly influential and strategic body. Meanwhile in Christchurch, an Anglican vicar with a passion for biblical preaching, William A. Orange, recruited a remarkable group of evangelical ordinands—the "orange pips"— who challenged the dominant tone of the New Zealand Anglican Church. Meanwhile small fundamentalist churches—Brethren, Baptist and Salvation Army—gradually increased their following in society.

English institutions were very influential in Australia and New Zealand. The newly founded Inter-Varsity Fellowship sponsored the visit of Howard Guinness to Australia and New Zealand. Guinness challenged the very liberal emphasis of the Student Christian Movement and created "Evangelical

Unions" in many cities in the two dominions. These unions birthed an educated elite for the future, distancing themselves along the way from Kemp's sharpness. Meanwhile, the Scripture Union sponsored the growth of an evangelical movement of state-school Christian clubs called Crusaders. By the time of World War II, there was a movement that on the whole eschewed the tone of fundamentalism for a more positive evangelistic outlook.

Another form of evangelicalism emerged with the beginnings of Pentecostalism. Its origins in Australia may be dated back to 1870, long before the Azusa Street revival in Los Angeles to which Pentecostalism is usually traced.[17] But the expansion of Pentecostalism in Australia is due primarily to the visits in 1920 and 1921 of the British Pentecostal evangelist Smith Wigglesworth, whose missions reported scores of miracles, and the American female evangelist Aimee Semple McPherson, whose meetings were attended by huge crowds. In New Zealand, Smith Wigglesworth effectively laid the foundations of Pentecostalism in two visits in 1922 and 1924. The 1922 mission in particular was marked by healing meetings that attracted very large crowds in the aftermath of the influenza epidemic of 1919. A Maori spiritual healing movement led by T. W. Ratana had success at exactly the same time, but it was not evangelical. In Wellington and Christchurch, Pentecostal congregations were founded, and although the movement proved very unstable, there was a provocative evangelistic energy about it that laid strong roots for the future.

THE 1950S

The bridge decade from an evangelicalism *contra mundum* (against the world) to one committed to reaching and engaging with the world was the 1950s. Churchgoing in Australia and New Zealand grew rapidly and peaked in the early 1960s. Key to this growth was the model of Billy Graham, who moved American evangelicalism away from its fundamentalist defensiveness to what became known in America as "the new evangelicalism." The Billy Graham crusades in 1959 brought Australia and New Zealand as close to nationwide awakenings as they have ever been.[18] During the three and a half

---

[17]Stuart Piggin, *Evangelical Christianity in Australia* (Oxford: Oxford University Press, 1966), pp. 64-66.
[18]Ibid., chap. 7, which discusses the proposition that Australia experienced revival in 1959.

months of the Southern Cross Crusade, which took place in Australia and New Zealand, nearly 3,250,000 people attended meetings—one quarter of the entire population. Of these, 150,000 decided for Christ. In Australia, 130,000 people (1.24 percent of the Australian population) responded to Graham's invitation. The New Zealand figures were somewhat lower but still very significant. The Billy Graham team had learned to be cautious about making extravagant claims for attendances, but they were still very interested in numbers, and they believed that the Australian figures were among the largest crowds that had ever heard the preaching of the gospel to that date.

In retrospect, however, the 1959 Billy Graham crusade was seen to have reaped the harvest of evangelical influence in Australia and New Zealand rather than being the means of producing bigger crops in the future. It was the high point of fifteen years of very active growth in the evangelical wing of the churches. This growth was typified in Australia by Alan Walker's "Mission to the Nation" in the early 1950s, and highly successful parish missions of evangelical Anglican churches, especially in Sydney, along with the fruitful missions of Presbyterian evangelist Harold Whitney. The Presbyterian Church in New Zealand took important steps back toward a conservative and evangelical tone, with a plan to extend the church by planting new churches through the New Life Movement, which was founded by the Bible Training Institute–trained Norman Perry. The result was a very extensive expansion of the denomination. Perry had worked among Maori, and the denomination, lacking the baggage of colonial missions to the Maori, promoted very significant evangelism in the central North Island. It was a decade of rapid urbanization of Maori, and evangelical churches and missions (notably the United Maori Mission and Maori Evangelical Church) provided hostels and support for many young Maori.

REFORMED AND CHARISMATIC DEVELOPMENTS

In the 1960s, the "new evangelicalism" of the United States with its briskly modern image did not receive great support in the Pacific, although it certainly had a very positive impact among the educated classes. InterVarsity Christian Fellowship and a host of new agencies (Youth for Christ, for example) did well, as conservatives drifted closer to evangelicalism in reaction to the growing liberalism of their denominations. Moreover the 1960s was an era of successful youth evangelism, although not for mass evangelism. A return visit by Billy Graham to both Australia and New Zealand in 1968 and 1969 proved disappointing, and subsequent crusades and rallies have never proved particularly successful by the standards of 1959.

The most striking feature of evangelicalism from the 1960s in New Zealand, which may be contrasted with its Australian experience, was its rapid movement in a charismatic direction. Beginning in the South Island in 1960, a group of young men whose message was unwelcome in their Sydney home territory began a new charismatic movement in New Zealand. The style was somewhat different from the old-style Pentecostal preaching. It was not sectarian; rather, friendly contacts were forged right across the theological spectrum with no call to "come out" from their old denominations. It was not particularly fundamentalist, but instead emphasized new experience, an existential encounter with Christ in holiness and power. The tongues were the signs following, proof of the reality of God, and not capable of rational explanation. Charismatic evangelists began to attract new believers and more ardent Christians from many of the more formal wings of the church.

In 1972 news of the Jesus Movement in the United States and concern at moral trends in New Zealand sparked a series of marches for witness—"Jesus Marches"—in the main streets of most cities, and showed the potential of the charismatic movement to create a broad and highly political front. They were both evangelistic expressions and "marches for righteousness" against the liberal agenda of secular government. Younger evangelicals were reenergized by these trends. Older evangelicals were generally suspicious of the charismatic movement, and the Brethren in particular excoriated this rival lay movement. As a result, the Brethren lost many of their younger leaders to the new movement; these young people used their biblical and fundamentalist training to ensure that the new movement—with a few exceptions in the high church and Catholic worlds—became very much a wing of evangelicalism. It took twenty years for the two sides to accept one another, and by that time old-style evangelicalism was much weaker.

In the last three decades of the twentieth century, both Reformed evangelicalism and its revivalist offshoot, the charismatic movement, burgeoned in Oceania. They were sometimes in competition with each other, yet hindsight shows that this need not have been. For example, the Queensland

Kanaka Mission had revivalistic origins, and its missionaries always encouraged fervency and the expectation of spiritual revival and prayed for
spiritual cleansing. In 1936 there was a renewal movement. After World War
II the South Seas Evangelical Church was formed, but spiritual life, as so
often occurs in erstwhile mission churches, was subdued through involvement in politics. Then Muri Thompson, a Maori evangelist affected by
the charismatic movement in New Zealand, held evangelistic meetings in
Papua New Guinea and throughout the Solomons. These meetings were
marked by highly emotional results, with tears, visions, spiritual gifts and
confession of sins. In a sense the charismatic movement helped the evangelical message to extend itself more deeply into the island cultures.

One highly significant outcome of traditional evangelical missionary
work combined with new charismatic insights was the Aboriginal Revival,
which began in the Uniting Church in Elcho Island (now Galiwin'ku), five
hundred kilometers east of Darwin, on March 14, 1979. Few on the island
were left untouched. Worship became more spontaneous and meaningful.
Backsliders and fence-sitters fell on their knees and implored those who had
been liberated to pray for them. Not only was the worship more emotional,
but there was also a change in the tone of the community: less drunkenness,
petrol sniffing and fighting; greater conscientiousness in work; and an increased boldness in speaking out against social injustices. Males took over
leadership of the church from women and of the singing in worship, a factor
with great significance in Aboriginal communities where churches had been
almost entirely without adult male members. The Elcho Islanders took their
emphasis all over Arnhem Land, north and northwestern Australia, and
perhaps most effectively, the central south of western Australia.

Revival is sometimes the agency for the indigenization of Christianity in
minority cultures, leading to the empowerment of adherents of those cultures that had previously been demoralized. It was one of the means by which
Aboriginal people were able to persevere in their campaign for land rights
and for a just recompense for the land from which they had been dispossessed. On June 3, 1992, in the case of *Mabo v State of Queensland*, the High
Court of Australia buried the fiction that, at the time of white settlement,
Australia was *terra nullius* (belonging to no one). The judgment found that
indigenous peoples had a legal communal title to land. The Aboriginal people,

together with the churches, have been in the vanguard in the matter of land rights. Together they have changed the views of many Australians toward a desire for reconciliation between aboriginals and white people and for making restitution for past wrongs. But the cultural clash between Western civilization and that of the indigenous peoples of Australia has been one of the nation's most intractable problems. For two centuries evangelicals—both white and Aboriginal—have been at the forefront of attempts to address the issue, but the record has been one of many failures and few successes. Bringing life and hope to displaced and dispossessed peoples remains one of evangelicals' greatest challenges across the globe.

These challenges of finding ways to express evangelical faith in indigenous forms has continued to be a burning issue in many other parts of the Pacific. The old mission churches have proved highly unreceptive to the emphasis on personal spiritual experience. They maintain their original evangelical theology at least in name, but cultural and political identification with the maintenance of the traditional status systems of the islands make them resistant to any spiritually democratizing emphasis. Consequently, particularly in Tonga, where church splits have been common over the last hundred years, and where concern at the growth of the Mormons has been high, a series of splits have occurred. Out of this splits emerged the charismatic New Fellowship. Likewise, in other places, various charismatic denominations gained a strong following. When the Pacific peoples came to New Zealand, and to a lesser extent to Australia, during the 1960s to 1990s, their churches were among the most mobile organizations that helped to provide social identity for them. However, the churches were the focus of cultural conservatism, and while they supported the conservative moral agendas of evangelicals in the Congregational, and then after a merger, in the Presbyterian and Methodist churches that welcomed them, they were rarely interested in the other dimensions of evangelicalism. There emerged streams of Tongan, Samoan and Cook Islands native-speaking charismatic congregations. The same phenomenon has not really happened—at least not to the same extent—within the Maori community. Evangelicalism in Oceania has much yet to clarify in its relationships to indigenous peoples. Yet there are signs that indigenous ministries have much to offer in the reawakening of the spiritual power of the movement.

In the observably rapid current decline of Christian influence among Western people there are opportunities for new growth in evangelicalism, with some very creative movements developing in Australia and New Zealand. Globalized evangelicalism is being nourished by its Southern constituents. Within the Pentecostal branch of the movement, the Hillsong churches (the founder of which came from New Zealand) have become Australia's largest church communities and are now being exported to Europe and North America. And the most distinctively Australian Reformed evangelicals, the Sydney Anglicans, have joined and significantly shaped GAFCON, the Global Anglican Future Conference, which first met in Jerusalem in 2008 and which represents a large number of Anglicans worldwide.

FURTHER READING

Breward, Ian. *A History of the Churches in Australasia.* New York: Oxford University Press, 2004.

Chant, Barry. *The Spirit of Pentecost.* Lexington, KY: Emeth Press, 2009.

Davidson, Allan K., ed. *A Controversial Churchman: Essays on George Selwyn.* Wellington: Bridget Williams Books, 2011.

Lange, Stuart M., *A Rising Tide: Evangelical Christianity in New Zealand 1930–65.* Dunedin: Otago University Press, 2013.

Lange, Raeburn. *Island Ministers: Indigenous Leadership in Nineteenth Century Pacific Islands Christianity.* Christchurch and Canberra: University of Canterbury and Australian National University, 2006.

Linder, Robert D. *The Long Tragedy: Australian Evangelical Christians and the Great War, 1914–1918.* Adelaide: Openbook, 2000.

Lineham, Peter J. *Bible and Society: A Sesquicentennial History of the Bible Society in New Zealand.* Wellington: Daphne Brasell Associates, 1996.

Newman, Keith. *Bible & Treaty: Missionaries Among the Maori—A New Perspective.* Auckland: Penguin, 2010.

Piggin, Stuart. *Evangelical Christianity in Australia: Spirit, Word and World.* Melbourne: Oxford University Press, 1996.

Sivasundaram, Sujit. *Nature and the Godly Empire: Science and Evangelical Mission in the Pacific, 1795–1859.* Cambridge: Cambridge University Press, 2005.

Stenhouse, John, and Jane Thomson, eds. *Building God's Own Country: Historical Essays on Religions in New Zealand.* Dunedin: University of Otago Press, 2004.

PART THREE

ISSUES IN EVANGELICAL
ENCOUNTERS WITH
CULTURE

9

ECUMENISM AND
INTERDENOMINATIONALISM

David M. Thompson

EVANGELICAL CHRISTIANS PLACE THEIR primary emphasis on personal commitment to Jesus Christ as Lord. This personal commitment has often been regarded as more important than the formal marks of church membership, and consequently evangelicals have usually regarded such commitment as more important than differences between denominations.

The word *denomination* was first used in English to describe those Christians who dissented from the Church of England, but the underlying belief that the true church was invisible meant that visible differences between different groups were less important. Furthermore, the international character of the Great Awakening meant that it was quite natural for evangelicals in different countries to communicate with one another, which deepened their sense that they all belonged to the same church.

The main impetus to evangelical cooperation came from the belief that new kinds of action were necessary to proclaim the gospel, beyond what local congregations, whether Anglican parish churches or Dissenting meetings, had done in the past. This led to the formation of new kinds of organizations—societies with specific purposes such as the support of traveling evangelists or the production of religious tracts or copies of the Bible. The existing structures of the established Churches of England and Scotland had no real parallel for such societies. This meant, on the one hand, that there was no competition with existing church structures in their formation, and on the other hand, that the model adopted was essentially that of a voluntary society of subscribers (financial supporters), run by an elected committee, which made an annual report. The annual meetings became occasions on which reports of progress and efforts to recruit new subscribers were made.

Although the majority of such societies formed at the end of the eighteenth century were evangelical in inspiration, the model was in fact originally high church in inspiration. The Society for Promoting Christian Knowledge, formed in 1698, was the first such society, and as its title indicates, its aim was to make available cheaply printed Christian literature. The Society for the Propagation of the Gospel was likewise the first Anglican missionary society, formed in 1701.

John Wesley's societies followed a similar model, as did those of the Countess of Huntingdon, the patron of the Calvinistic Methodists. Furthermore, the experiences of both the Wesley brothers and George Whitefield in America meant that they were exposed to situations in which Christians of various traditions lived side by side in the same communities. Not that this meant that there were to be no controversies: the so-called Calvinist controversy between Whitefield and Wesley that began in 1740 and reappeared in 1770, after Whitefield's death, was an example of a continuing tension point between evangelicals.

In addition to the concern to spread the gospel, the other impulse behind evangelical interdenominational organization was political. The campaign against the slave trade (and then slavery itself), which began in Britain in the last third of the eighteenth century, brought together evangelicals of varying persuasions. Again the model of a society of subscribers was used. The campaign against slavery also prompted an interest in and concern for the slaves on the sugar plantations in the Caribbean, and then in the parts of Africa from which the slaves were drawn. This was one of the reasons for missionary activity there, and the momentum behind this movement was different from that directed toward India—though it also drew on the experience recorded by Jonathan Edwards of attempts to convert Native Americans.

The overseas missionary societies formed in England in the 1790s have always been seen as a manifestation of evangelical activity. However, they were not for the most part interdenominational. The first was the Baptist

Missionary Society in 1792, which was quite definitely Baptist in conviction and practice; the second was the London Missionary Society in 1795, which did at first include representatives of several denominations (although all believers in infant baptism) and had an explicitly nondenominational goal; but the third, the Church Missionary Society, founded in 1799, was specifically founded because the London Missionary Society was not felt to give sufficient emphasis to the importance of bishops in its doctrine of the church (even though the CMS's first missionaries actually came from German nonepiscopal churches).

Less often noticed, but equally important, were missionary societies at work in Britain. Those domestic societies established to support traveling preachers in the British Isles were almost without exception denominational in their structure—indeed they formed the pattern for the kinds of denominational organization that subsequently became normative. So although they were clearly evangelical, they were equally clearly denominational. On the other hand, domestic city and town missions were commonly organized on an interdenominational basis. The London City Mission, founded in 1835 by David Nasmith, was the model for such societies and was decidedly interdenominational. At a local level, throughout Britain and subsequently throughout the British Empire, city and town missions were a key area of interdenominational cooperation.

Where else was interdenominational cooperation found? On the American frontier at the beginning of the Second Great Awakening, different denominations joined in the new camp meetings. The famous Cane Ridge revival in Kentucky, August 6–12, 1801, was the culmination of four months of religious excitement in northern Kentucky. It began with a Presbyterian "Communion Season" preparatory service at Barton W. Stone's meetinghouse. On the following day crowds arrived, estimated at between ten and twenty thousand, with between 125 and 148 wagons drawn around the meetinghouse. Methodist and Baptist preachers joined the crowds and spoke from their own platforms. Preaching continued for several days. All were refreshed by the experience and estimates of those receiving assurance ranged from five hundred to one thousand. It was the beginning of mass revivalism in the early nineteenth century. With the passage of time, revivals were more commonly organized by a single denomination, but the inter-

denominational history lay behind the later success of preachers like Dwight
L. Moody and even Billy Graham.

From the mid-nineteenth century, a series of missionary conferences
were held, at first in Great Britain, but culminating in a grand international
conference in New York in 1900 to survey the prospects for a new century.
These formed the essential background for the more famous Edinburgh Missionary Conference of 1910, which was, in fact, the *third* World Missionary
Conference. The Edinburgh conference is remembered for three reasons: it
established a Continuation Committee, which subsequently established the
International Missionary Council in 1921; it involved Anglo-Catholic missionary societies for the first time; and it led to the establishment of the Faith
and Order movement. This movement became one of the constituent elements of the World Council of Churches when it was formed in 1938, and
was formally constituted ten years later at its first Assembly after the Second
World War in Amsterdam in 1948.

Another dimension of evangelical interdenominational cooperation was
the British and Foreign Bible Society founded in 1804, with the American
Bible Society following in 1814, as well as series of Bible societies in other
countries of the world. These societies had a manifold significance. First, the
idea of cooperating to produce cheap copies of the Bible, and individual
books of the Bible, in a variety of languages represented in the clearest possible way the assumption of a common biblical basis for evangelical Christianity. The publication of evangelical tracts was not to be a primary means
of disseminating evangelical principles; the primary means was the publication of the Scriptures themselves, traditionally "without note or comment."
Second, the emphasis on putting the Bible into the hands of the people was
also fundamental to the method of evangelical testimony. Just as the publication of the Bible in the vernacular was seen as a powerful weapon in the
publicizing of Reformation principles in the sixteenth century, so three centuries later was it felt necessary to catch the rising tide of popular literacy
and to ensure that the field was not left open solely to advocates of revolutionary political ideas. Third, cooperation for the publication of Bibles was
something difficult for the established Churches of England and Scotland
to resist; yet equally this presumed an equality among different Christian
traditions in Britain that the established churches did not greet with enthu-

siasm. In fact, however, local branches of the Bible Society have proved to be one of the most durable local manifestations of interdenominational activity among the British churches. Fourth, the somewhat depressing "Apocrypha controversy" of the 1820s, when certain evangelicals protested against the fact that the Bible Society was publishing Bibles that contained the Old Testament apocryphal books for sale in Catholic countries in mainland Europe, illustrated the extent to which the Bible Society became associated with a decidedly Protestant position.[1]

In fact, evangelical cooperation in the early nineteenth century was increasingly associated with an anti–Roman Catholic position. From one point of view this was not surprising. Protestant Christianity in Europe was decidedly anti-Catholic in the eighteenth century. After all, the later seventeenth century had seen a strengthening of the Roman Catholic Church in a number of countries where the Reformation had been initially popular. From another point of view, however, in Britain and the United States the development of evangelically minded Protestant denominations had depended on the acceptance of a position of religious toleration and the right of private judgment that logically entailed the concession of the same rights to Roman Catholics. Thus in early nineteenth-century English politics, anti-Catholic feeling tended to be stronger among Anglican evangelicals than among nonconformists; for the latter, the attainment of full civil equality with members of the established church made it difficult to deny the same rights to other Christians simply because they were Roman Catholics. The founding fathers of the United States likewise adopted a position of denominational neutrality.

This difference of view is well reflected in the background to the formation of the Evangelical Alliance in 1846. The context in British religious politics in the early 1840s was complex. In 1841, John Henry Newman wrote in *Tract 90* (a part of the high-church Tracts for the Times series) that subscription to the Thirty-Nine Articles of the Church of England was not incompatible with the teaching of the Council of Trent—the sixteenth-century

---

[1]Alongside the interdenominational efforts of the Bible societies in both Britain and America was the work of the Religious Tract Society and the American Tract Society, both of which operated on an interdenominational basis. Throughout the nineteenth century these societies produced not only short tracts, but also published books. These societies were the handmaidens of evangelical missions efforts throughout the nineteenth century.

council of the Roman Catholic Church that had decisively rejected Protestant teaching. The tract provoked a fierce outcry, and was condemned by the bishops of the Church of England. Nevertheless it led many evangelical nonconformists and even Anglican evangelicals to fear that there was a definite move toward Rome on the part of significant voices in the Church of England. In May 1842 at the annual assembly of the Congregational Union in London, Rev. John Angell James of Birmingham, when welcoming other Christians from Scotland, Wales, Canada and Germany, pleaded that steps be taken to promote union among evangelical Christians who supported the voluntary principle (that is, those who opposed state churches and endorsed the belief that churches should be supported by the will of the people), and he published a "Proposal for a General Protestant Union" in the *Congregational Magazine* for July 1842. The result was a packed meeting of more than ten thousand people in London on June 1, 1843, which passed several resolutions in favor of Christian union.

The Disruption of the Church of Scotland in May 1843, when some four hundred evangelical ministers of the church left in protest against what they regarded as illegitimate legal interference in the spiritual life of the church, led many evangelical nonconformists in England and Wales to see the moment as an auspicious one to launch a renewed campaign for disestablishment (the removal of state support of and links with a "national" church) on the ground that the state could no longer be trusted to defend an essentially Protestant position. When the government proposed in 1845 to increase its grant to the Roman Catholic seminary at Maynooth just outside Dublin in Ireland, this also resulted in a more concerted effort by many evangelicals to establish a movement to unite all evangelicals. As a result of a letter from the veteran Scottish leader Thomas Chalmers, a preparatory meeting was held in Liverpool in October 1845, which agreed to form an Evangelical Alliance for the British Isles. Here a key decision was that membership would be open to individual Christians or congregations, but there was to be no attempt to form any kind of union or federation of separate churches or denominations. An international conference was held in London in August 1846, at which the international Evangelical Alliance was founded. It was attended by some eight hundred Christian leaders from eight European and North American countries, including men such as Adolphe

Monod from France, August Tholuck from Halle University in Germany and Johann Oncken, the leader of the German Baptists. Other national Alliances were founded in Canada in November 1846, Germany and Switzerland in 1847, India in 1849, Turkey in 1855 and the United States in 1867.

The Alliance formalized international cooperation among evangelicals in a new way. Its setting aside of a week for united prayer beginning on the first Sunday in the year brought Christians of different traditions together on a regular basis for the first time. The idea of international Christian conferences, on wide-ranging themes, was developed by the Alliance; eleven such conferences were held between 1851 and 1907. It is significant that 10 percent of the delegates at the founding conference were from North America at a time when transatlantic travel had scarcely entered the steamship era. (However, the American representatives were less happy with the antislavery position taken by those in Britain, and this impeded the progress of the Alliance in the United States until after the Civil War.) The journals associated with the local branches of the Alliance, such as *Evangelical Christendom* in Britain, provided a more sophisticated network of information about the churches of the world—something that had not previously existed. The theme of missions was always prominent, and the plan for the first international missionary conference in 1854 was first proposed at the annual meeting of the British Evangelical Alliance. Finally, the defense of religious liberty was a constant theme—and one that alienated the European state churches. It was one thing to defend the rights of Protestant minorities in Catholic countries, such as the Waldensians in Italy, for example; it was quite another to defend the rights of Protestant minorities in countries with Lutheran state churches like Germany and Sweden. However, the great weakness of the Alliance was that it remained a union of individual Christians rather than churches. Indeed, if anything, its reluctance to consider any attempts at a formal confederation of churches increased with the passage of the years.

The Evangelical Alliance was the result of the initiative of ministers. At about the same time, an initiative among lay people produced two other rather different organizations. The Young Men's Christian Association (founded in 1844) and the Young Women's Christian Association (founded in 1854) were originally intended to provide Christian lodgings for young men, and later women, living away from home from the first time. In Great

Britain and later in Europe, the work of these organizations was primarily to serve working young people, often in the mushrooming clerical jobs associated with the spread of industry and commerce. In North America that work was supplemented from an early stage by work in the rapidly growing colleges that were founded as the United States frontier moved steadily westward. The YMCA was also a focus of interest for men who had an even broader vision of Christian cooperation. Henri Dunant of Switzerland went on to found the Red Cross, whose Christian origin was clearly indicated by its symbol.

Dwight Lyman Moody (1837–1899), who began adult life as a successful shoe salesman, worked under the YMCA organizing Sunday School Teachers' Conventions. His gift for evangelism led him to make a preaching tour in Britain from 1872 to 1875, accompanied by the singer Ira D. Sankey (1840–1908). This was followed by similar missions in North American East Coast towns. The deliberate use of musical solos and easily sung gospel songs to drive home the message was one of Moody's innovations. Another was the "Enquiry Room," where potential converts could receive further instruction after the meeting (instead of coming forward to make a confession of faith immediately), which became a standard feature of later nineteenth-century revivals. Moody had stirred up revival in American colleges, and on his second British tour in 1881–1884 he visited universities there. As a result of his meetings in Cambridge, several students offered themselves for missionary work overseas, in particular with Hudson Taylor's new interdenominational China Inland Mission. Moody strongly influenced the American Methodist layman John R. Mott (1865–1955), who was a central figure in student and mission work, including the YMCA, Student Volunteer Movement, World's Christian Student Federation, Edinburgh World Missionary Conference and Continuation Committee. Mott participated in the major ecumenical meetings and was named honorary president of the World Council of Churches. The link between the student and missionary movements was crucial for the development of the twentieth-century ecumenical movement.

An important development in late nineteenth-century Britain was the Keswick Convention, an annual gathering of Christians at Keswick in Cumberland (now Cumbria) begun in 1875 at the invitation of the Vicar of Keswick, Rev. T. D. Harford-Battersby. It is known particularly for its emphasis on holiness or entire sanctification, which was always a controversial view among Anglican evangelicals. Less known is how significant the Keswick gatherings were for ecumenism. These meetings drew together evangelical Christians from many denominations on a regular basis, and the friendships created and fostered therein were to be important well into the twentieth century. In fact, Keswick held an appeal to a wider group than only those who believed in the holiness doctrine of "entire sanctification." Thus it was a place where the influence of many notable evangelical women could be felt, including Charlotte Elliott (1789–1871), Fanny Crosby (1820–1915) and Frances Ridley Havergal (1836–1879), who regularly attended in person. It was also a place where premillennial doctrines were regularly preached and where a conservative view of Scripture was fostered, against what were felt to be the threats of modern biblical scholarship. Symbolically, the Keswick Convention acted as a rallying point for the conservative elements among British evangelicals in the late nineteenth century.

The early twentieth century saw the emergence of a movement popularly known as "fundamentalism," which became the focus for conservative theological groupings. It has never been right to identify evangelicalism with fundamentalism, although this charge has often been made. Undoubtedly, however, fundamentalism did appeal to a conservative evangelical constituency. It was initially a protest against what was often called "modernism" in early twentieth-century theology—a term never precisely defined except by its enemies—by which was meant the attempt to accommodate Christian doctrine to modern philosophical and scientific thinking, especially in relation to Scripture. One reaction to modernism was the publication in the United States of a series of pamphlets titled *The Fundamentals* (1910–1915), which defended what were regarded as fundamental doctrines of the Christian faith. Although this series led to the use of the term *fundamentalism*, the usage was always less precise. Most often it referred to an understanding of the inspiration of Scripture as verbally inerrant. Fundamentalism was also closely associated with premillennial, and specifically dispensational, views, which had gained ground rapidly in the previous hundred years. Since this association involved criticism of the postmillennialism that had inspired much social involvement by Christians and the churches in general, it was also linked to opposition to the so-called social gospel, which was regarded by premillennialists as naively optimistic in linking the understanding of the kingdom of God with improvement in social conditions.

The result of the fundamentalist-modernist controversy was an increasing, and often bitter division between conservative and liberal evangelicals (particularly in the United Kingdom and North America) during the first half of the twentieth century. By the 1890s the Evangelical Alliance had become virtually defunct in North America. In 1942 a new National Association of Evangelicals was established in the United States, and it was an American initiative that led to the formation of the World Evangelical Fellowship at a meeting in Wondschoten, Zeist, Holland, in August 1951. One characteristic of the conservatives was criticism of the ecumenical movement, particularly organizations like the National Council of Churches of Christ in the United States and the World Council of Churches. It was particularly associated with Carl McIntire and his American Council of Christian Churches. On the other hand, the same antagonism was not shared so much in Africa and Asia, where evangelical Christians supported the movement to make their churches self-governing and free of control by Western missionary societies.

A rather different movement, which was destined to be significant for twentieth-century evangelicalism, was Pentecostalism. Essentially Pentecostals were Christians who declined to believe that baptism in the Spirit, and particularly speaking in tongues, were experiences of the early church alone. There had been occasional claims of speaking with tongues since the time of the eighteenth-century revivals. These were renewed in California in 1905–1906 as reports of the Welsh Revival were received. In the next few years several new Pentecostal groups emerged, sharing adventist beliefs and proclaiming a simple "back to the Bible" gospel. On the whole these groups were spurned by conservative evangelicals in Britain and the United States in the first half of the twentieth century. However, charismatic renewal affected the whole range of churches from the 1960s, including the Roman Catholic Church. By the 1990s, Afro-Caribbean churches in Britain, which often had links with Pentecostalism, were becoming fully involved in interdenominational activities with white evangelicals. Furthermore, Pentecostalism became increasingly important outside Europe. It affected a number of African-instituted churches and was particularly influential in Latin America, where it grew more rapidly than anywhere else in the world in the last quarter of the century.

In the first half of the twentieth century, evangelicalism had been fragmented, often acrimoniously. In the second half, a greater sense of unity was recovered. After 1945 the significance of denominations declined sharply in the United States. By the end of the century, many American evangelicals were attending megachurches, few of which were denominationally aligned, or if they were denominationally aligned, they often played down that fact in an effort to attract as broad a following as possible. The phenomenal growth of Christian schools and of home schooling as options for many evangelical parents created links across denominations. The rise of large interdenominational youth ministries—Youth for Christ, Young Life, Navigators, Campus Crusade, groups associated with the International Fellowship of Evangelical Students and Youth With a Mission and Operation Mobilization abroad—eclipsed virtually all the denominationally based organizations aimed at young people. Likewise, as evangelicals became involved in international aid work, they by and large did so by creating interdenominational agencies like World Vision, Food for the Hungry and a host of similar organizations rather than use denominational channels. Furthermore the emergence of large interdenominational seminaries—Fuller Seminary, Trinity Evangelical Divinity School, Dallas Theological Seminary and Gordon-Conwell Seminary in the United States, and Tyndale Seminary and Regent College in Canada—impacted the training of large numbers of evangelical ministry candidates: students from these schools often reentered denominations with a much stronger commitment to transdenominational evangelicalism than did their peers who had trained in strictly denominational schools. By the end of the twentieth century, American evangelicals sat far more loosely to denominations than did British evangelicals, or than their American forbears had at the start of the twentieth century.

One of the visibly uniting factors in America was the Baptist evangelist Billy Graham. After establishing his reputation in the United States, he held three mass crusades in Britain in 1954–1955, 1966–1967 and 1984–1985. The opening week in 1954 in the Harringay Arena, London, attracted over eighty thousand people. In some respects he was like Moody, without Sankey—in that there was little by way of innovation. One of Moody's greatest British followers, the Congregational minister George Campbell Morgan, had been more successful in the United States than Britain in the early 1920s. Graham showed that mass evangelism could still bring results in Britain, but on balance he was more successful elsewhere. His significance, however, is that he was able to draw on support from most of the major Protestant denominations; the same was true elsewhere in the world.

Another unitive figure was the Anglican cleric John Stott (1921–2011). After a distinguished career at Cambridge, he became first curate and then rector of All Souls' Church, Langham Place, London. He drafted the basis of the World Evangelical Fellowship when it was formed in 1951, and he was a key supporter of Billy Graham's evangelistic campaigns. Indeed, he himself conducted successful university missions at Oxford and Cambridge, as well as providing a model of a successful evangelical Anglican parish church. In the 1960s he became an influential world figure through his international speaking tours and his writings. He was anxious to affirm the position of evangelicals within the Church of England's governing structures, and he publicly opposed the suggestion at a famous 1966 meeting by Martyn Lloyd-Jones, minister of the independent Westminster Chapel in London, that evangelicals should leave the mainstream churches. In the following year, at an important meeting held at Keele, Anglican evangelicals endorsed Stott's position, and this led to evangelicals taking an active part in the new General Synod of the Church of England, which was initiated in 1970. Sir Norman Anderson, a leading evangelical, became the first Chairman of the House of Laity.

Stott was also a key figure at the Lausanne International Congress on World Evangelization in July 1974, and his drafting skills were once again called upon for the Lausanne Covenant. The initiative for Lausanne came significantly from Billy Graham, rather than the World Evangelical Fellowship. There had been a regional congress in Berlin in 1966, but the world meeting attracted nearly 2,500 participants from 150 countries and 135 Protestant denominations. The significance of Lausanne was that it marked the point at which evangelicals from outside Europe and North America began to exercise the influence that their numbers warranted. This was reflected in the fact that the Covenant committed evangelicals to sociopolitical involvement, eliminating any dichotomy between evangelism and social work. The Covenant also emphasized transdenominational evangelical unity: "Evangelism summons us to unity, because our oneness strengthens our witness." It also entertained the possibility of indigenization, with its statement that the Holy Spirit illumines the minds of God's people in every culture to perceive truth freshly through their own eyes. So those involved at Lausanne called for a change of mind and heart among evangelicals.

This explains some of the tension between the Lausanne Continuation Committee and the World Evangelical Alliance, which was still dominated by antiecumenical North American figures. When the Lausanne Committee held a meeting with Roman Catholic representatives in 1980, it touched another lingering fear in more traditional American and European evangelical groups. In these ways the Lausanne movement was able to make links with the Commission on World Mission and Evangelism of the World Council of Churches. This had been created in 1961 when the International Missionary Council became part of the World Council. Hence its conferences on mission and missionary work continued under a new heading. One of the striking characteristics of Christians in Africa, Asia and Latin America was that they tended to support both evangelical and ecumenical initiatives, whereas in Europe and North America there tended to be more division. Global evangelicalism today has no great enthusiasm for or sense of urgency about bringing separated churches together. To date, cooperation in mission has been sufficient for evangelicals.

FURTHER READING

Briggs, John, Mercy Amba Oduyoye and Georges Tsetsis, eds. *A History of the Ecumenical Movement, Vol. 3: 1968–2000*. Geneva: World Council of Churches, 2004.

Fey, Harold E., ed. *The Ecumenical Advance: A History of the Ecumenical Movement, Vol. 2: 1948–1968*. London: SPCK, 1970.

Harmon, Steven R. *Ecumenism Means You: Ordinary Christians and the Quest for Christian Unity*. Eugene, OR: Cascade, 2010.

Lossky, Nicholas, et. al., eds. *Dictionary of the Ecumenical Movement*. 2nd ed. Grand Rapids: Eerdmans, 2002.

Martin, Roger H. *Evangelicals United: Ecumenical Stirrings in Pre-Victorian Britain, 1795–1830*. Metuchen, NJ: Scarecrow, 1983.

Rouse, Ruth, and Stephen Charles Neill, eds. *A History of the Ecumenical Movement 1517–1948*. Philadelphia: Westminster, 1954.

10

EVANGELICALS AND GENDER

Critiquing Assumptions

Sarah C. Williams

> On the verge of the crowd hung a dark Irishman and seeing the anxious gaze I grasped his hand with the blunt enquiry whether all was well with his soul. Conversation followed and the stern man melted to tears. He was a Roman Catholic but had never had the claims of Christ put point blank in the manner of my question and the attic which served him for a home was squalid and wretched through the conduct of drunken parents and neglected children. But the Saviour's transforming power laid hold upon O'Connor's heart and re-formed his life and renewed his home. Today in a clean and comfortable cottage he lives upon his frugal Dockers wage but his home is a credit to the district and he has proved how true it is that, "Godliness is profitable unto all things."[1]

The description given here of the conversion of a London docker in the *British Workman Annual* of 1906 provides a glimpse of the way in which evangelical belief impacted understandings of self, gender, sexuality and society. Part of the outworking of evangelical conversion was an alteration of ideals of masculinity and femininity and the expectation that certain gender traits would follow as part of the pursuit of godliness. The case of O'Connor is typical of a recurrent pattern in late-nineteenth-century conversion narratives: a penitent heart is linked to a reformed life and a renewed home, all of which are signified most fully in changed attitudes toward manhood, fatherhood and, above all, the ongoing demonstration of reliable breadwinning. In this way gender and spirituality are deeply interwoven in

---

[1] *The British Workman Annual* 1906 (vol. 51), p. 39.

the assumed practices of everyday life. Both function as signifiers of allegiance and both are markers of evangelical identity.

However, the interconnections between the two have as yet been little explored in evangelical scholarship. Historians have been quick to point out significant shifts in perceptions of Christian piety in the period from the late eighteenth century through to the twentieth century. They have noted the ways in which these shifts in turn produced wide-ranging changes in Victorian culture, society and politics. Moreover, few historians would disagree that at the epicenter of these changes were the outworkings of the evangelical revival. Yet historians have been slower to recognize the complex but formative interactions between evangelical beliefs and cultural constructions of masculinity and femininity. It is unquestionably the case that evangelicalism had a vast impact on the intricate fabric of social relationships between men and women. As the O'Connor narrative illustrates, evangelicalism was a vital site for debate about men's and women's roles. Yet Christian scholars have in general neglected gender as a facet of the relationship between religion and culture. This research area has been left, hitherto, to secular historians, many of whom approach this topic from a strongly ideological point of view. Given the contentious nature of this topic, it is hardly surprising that scholars have been vulnerable to the temptation to jump straight into the material, imposing twenty-first-century agendas and categories onto the past. In many cases the autonomy of the past has been collapsed and there has been little recognition of the possibility that the ideas of gender that dominate our own age may not in fact be historically normative. For history to be instructive we need to treat the ideas and thoughts of any given period within their own terms of reference, however discomforting they may be to our contemporary sensibilities. Yet when it comes to questions of gender, it seems to be particularly difficult for historians to exercise the disciplined art of listening. We have been susceptible to making the past into a sounding board from which we catch nothing but the echo of our own voices.

This chapter is an attempt to look again at the relationship between gender and evangelicalism in the modern period. It is my contention that five underlying assumptions have shaped mainstream historiographical interpretations of the relationship between gender and evangelicalism. Each of these assumptions, for differing reasons and to varying degrees, inhibit and distort our understanding of the range and depth of evangelical influence on historical structures of thought and patterns of life. I will examine each of these assumptions in turn to demonstrate the ways in which they continue to impact our reading of this subject area. In so doing my hope is to suggest ways in which to reframe analysis, to reconsider the scope of religious influences on modern culture, and to build bridges between ongoing mainstream interpretations of this topic and scholarship produced within the Christian academy.

ASSUMPTION ONE: WHO IS IN CHARGE?

The first assumption centers on the question, *who is in charge?* The contours of this field of study were defined in the 1970s and the early 1980s by the feminist reaction to the historical silence of male historians on the topic of women and religion. The scholarly agenda was shaped by the assumption that Christianity, and evangelicalism in particular, was and is unremittingly patriarchal. Evangelicalism is presented in the pages of such history books as a force that subordinated women to male domination in church and society.[2] As a result, subjects such as female leadership in the church have become highly charged and adversarial, which often obscures the vital and creative interweaving of Christian spirituality and constitutive social ideals based on relations between as well as within the sexes.[3] The word *gender* itself carries connotations of power, and early studies of this topic were concerned above all with the relative distribution of power between men and women within the structures of church leadership. This view was part of a wider tendency within the discipline of history to centralize great people, great events, and political and ecclesiastical aspects of religious history. As Gail Malmgreen notes, "Church history has been preoccupied with clerical heroes and with matters of governance and doctrine all of which normally results in a male bias."[4] The notable absence of any mention of women on the pages of classic church history tomes was a particular irritant to feminist

---

[2]See, for example, Philippa Levine, *Victorian Feminism, 1850–1900* (Gainesville: University Press of Florida, 1994).

[3]For further discussion of this debate see Susan Morgan, ed., *The Feminist History Reader* (London and New York: Routledge, 2006), p. 6.

[4]G. Malmgreen, ed., *Religion in the Lives of English Women* (London: Croom Helm, 1986), p. vi.

historians of this first generation,[5] and it spawned a series of studies that attempted to highlight the significant leadership roles carried by women in various denominational settings.[6] Studies of women such as Elizabeth Fry, Josephine Butler and Catherine Booth have all contributed significantly to extending our understanding of female leadership in the church.

Yet the redressing of imbalance does not deal fully with the issue of whether *who is in charge?* is in fact the best question to be asking the material. To employ such a narrow analytical lens is not only limiting, but it also tends to impose our own contemporary preoccupation with power relations between the sexes at the center of the scholarly agenda, irrespective of the degree to which this question preoccupied the historical actors themselves. The question *who's in charge?* was not the primary question in most evangelical nonconformist communities in the nineteenth century; rather, deliberate emphasis was placed on the priesthood of all believers and the active responsibility of participation as a result of conversion. The consequence of this line of thinking has been the downplaying of myriad and subtle ways in which influence is wielded—not only among women, but also among men—as lay members of congregations. It is all the more problematic given the universal recognition among historians of the disproportionately high number of female church attenders in the Victorian period; a pattern so widespread that it has been dubbed the *feminization of religion.*

Historians are agreed that one of the key themes of modern religious history is the increasing association of religion with women and all that is feminine. Historians Hugh McLeod and Callum Brown are both advocates of the strong impact of the *feminization of religion* on the character and role of the modern church. In the first chapter of Brown's acclaimed book *The Death of Christian Britain* (2002), he outlines Western Christian history on the basis of this concept. In the Middle Ages and for much of the early modern period, he argues, female piety was understood in terms of the religious woman becoming male. Icons of female piety such as martyrs and

---

[5]Ibid., pp. 1-2.
[6]Olive Anderson, "Women Preachers in Mid-Victorian Britain: Some Reflections on Feminism, Popular Religion and Social Change," *Historical Journal* 12, no. 3 (1969): 457-85; D. Valenze, *Prophetic Sons and Daughters* (Princeton: Princeton University Press, 1985); Martha Vicinus, *Independent Women* (Chicago: Chicago University Press, 1985); Brian Heeney, *The Women's Movement in the Church of England, 1850–1930* (Oxford: Oxford University Press, 1980).

ascetics were represented essentially in masculine forms, while femininity, menstruation and childbirth were all regarded as polluting and even dangerous to piety. According to Brown, this dominant discourse lasted until the end of the eighteenth century when, under the influence of evangelicalism, there was "a gender shift in the centre of religiosity."[7] Brown follows McLeod[8] in arguing that in the wake of the evangelical revival Christianity was feminized and depictions of women as avaricious, greedy, lustful and sexually predatory gave way to the venerated female spirituality of the Victorian woman, depicted so graphically in Coventry Patmore's famous 1854 poem, "The Angel in the House." If women do indeed predominate in every area of religious life except in formal leadership, then it makes little sense to limit the scope of enquiry to officially designated institutional leaders, as if it is they who lead exclusively and they who necessarily carry the tone and emphasis of community life.

The limitations of narrowing the focus to *who's in charge?* were brought home to me while researching popular religion among the inhabitants of the London Borough of Southwark. My research centered on the nature and character of religious belief among communities of ordinary working people in this part of London during the period circa 1880–1939. I was deeply impressed by a handwritten recollection of one elderly gentleman by the name of Stan Hall. Stan Hall's family lived at the northern end of Newington Butts not far from the Elephant and Castle in South London. Stan grew up among the mixed population of this area, a population of mechanics, laborers, street traders and charwomen. His family only attended church for churchings, christenings, weddings and funerals, but they nonetheless insisted that Stan attend the local Sunday school on Borough Road every Sunday. It was clear from Stan's reminiscences that all his associations with Christianity were connected to the formative memory of his dearly loved Sunday school teacher Miss Webber. Stan described her as a "true believer," and for the rest of his life all encounters with Christianity were refracted through the memory of this woman's kindness. Miss Webber was a single woman who had lost her fiancé during the First World War. She had devoted her life subsequently to the care of the community in the Borough. As Stan Hall put it, "I think Miss

---

[7]Callum Brown, *The Death of Christian Britain* (London and New York: Routledge, 2001), p. 59.
[8]H. McLeod, *Religion and Society in England, 1850–1914* (New York: St. Martin's Press, 1996).

Webber had settled that . . . she would give love to those who had suffered as
she had and be with the young children in place of those she would never
now have."[9] Her devotion was proved by her kindness and the way in which
she invited the children in her Sunday school class to her one-roomed home,
spending her weekly allowance on providing them with food:

> She would in turn invite us in twos or threes; in groups of boys and girls to
> her flat for tea. Her flat was in fact one room in which she had a bed, a table,
> three chairs and a piano. . . . Miss Webber would serve tea with bread and
> butter (if butter could be had), some cake and after that we would gather
> around the piano and sing hymns and songs and then a simple game and we
> would always leave with a few sweets. How she must have gone without to
> give those little tea parties.[10]

Her kindness did not stop there; if any children were in trouble she would
visit them in their home, and when each of them had a birthday she would
send them a card. Stan Hall pointed out that these were not ordinary cards
that could be purchased for one or two shillings but a hand-painted card of
flowers that cost at least four shillings.

Figures such as Miss Webber were not merely mythical ideals; they had
substance among the ranks of devout working-class believers who are frequently ignored in studies of religion in this period. Stan Hall's recollections
were typical of many of the interviews I carried out with elderly inhabitants
of this area. In reconstructing a picture of the religious beliefs and the ways
in which these beliefs were expressed in the community, it was crucial to
explore the connections made between events, symbols, values and beliefs.
Repeatedly, memories of Sunday school triggered memories of specific
hymns, which in turn evoked a sense of nostalgia associated with the home
and particularly with the mother or some other close female friend, relative
or teacher such as Miss Webber. The context or atmosphere in which religious beliefs were forged is a vital part of understanding how those beliefs
operate within the mental framework of infrequent church attenders. It is
abundantly clear that for Stan Hall, it was Miss Webber who set the tone for
Christian influences in his life. The vicar of the parish church—who had

---

[9]A. S. Hall, "Reminisinces" (1988), unpublished, p. 24, in South London Studies Library.
[10]Ibid.

undoubtedly appointed Miss Webber to her position as Sunday school teacher—was never mentioned. The subtleties of this kind of evidence can be overlooked when we rely on too narrow a definition of what constitutes leadership and influence in Christian communities.[11]

There is no doubt that the primary source material is at least partially responsible for the adoption of this more limited lens. Much of the material upon which we depend as historians is written from the male perspective and more often than not from the vantage point of the pulpit rather than the pew. Returning to the example of Southwark, much of the material upon which historians have relied is drawn from the extensive observations made by the sociologist Charles Booth in his pioneering survey titled *Life and Labour of the People of London* (1889, 1900 and 1902). Yet Booth makes it clear at the start that he is deliberately relying on the perspective of male heads of house to glean the beliefs and religious practices of the household as a whole.[12] This is highly problematic when in most cases it was the mothers in working-class families who were more devout, who attended the regular mothers meetings, taught their children to pray at night and organized familial participation in ecclesial rites of passage. If we rely singularly on a source such as Booth and we fail to bring corroborative evidence alongside, it is easy to get a distorted and partial picture.

The postmodern linguistic turn within the mainstream academy has proved to be a helpful theoretical watershed when it comes to the widening of the lens of study. During the 1980s and 1990s, a second generation of historians working on this topic was shaped by the so-called movement of history "from below." This generation has listened more carefully to the voices of the marginalized, has drawn on a wider variety of source material, and has extended the boundaries of what has traditionally been called church history. The work of Gail Malmgreen—*Religion in the Lives of English Women, 1760–1930* (1986)—has been pivotal in this respect. Malmgreen's work was an attempt to look at the many and varied ways in which women were involved in the religious life of this period. She attacks the feminists

---

[11]For further details, see S. C. Williams, *Religious Belief and Popular Culture* (Oxford: Oxford University Press, 1999).

[12]C. Booth, *Life and Labour of the People of London,* 3rd series: *Religious Influences* (London: Macmillan, 1902), p. i.

who have either left religion out of their considerations of women or have seen religion as an altogether confining force. She argues for the need to look at religious influence on the lives of women in a sustained manner. Malmgreen established the agenda for a new wave of historical research in the '80s and '90s. As a result, investigation into the activities of women from a historical perspective has increased dramatically over the last two decades. The concurrent rise of social history has also tended to break down the old "great men" and "great events" approaches and given way to an increased sensitivity on the part of historians to the ordinary and the mundane.

ASSUMPTION TWO: IT'S ALL ABOUT WOMEN

However, despite the quality and breadth of this revisionist historiography, the debate remains inhibited by a second interrelated assumption: the assumption that it is all about women! The traditional neglect of women in historical discussions of religious influence pushed the historiography so decisively in the direction of a kind of corrective women's history that it has led to a scholarly neglect of masculinity and the formative construction of male and female cultural identities in dialogue with one another. Once again, this is particularly problematic when it comes to the study of evangelicalism. Within ecclesial communities impacted by the eighteenth-century revival, masculinity was central to understandings of spirituality. Norman Vance, in his study *Sinews of the Spirit: The Ideal of Christian Manliness in Victorian Literature and Religious Thought* (1989), argues that for members of the evangelical Clapham Sect—men such as William Wilberforce, Henry Venn and Zachary MacCaulay—masculinity represented a concern with the successful transition from Christian immaturity to maturity. To be spiritually mature was to display earnestness, selflessness, integrity, virility, hardiness and endurance with the benevolent magnanimity of the father. Indeed religious devotion itself was woven together with ideals of manliness, which had by the 1850s established an iconic status in Victorian society. Vance goes so far as to argue that these ideals of manliness were an inescapable and pervasive feature of middle-class existence in both Britain and North America from the mid-nineteenth century right through to the 1940s. Thus, in literature, education and politics, a particular concept of maleness was promulgated in which evangelical Christianity attached itself to a recognized code of conduct that ultimately formed the backbone of ideas of national identity and late Victorian nationalism.

J. A. Mangan and J. Walvin establish a related but distinct argument in their book *Manliness and Morality: Middle Class Masculinity in Britain and America, 1800–1940* (1987). For these writers, Christian manliness was defined in deliberate contradistinction to the cluster of traits, behavior and values that predominated in Victorian society at large. They argue that spirituality involved a series of cultural choices made from an array of possible masculine identities in an industrializing society. They also point to the distinctive values of the Clapham Sect (the group of talented and powerful leaders associated with William Wilberforce in England) as an inherent critique of the predominant norm of "masculine achiever" who epitomized contemporary masculine ideals. The "masculine achiever" is defined as a cultural ideal that presented the male sex as naturally active, strong, dynamic and enduring. This ideal rested on the belief that persevering energy and industry were even more important than talent in determining how high a man could rise. If a man wished to make his way in the world he had to break free of the restraints of home and of community and take the path of economic independence and self-reliance. In this way Mangan and Walvin argue that the ideal of the "masculine achiever" encouraged the identification of men with their actions—in contrast to their consciences, sensibilities or virtues.

The "Christian gentleman," on the other hand, exerted effort to maintain moral order at a time when communal values were threatened by unbridled individualism and the competitive impulse of early industrialization. He was expected to reject self-seeking of all kinds, including material gain, and to display instead benevolence, lovingkindness, compassion and philanthropic concern. It was well known, for example, that Henry Thornton gave away five-sixths of his income during bachelorhood, and this was considered an exemplar of moral manhood among the Clapham evangelicals. Likewise, Wilberforce noted in his *Retirement Memorandum* of the first of February, 1825, that his decision to retire was the result of the particular needs of his family at that juncture.[13] The historian John Tosh, in his im-

---

[13]As quoted in R. Furneaux, *William Wilberforce* (Vancouver: Regent College Publishing, 2005), p. 422.

portant work *A Man's Place: Masculinity and the Middle Class Home in Victorian England* (1999), has shown how imperative it is that we reclaim masculinity as a complex historical identity in relation to femininity rather than in isolation from it. To study either at the exclusion of the other gender is to do an injustice to the material and to contemporary understandings of the family as a complex web of relationships.[14] To argue in this way is to encounter a third problematic assumption that has shaped the study of gender and evangelicalism in the modern period.

ASSUMPTION THREE: THE SEPARATION OF MALE AND FEMALE SPHERES

Typically, discussions of gender have been mapped onto an analytical framework that assumes the binary opposition of public and private spheres. This "separate spheres theory" rests on the idea that the Industrial Revolution created distinct highly gendered subcultures for men and women. As industrialization forced the retreat of women from economic production of all kinds, bourgeois mothers redirected their energies toward creating a separate sphere rooted in reproduction and womanhood within the context of the home. Men, on the other hand, centered their understanding of identity on the sphere of acquisition and competition. The most important advocates of this separate-spheres argument are Deborah Gorham, Leonora Davidoff and Catherine Hall.

Gorham, in her book *The Victorian Girl and the Feminine Ideal* (1982), argues that domestic ideology (by which she means a social arrangement in which true women are understood to be gentle, protected and pious wives and mothers at the nurturing center of the home) was the natural outcome of the Industrial Revolution and specifically of the creation of the middle class. For the middle class to function as a social group it had to develop its own value system. This included certain ideas of masculinity and femininity, which were institutionalized within cultural ideals of the family as a way of allaying tension and uncertainty in a society marked by economic flux. Thus she writes,

---

[14]J. Tosh, *A Man's Place: Masculinity and the Middle Class Home in Victorian England* (New Haven: Yale University Press, 1999).

> The cult of domesticity helped to relieve the tensions that existed between the
> moral values of Christianity, with its emphasis on love and charity and the
> values of capitalism which asserted that the world of commence should be
> pervaded by a spirit of competition and a recognition that only the fittest
> should survive. By locating Christian values in the home and capitalist values
> in the public world of commerce the Victorians were able to achieve an effi-
> cient moral balance.[15]

In other words, Gorham argues that the world became bearable through the
idealization of the home as a retreat from that public world.

Gorham's thesis was further refined by subsequent research, most notably
that of Leonora Davidoff and Catherine Hall in their profoundly influential
book *Family Fortunes: Men, Women and the English Middle Class* (1987). The
core argument made by Davidoff and Hall is that during the period from
1780 to 1830 the newly emergent configurations of class produced by industrial change took on a specifically gendered form. For the new middle class
an idea of separate male and female spheres was integral to the creation of
their distinctive cultural values. Davidoff and Hall argue that men and
women of the provincial middle class established their power in the early
nineteenth century by claiming for themselves moral power. This claim was
fuelled by their religious belief and their ardent evangelicalism. Crucially,
this middle-class moral value system depended on the recodification of
ideas about women and men. It redefined lifestyles and ethics and provided
a theological framework for a culture of female domesticity. It is this model
that has become the paradigmatic explanation for understanding cultural
configurations of gender in nineteenth-century Britain and North America.
It has left a significant analytical legacy.

However, by separating the public male and the private female spheres
from one another, the model fosters a neglect of the complex and multiple
ways in which these spheres intersect and interweave. John Tosh's work is
one example among a number of mainstream secular scholars who have
suggested that these kinds of polarities are deeply unhelpful ways in which
to reconstruct the history of gender and Christianity in this period. In his
two works, *A Man's Place: Masculinity and the Middle-Class Home in Vic-*

---

[15]D. Gorham, *The Victorian Girl and the Feminine Ideal* (London: Croom Helm and Indiana
University Press, 1982), p. 4.

torian England (1999) and *Manliness and Masculinities in Nineteenth-Century Britain: Essays on Gender, Family, and Empire* (2005), Tosh argues that a man's life was defined as much by his home and private life as it was by his public action. In fact it was the concern of much evangelical literature addressing men in this period to cultivate a definition of integrity that required a coherence of life between the two arenas. To be a mature man was to establish a home, to protect it, to control it and to train one's sons to responsible manhood within it. All of these expressions of masculinity affected a man's standing with his peers and the degree to which he was or was not understood to be Christian. The domestic sphere was in this way integral to the social construction of masculinity and the most important expression of individual interiority to develop since the Enlightenment.

Tosh's work points the way forward in research. But recent scholarship is doing more than just adjusting the balance between public and private; it is also calling the basic analytical distinction into question. In recent years the structural analysis of women's history has been thoroughly reworked and a subtle picture has emerged of the many, various and at times conflicting ways in which male and female identities are constructed during this period. Gender historians have begun to ask different and challenging questions about culture and identity, and they have started to collapse and reconfigure binary distinctions between the public and private spheres.[16] Inga Bryden and Janet Floyd, for example, have looked again at the physical and material environment of the middle-class home as it was imagined in nineteenth-century domestic discourse.[17] They question the way in which scholars have read domestic ideology into their analysis of physical space and thus reiterated the image of the middle-class house as a highly structured, confined and enclosed space acting physically to reinforce the strict hierarchies of gendered power. Bryden and Floyd point to disparate forms, conflicting ideals and competing layers of domestic discourse within the material ordering of the household. Furthermore, they highlight the different uses of the home, ranging from workplace to place of leisure, as well as a context for

---

[16]A. Vickery's work is crucial here; see, for example, "Golden Age to Separate Spheres? A Review of the Categories and Chronology of English Women's History," *Historical Journal* 36 (1993): 383-414.

[17]Inga Bryden and Janet Floyd, eds., *Domestic Space: Reading the Nineteenth Century Interior* (Manchester: Manchester University Press, 1999).

charged encounters between classes and races. Relatives, lodgers, cooks, maids, nannies and footmen crowd the private picture and add layers of meaning to the concept of keeping house.[18] In this way texture, subtlety and contradiction are now being injected into our understanding of the modern home and family. Far from operating as a private sphere alone, it is a complex mixture of both public and private.

Historians working on material acquisition in the Victorian period make a similar point. Objects inside the so-called private sphere were in fact designed for public display. Furniture, drapery and servant keeping were understood within nineteenth-century culture to be "a guide to a man's wealth and a mirror of his moral character."[19] Deborah Cohen's recent book *Household Gods: The British and Their Possessions* (2006) picks up on the interrelated themes of the material culture of the home, gender and religion. Cohen traces the competing claims of God and Mammon in the middle-class home during the period from 1830 to 1930. She argues that at every stage the relationship between families and their possessions was charged with moral and religious meaning as well as specific gender overtones. She establishes a trajectory of change in which the austerity of the early century gives way during the height of Victorian affluence (from the 1840s through the 1870s) to a situation in which "things themselves" were ascribed "moral qualities." This, she argues, allowed the Victorians to incorporate material acquisition with demonstrations of godliness in the act of furnishing.[20] Lynne Walker and Vron Ware draw out a similar point in their study of the material culture of abolitionism and its presence within the American anti-slavery household. They argue that women participated in and identified strongly with the abolitionist movement through the decoration of their homes with emblems of slavery.[21] The decoration of the female body and female domestic space with political images challenges the binary divisions of space and culture into public and private. These practices not only

---

[18]Ibid., p. 7.

[19]Tosh, *A Man's Place*, p. 24.

[20]D. Cohen, *Household Gods: The British and Their Possessions* (New Haven: Yale University Press, 2006).

[21]L. Walker and V. Ware, "Political Pincushions: Decorating the Abolitionist Interior, 1787–1865," in *Domestic Space: Reading the Nineteenth Century Interior,* ed. Inga Bryden and Janet Floyd (Manchester: Manchester University Press, 1999), pp. 80-102.

mapped the home as a legitimate arena for political action but also created a power base in the nineteenth-century home for activities previously considered the terrain of masculinity in the public realm. Such work calls into question the analytical distinctions between "public male" and "private female" spheres.

Public and private distinctions are challenged all the more so when it comes to studies of the church. Linda Wilson's work *Constrained by Zeal: Female Spirituality Amongst Nonconformists, 1825–1875* (2000) has also highlighted how blunt public and private spheres are as analytical distinctions when studying Baptist, Congregationalist and Methodist communities. While she agrees that the private sphere of the home was a vital site for the expression of female spirituality, she notes that evangelical church communities operated like extended households for women. Churches were neither fully public nor fully private; rather, they are best thought of as a kind of third sphere or middle space that overlapped with and transcended both. Wilson's research highlights the way in which the church offered an environment where men and women received teaching that emphasized the common pursuit of Christ rather than the bifurcation of practice on the basis of gender. Wilson's study, with its careful comparison of four different denominational settings, also challenges a fourth assumption that has dominated the literature on gender and evangelicalism in this period.

ASSUMPTION FOUR: HEGEMONIC EVANGELICALISM

Historians have generally assumed that evangelicalism was a hegemonic movement about which one can easily generalize. Callum Brown's work is a clear example of this assumption at work in the basic analytical framework of his argument. Brown's argument centers on the close relationship between evangelicalism and gender in what he calls "discursive Christianity."[22] By this he means religiosity based on peoples' subscription to protocols of personal identity, which they derive from Christian expectations or discourses. Protocols are rituals or customs of behavior, economic activity, dress, speech and so on that are collectively promoted as necessary for Christian identity. These are prescribed in a discourse of Christian behavior,

---

[22]Brown, *Death of Christian Britain*, p. 12.

which can be heard by the historian in reported speech, oral testimony or autobiography. Individual and communal subscription to public discourse creates, Brown argues, a compelling religious culture, which shapes the construction of social attitudes in society at large. What made Britain Christian, according to Brown, was the way in which a Christian discourse infused public culture and was adopted by men and women in forming their own highly gendered identities.

At the heart of this narrative Brown identifies particular encompassing definitions of masculinity and femininity that emerged after 1800 to constrain behavior and shape cultural expectations. Women were at the center of these ideals. It was their responsibility to instruct at the fireside, impress their families with Christian teaching, watch over the sanctity of the family and in this way reinforce the validity of evangelical sensibilities in society as a whole. "Theirs was," as Brown puts it, "a privileged and pivotal religiosity."[23] Women were the pivots not only for individual moral reformation within the family but also for the moral regeneration of the nation. Brown traces this feminized piety through an analysis of the obituary columns of religious magazines, concluding that female religiosity was relatively unproblematic for the evangelical. If women were by nature pious, then their capacity to confer piety required their judicious separation from "the world," an arena Brown interprets as synonymous with the public sphere.[24] Conversely, just as female piety was centrally located in the home, so masculinity was constructed in opposition to the stability, order and spirituality of the hearth. Indeed, Brown argues that from 1800 to 1950 masculine identity formed in antithesis to religiosity. He argues that within the evangelical and popular press, definitions of masculinity revolved around the susceptibility of the male to worldly temptations and his need of a mother or wife to rein in his willfulness and avert his natural tendencies to undermine the family and society. From the 1840s right through to the 1960s, these two dimensions of gender and piety/impiety became what Brown calls "mutually enslaved discursive constructions."[25]

Brown's approach is helpful in many respects, but it relies on the as-

---

[23]Ibid., p. 59.
[24]Ibid., p. 61.
[25]Ibid., p. 68.

sumption of a unitary and dominant Christian discourse. Brown's understanding of discursive Christianity, shaped as it is by an ideal type of highly gendered church-based evangelicalism (or Puritanism, as he calls it from time to time), is applied as a singular definition of Christian discourse across a variety of social contexts without reference to the detailed varieties of belief and social expectation that existed in different regions, in different denominational settings and across time.

When we look closely at religious cultures in this period—even those within the broad category of evangelicalism—far from finding a coherent core discourse arising from a single "puritan" stance, we actually find a variety of religious idioms, which intersect with but also extend beyond the stylized version of evangelical Christianity adopted by Brown. Evangelicalism on its own is an inadequate umbrella category to express the varieties of theological positions, ecclesiological structures, religious dispositions and denominational milieu that coexisted throughout this period and that together shaped the religious culture of the nation. Moreover, to deploy one singular Christian discourse about gender as encompassing and typical is at best to simplify and at worst to gravely misrepresent the diverse spectrum of ideas about gender, many of which were theologically, locally, denominationally and even occupationally specific.

Nonconformist evangelical groups in England, for instance, had different expressions not only of worship and devotion but also of family life and male-female relationships from evangelical streams within the established Anglican Church. William Kent, in his autobiography, *The Testament to a Victorian Youth* (1938), describes how the Methodist community in which he was raised operated as a "whole sub-society."[26] Kent's description of his strong Methodist upbringing in late-nineteenth-century suburban Kennington depicts a family culture that revolved in every dimension around the local chapel community. The family socialized with other members of the community and used the same practices of prayer as others in the wider "church family." Meal times and customs were constrained by chapel conventions, and the boundaries between home and chapel were further blurred through the practice of taking in successive lodgers from among the single

---

[26]William Kent, *The Testament to a Victorian Youth* (London: Heath Cranton, 1938), p. 23.

male population of the church. The Methodist W. H. Lax also encapsulates this idea of parallel culture in his autobiography:

> There is in my opinion a distinction between the Methodist type of family life and all others. Just as Methodism presents its own form of evangelicalism among the churches so it has introduced to the world a specific type of family life.[27]

Lax goes on to describe a family life centered on prayer, Bible reading and weekly chapel attendance. It is clear that even with Methodism there were important varieties of religious expression, which shaped the nuance of gender relations both in the church and in the home. Methodist groups influenced by the holiness movement and the transatlantic revivalism of the late 1850s were far more open to female preaching, for instance, than traditional Wesleyan Methodists. Catherine Booth situated herself squarely within the Methodist tradition, but her understanding of the mutuality between man and woman in marriage and the necessity of obedience to the special calling of God to preach in times of renewal was at odds with strands of her own tradition since the prohibition of women preaching among Wesleyan Methodists in 1803.[28]

Linda Wilson, in *Constrained by Zeal* (2000), evokes a similar world of strong denominational allegiance among Particular Baptists, Congregationalists, Wesleyan Methodists and Primitive Methodists. She concludes that the primary shaping force in constructing domestic ideals of femininity, norms of behavior and customs of child rearing was denominational culture, and the specific cultures embedded practices that varied with subtle but important distinctions. In this way Wilson's study cuts across a more typical reliance on a highly stylized and regionally undifferentiated evangelicalism that surrenders nuanced theological subcultures to a general definition that supposedly holds across time and space.

Much work is yet to be done to unpack the detailed integration of evangelicalism and gender on the ground. This need is heightened still further when we consider evangelical mission in the non-Western world.

---

[27]W. H. Lax, *Lax and His Book: An Autobiography* (London: Epworth Press, 1937), p. 54.
[28]C. Booth, *Female Ministry; or Woman's Right to Preach the Gospel* (London: Morgan and Chase, 1859).

The second half of the nineteenth century witnessed an unprecedented willingness to envisage the possibility of missionary careers for single women abroad as agents of "woman to woman" mission.[29] Laura Lauer has argued that while the Baptist denomination in general was unwilling to recognize women's authority in church matters in the home context, in India Zenana missionaries were able to carve out a place of independent leadership for themselves within the Baptist polity. (The *zenana* was the area of Indian homes reserved for women.) This resulted in Baptist missionary women engaging in a much wider sphere of feminine involvement, which transgressed many of the norms of denominational life in their sending churches.[30]

Moreover, it is often the case that when evangelicalism is applied too broadly there is no attempt to understand qualitative layerings of belief and fervency over time. Davidoff and Hall, for example, comment on the difference between first, second and third generations of evangelicals. By the 1840s most evangelicals were brought up within the faith rather than converted to it in adulthood. Both are designated evangelical without careful consideration of the ways in which customary tradition and theological practice can become confused and conflated in the process of generational transmission. Davidoff and Hall point out that tract writers of the 1830s and '40s tended to extract the moral content of teaching on the role of women and leave to one side strongly Christian and theological elements. In this way practices may still be referred to by historians as "evangelical" when in fact there is only a tenuous link between societal custom and fervently held religious belief. To associate evangelical theology too straightforwardly with these positions is problematic, particularly because evangelicalism was a theological culture that attended carefully to issues of faith transmission between generations, prizing the central role of personal conversion over and above mere communal belonging as a criteria of spirituality. To ignore what we might call the fervency dynamic is thus to negate a central feature of the movement. It is often the case that individuals and communities of

---

[29]See the work of Laura Lauer, "Opportunities for Baptist Woman and the Problem of the Baptist Zenana Mission, 1867–1913," in *Women, Religion and Feminism in Britain, 1750–1900*, ed. S. Morgan (Basingstoke, Hampshire, and New York: Palgrave Macmillan, 2002).
[30]Ibid.

live and active faith sit on the vanguard in critique of formalized and potentially constraining definitions of both men and women, even within the
mainstream of particular denominational groups. Pamela Walker's excellent
work on the Salvation Army, for instance, demonstrates the vitality of urban
mission within the movement but also the overturning of norms regarding
customary female behavior in the practices of the "Salvation Lassies"[31]—
practices that would have been frowned upon by the majority of Methodists.

ASSUMPTION FIVE: THE CORRELATION BETWEEN SOCIAL AND POLITICAL CONSERVATISM

One final assumption must be added into this thematic mix: the assumption
that social conservatism and political radicalism are mutually exclusive categories. We began this chapter by noting how scholars have often held evangelicalism responsible for the prevalence of constraining social norms and
conservative restrictions on male and female behavior. It is often assumed
that the prescription of a domestic role for women and a sharp delineation
of masculinity and femininity imply a necessary political quietism and an
entrenched attachment to the status quo. Yet what these connections fail to
recognize is the dynamic role of evangelical belief in providing a theological
language through which to engage in cultural and political critique. The
religious writer, educationalist and philanthropist Hannah More is a helpful
example in this respect.

Hannah More is often held up as paradigmatic of moralistic evangelicalism, which instills passivity and political detachment among the faithful.
Her writings certainly formed part of what has been called the "conservative
reaction" to the French Revolution. Her widely read tract *Village Politics*
(1792) was written specifically to counter the radical pleas of Thomas Paine's
The Rights of Man (1791). Likewise, her *Thoughts on the Speech of M DuPont*
(1793) denounces the anticlericalism of the French Revolution and calls
upon the church to reinhabit its traditional societal role. Yet her concerns
were profoundly politically engaged. All of her work reflected the unique
combination of passions found in the Clapham Sect—political focus, philanthropic involvement, active engagement with the poor, education and

---

[31]P. Walker, *Pulling the Devil's Kingdom Down: The Salvation Army in Victorian Britain* (Berkeley:
University of California Press, 2001), pp. 206-44.

communication with the expressed purpose of effecting change in society.

In *Village Politics*, More asserted that the Revolution posed a grave threat to the moral and civil liberties of the English people. In such conditions it was imperative that the moral character of the British people be strong and resolute to resist the tide of evil radiating from France, with which the British were at war from 1793. More argued passionately that the trivializing of women's lives was ultimately a danger to the nation. In her introduction to *Strictures on the Modern System of Female Education* (1799) she argued that

> it is a singular injustice which is often exercised towards women first to give them a most defective education and then to expect from them the most undeviating purity of conduct.[32]

Inadequate education for women, a focus on appearance, affectation and mere ornamental accomplishment rendered women prey for immoral whims. Women, she argued, needed true moral fiber to withstand the onslaughts of the French Revolution and shore up the courage and tenor of the nation as a whole. Therefore, to regenerate the nation required improvements in the education of women as well as men. These points were reiterated in later writings such as *Hints Towards Forming the Character of a Young Princess* (1805) and the novel *Coelebs in Search of a Wife* (1808).

There is no question that the education for which More advocated was carefully circumscribed. Writing was not taught in case it bred sedition. But women of all social orders were encouraged to read in the schools More established in villages near Bristol. They were taught knitting and sewing, and they were encouraged to participate in community activities such as building a communal bread oven. The women More wrote about were primarily trained to inhabit the home, but not before they were simultaneously equipped with the ability to access political and social debate and skills with which to aid the economic resilience of the family. Moreover, from the beginning More placed the leadership of her schools in the hands of women. Sarah Baber, for example, led the school in Cheddar. She was a widow and she taught in the Cheddar school with her daughter. She was a deeply devout

---

[32]Hannah More, *Strictures on the Modern System of Female Education* (London: Cadell and Davies, 1799), 1:ix.

evangelical. When she died suddenly in 1794 the community was devastated. Hundreds of people lined the streets at her funeral. More's biographer, Anne Stott, notes how, in a letter to William Wilberforce, More reflected on Baber's life after the funeral. In the letter she compares the life of Baber to the life of the Earl of Cornwallis, former Governor General of India. She writes, "But how little in my estimation are the most brilliant Heroes when compared to this dear woman, who has turn'd *many*—I had almost said *hundreds*—to righteousness."[33]

More is a highly ambiguous figure. She was both radical and conservative, feminist and antifeminist. What cannot be said of her, however, is that her social conservatism lacked political edge. She has received a great deal of new interest recently by feminist historians such as Patricia Demers[34] and Anne Stott.[35] These historians have challenged earlier depictions of More stressing her agency in elevating the status of women from passive objects to contributing members of society. More's legacy was to establish the place of education in the formation of serious moral and religious character among women. Her reforms opened the door to female education, which could then move in many creative directions through the course of the nineteenth century. Above all, her work established a crucial link within evangelical culture as a whole between the values inculcated in the home and the maintenance of national identity, stability and order. In this way homes came to be seen not only as places of individual moral formation but also as the training grounds for citizens. The famous evangelical public figure Lord Shaftesbury, who fought against exploitative labor practices that hurt women and children, put it like this:

> There can be no security to society, no honour, no prosperity, no dignity at home, no nobleness of attitude towards foreign nations unless the strength of the people rests upon the purity and firmness of the domestic system. At home the principles of subordination are first implanted and the man is trained to be a citizen.[36]

---

[33]More to William Wilberforce, 1795, *Memoir of Mrs Hannah More*, 1:466. Quoted in Anne Stott, *Hannah More: The First Victorian* (Oxford: Oxford University Press, 2003), p. 466.
[34]Patricia Demers, *The World of Hannah More* (Lexington: Kentucky University Press, 1996).
[35]Stott, *Hannah More*, p. 163.
[36]Anthony S. Wohl, *The Victorian Family: Structure and Stresses* (New York: St. Martin's Press, 1978), p. 9.

What we see time and again in evangelical writings is the idea of the family as a microcosm of wider social and political relationships. These relationships by their very nature were gendered, and social ordering between the sexes was a deeply politicized act in evangelical culture. The mark of a fully evangelical household—whether Anglican or Dissenting— was the bolstering of the faith of each member through the enforcement of certain common disciplines such as early rising, Sunday as the family day, family prayers and grace at meal times. Typically, the husband would lead the prayers, and the earthly authority of the father was seen as the microcosm of the divine authority sanctified by God himself. Even Nonconformists who held a rigidly antisacerdotal interpretation of ecclesial ministry referred to the household head as a priest. The husband's sacred authority was seen to combine in marriage with the woman's spiritual purity and morality.

These ideas even influenced the physical layout and architecture of houses. The ideal in the middle-class evangelical home was a bedroom for each person so that everyone could carry out their own private religious devotions, which were vital to the faithful and upright performance of their work in society. As the locus of evangelical familial identity, the home contained and was seen to contain both public and private elements. Husband and wife in their union in the home were understood to image the relatedness and difference of elements of society. Political thinkers such as John Stuart Mill described authority relations within the home as expressions of the state; disorder in one boded ill for stability in the other.[37] Such an understanding of the home necessarily implied political critique. The sheltered place with its stability and order critiqued the restless pace of aggressive individualism in a rapidly industrializing society.

This dimension of critique was not lost on evangelical women. What we see during the course of the century is that domestic discourses, rather than constraining women, often became the primary conduit through which women found a radical political voice. As Levine concedes, domestic ideology became the weapon by which women began to challenge the norms and assumptions of their society. If women's purity made them

---

[37]J. S. Mill, *The Subjection of Women* (New York: D. Appleton, 1869).

custodians of women's religious teachings and values, then their effect on public life could only be uplifting. The idea of moral superiority of the woman became the fulcrum of women's challenge in this period. The ideology itself thus became a positive expression of female identity in the political sphere.[38]

Levine goes so far as to argue that the roots of the modern feminist movement are in the language of faith and theology. David Hempton and Myrtle Hill have argued much the same, suggesting that evangelical religion was far more important than secular feminist ideas in enlarging women's sphere of action during the nineteenth century. For instance, Claire Midgley and Kathryn Gleadle have also shown how women such as Charlotte Elizabeth Tonna drew on evangelical discourse and inflected it with a radical edge to sanction a political and public role for themselves.[39] Such historians have been quick to argue that the central force shaping feminism as it emerged within the nineteenth-century British context was evangelicalism itself, as its emphasis on mission, compassion and activism opened a radical dimension in women's lives. It disturbed the tranquility of the home by instilling a conscience. It opened the eyes of the evangelical man to a world of poverty and misery, which problematized the profit-oriented capitalism of the wealth-generating machine of empire and the images of masculinity associated with it. The engagement of evangelicals in philanthropy critiqued the growing bureaucratization, centralization and professionalism of the nineteenth century by retaining and refining paternalist models and voluntarism.

At the same time, the engagement of evangelical women in philanthropy extended women's moral vision. It developed a sense of sisterhood and suggested alternative visions or possibilities for the future by opening up avenues for fulfilling work, giving women skills, training and opportunity. You could say that the application of domestic ideology internally transformed itself within the heart of Victorian culture, altering the basic categories in which women were able to operate. Anne Summers, in her article "A Home from Home: Women's Philanthropic Work in the Nine-

---

[38]Levine, *Victorian Feminism*, pp. 57-81.
[39]K. Gleadle, "Charlotte Elizabeth Tonna and the Mobilization of Tory Women in Early Victorian England," *The Historical Journal* 50, no. 1 (2007): 101.

teenth Century," vigorously challenges the suggestion of older historiography that it was simply boredom that drove women into philanthropic work.[40] Summers suggests that it was the particular influence of evangelicalism that provided crucial motivation. Faith, she argues, galvanized women who may initially have held a conservative position on women's natural roles in the family. However, philanthropic involvement itself changed both women and men, making them aware of middle-class selfishness, stimulating them to question their value system and that of their family, and prompting heart searching as to how one could in fact justify staying at home when there was so much evil in the world and so much healing and caring to be given.

More than anyone else, the evangelical social purity campaigner Josephine Butler challenges the assumption of a correlation between social and political conservatism. Butler led the political opposition to the Contagious Diseases legislation passed in Britain in 1864, 1867 and 1869. Her faith provided a language for female political activism. From Scripture, Butler drew a radical critique of contemporary values. Alison Milbank, in her work on Butler, argues that it was her eschatology that led to an imperative emphasis on social and political involvement.[41] Butler did not share the glorification and idolization of the family that defined so many of her contemporaries; for her, the family needed redeeming from selfishness and from the distortions wrought internally by inequality of the sexes. Moreover, she called for the Victorian family to turn outward toward society, not inward in retreat from it. If, Butler argued, Victorian society preferred the family as its model of rightly ordered social relations, then why should this model not also be applied as the best model for the society as a whole—a model in which interdependence between men and women, mutuality and vulnerability dominated rather than competition, exclusivity and relegation to separate spheres? Butler's deep political and social engagement reinforces the point that religious discourse cannot be interpreted merely as part of the armory of conservative ideologies or as

---

[40]Ann Summers, "A Home from Home: Women's Philanthropic Work in the Nineteenth Century," in *Fit Work for Women*, ed. S. Burman (London: Croom Helm, 1979), pp. 33-63.

[41]Alison Milbank, *Beating the Traffic: Josephine Butler and Anglican Social Action on Prostitution Today* (Winchester, UK: George Mann, 2007).

a discursive system that shackled women to a narrow, passive, if morally exalted role in society. In fact, religious belief could and did encourage different and even oppositional ways of thinking about women's roles in society. In this way the consequences of religious commitment were and perhaps have always been paradoxical.

This chapter has challenged five problematic assumptions that have dominated the literature on the subject of evangelicalism and gender in the modern period. In considering each of these assumptions in turn it has become clear that the depth and breadth of evangelical influence on cultural constructions of masculinity and femininity is both profound and formative. When we look beyond formal institutional leadership to see expressions of evangelical influence in the wider life of the church, we see women involved in many areas of leadership and mission. When we begin to see the history of gender as a study of the complexity of interrelationships between men and women rather than focusing singularly on women's history, we are able to see how male and female relations mapped the political landscape and thus to break down the problematic polarization of human operations into separate public and private camps. In so doing we are able to reclaim the public sphere as a place of deep reflection on the ethical direction of modern economic development from a Christian perspective and the private sphere as a profoundly important basis for cultural and political critique. Evangelicalism from the Georgian period to the early twentieth century was quintessentially the religion of the family. As an expression of faith it recalibrated the intimate balance of male and female relationships, but in doing so it ensured that evangelicalism was not only the religion of the home but also of the wider culture and of the nineteenth-century state.

FURTHER READING

Brekus, Catherine A. *Strangers and Pilgrims: Female Preaching in America, 1740–1845.* Chapel Hill: University of North Carolina Press, 1998.

Cott, Nancy F. *The Bonds of Womanhood: "Women's Sphere" in New England, 1780–1835.* New Haven: Yale University Press, 1985.

Davidoff, Leonore, and Catherine Hall. *Family Fortunes.* New York: Routledge, 1982.

Hammond, Geordan, and Peter S. Forsaith, eds., *Religion, Gender, and Industry: Exploring Church and Methodism in a Local Setting*. Eugene, OR: Wipf and Stock, 2011.

Juster, Susan. *Disorderly Women: Sexual Politics and Evangelicalism in Revolutionary New England*. Ithaca, NY: Cornell University Press, 1994.

Ryan, Mary P. *Cradle of the Middle Class: The Family in Oneida County, New York, 1790–1865*. New York: Cambridge University Press, 1981.

Valenze, Deborah. *Prophetic Sons and Daughters: Female Preaching and Popular Religion in Industrial England*. Princeton: Princeton University Press, 1985.

GLOSSARY

apostolic: of or relating to the apostles; a variety of Pentecostal churches and denominations use the word to denote the continuity of their practices with the supernatural gifts of the New Testament church. Often used to refer to a set of twentieth-century *indigenous Christian movements in the Global South and the East that tend to be *Pentecostal and independent.

believer's churches: those churches or denominations that practice believer's baptism—only baptizing those who have come to a personal faith. In contrast to infant baptism, believer's baptism stresses the conscious and voluntary aspect of conversion. Thus, church membership is reserved for believers who have been baptized. The Baptist and Mennonite traditions are examples of believer's churches.

charismatic: a Christian or group of Christians who are not associated with *Pentecostal churches but nonetheless adopt some Pentecostal practices. Charismatics belong to the "Second Wave" of Pentecostal renewal, and during the second half of the twentieth century, charismatic movements appeared in many Protestant denominations as well as the Roman Catholic Church. Charismatics emphasize the direct presence of God through the Holy Spirit, and they typically attempt to maintain a link between their personal experience and traditional Christian theology.

contextualization: the process by which theology grows out of a particular historical, linguistic and cultural context. This term can refer to a wide swath of *indigenizing approaches and practices, from the translation of Scripture on the less controversial side of the spectrum, to the Christian-Marxist approach advocated in the 1970s—whereby experience and local traditions are given priority in the formation of theology rather than systematic or confessional bases—on the more controversial side.

conversion: the spiritual event wherein the human, empowered by grace, turns away from self and sin and enters into new life through Jesus Christ.

dispensationalism: a system of biblical interpretation that sees God as having acted in history through various dispensations, of which the age of the church is one. Pioneered by nineteenth-century theologian J. N. Darby, dispensationalism was widely popularized through the publishing of the Scofield Reference Bible in 1909. When it comes to *eschatology, dispensationalists are premillennialists—they believe in the physical return of Christ to the world to take believers to heaven before the millennial reign. Typically, dispensationalists in the late nineteenth and early twentieth centuries, based on their interpretation of scriptural prophecy, saw themselves as living in a time of apostasy immediately preceding Christ's second coming.

Dissenting churches: churches that separated from the Church of England during the sixteenth, seventeenth and eighteenth centuries; a group that includes Puritans, Quakers, Socinians and other Nonconformists. Typically, Dissenters opposed state influence on the church. The Act of Uniformity in 1662 required the use of the *Book of Common Prayer* and Anglican ordination, limiting the rights of Nonconformists and leading to their persecution. After the 1689 Act of Toleration, which restored a semblance of religious freedom to Nonconformists, those who took an oath of allegiance began to be called Dissenters. Over the course of the eighteenth century, many Dissenters became part of the broad evangelical movement.

ecumenism: efforts or initiatives that aim at bringing about greater unity and/or cooperation between all Christians and/or denominations.

eschatology: the theological doctrines related to last things, specifically, death, the final judgment, heaven and hell. Traditionally, three broad eschatological conceptions have been held: amillennialism, premillennialism and postmillennialism. The amillennialist view is that the "thousand-year" reign described in the book of Revelation is not literal, but refers to the period between Christ's first coming and his second coming, which will be a natural conclusion of the evangelization of the world. Premillennialism holds that Christ's second coming will usher in a great tribulation followed by a thousand-year period of peace. Postmillennialism is the position that the "thousand-year" reign began upon the ascension of Christ, and it progresses through the conversion of the world to Christianity.

established church: a particular church that is favored by and receives specific benefits from the state. Established churches receive official or public favor, and its values predominate in its society. An established church is usually, but not always, the *state church. Examples of established churches that were not state churches include the Lutheran churches in Weimar Germany and the Southern Baptist denomination in the late nineteenth and early twentieth centuries in the US South.

faith missions: an approach to missions that holds that if God has called a person to mission, then God would also provide the financial support needed for the mission. Typically a faith missionary is not supported financially by a denomination, but many faith missions have taken place through the work of missionary societies that may or may not have had denominational connections. Some faith missionaries, such as Hudson Taylor and George Müller, refused to solicit funds as an act of faith, simply praying for God's provision.

fundamentalist: a term first used in the early twentieth century for conservative evangelicals who opposed *liberalism and insisted on the infallibility of the Bible, the virgin birth of Christ, substitutionary atonement and the second coming. It later became used by some groups who separated themselves from other forms of Christianity—including not only Roman Catholicism and liberal Protestantism, but other varieties of evangelicalism. It is this separatist impulse that most clearly distinguishes fundamentalism from evangelicalism, as the two can have other central theological stances in common.

globalization: a term that encompasses the process of *modernization and worldwide spread of a common (Western) culture. Some argue that globalization serves to *homogenize cultures. See chapter three for a thorough discussion of the multilayered, contentious discussion among scholars as to what globalization actually means and the assumptions underneath this discussion.

Holiness movement: a nineteenth-century movement that drew on Methodist teachings on Christian perfection and emphasized the need for Christians to receive a "second blessing" of entire sanctification. This second blessing would remove temptation to sin and believers would achieve perfection. Some branches in the broader holiness movement, such as the Keswick Holiness movement, emphasized the "deeper life" of the believer rather than eradication of the sinful nature. Out of this movement, which was prominent both in America and Britain, grew a variety of denominations, including the Church of the Nazarene and the Christian and Missionary Alliance.

homogenization: the process by which elements are made uniform in substance or character; in reference to cultural realities, the flattening or reducing of diversity into a uniform culture or taste.

inculturation: the process by which Christian doctrines or teachings are adapted to specific cultural contexts and, in turn, the ongoing influence of that cultural context on those doctrines.

indigenous: native; characteristic of a particular culture or region. When used of churches, as in "indigenous churches," it refers to those led by people native to that particular culture or region. Indigenous churches are often marked by independence from external or Western structures, including funding, and develop their own unique forms of theology and practices.

individualism: an ideology or outlook that focuses on the individual person and his or her value. Individualism tends to value the independence, self-reliance and interests of the individual above societal or institutional interests.

itinerant: travelling from place to place; typically used of ministers or evangelists who traveled around to preach, often in open-air settings, rather than solely remaining in one parish or local church.

liberalism: in theology, the subjection of Christian theology to *rationalist and *modernist ideas. Liberalism rose to ascendency in the late nineteenth and early twentieth centuries. Typically it denied the supernatural elements of Christianity and sought to reinterpret traditional Christian doctrines, confessions and creeds in light of modern sensibilities and new science.

millenarianism: the belief that society will be radically transformed by a messianic figure. Millenarian groups can take a variety of social and political approaches, and they often involve a charismatic leader who self-identifies with a messianic role in order to bring about transformation.

millennialism: also known as premillennialism, millennialism is one form of Christian *eschatology that believes that Christ will return to earth and set up a thousand-year kingdom, after which will occur the final judgment. Millennialism is a type of *millenarianism.

modernism: a way of seeing the world through modern lenses that has its origins in Enlightenment thought. While the term is used for a broad spectrum of concepts or movements, here it specifically refers to naturalistic conceptions of the world, the preeminence of rationality above faith or revelation, the use of science to determine and bound reality, and secular *pluralism.

modernization: the social process involved in capitalist development that has as its goal the creation of a global consumer culture. Typically used to describe how societies transition from local, "traditional" cultures, infrastructures, customs and technologies to those of Western industrial and postindustrial societies.

Nonconformist churches: *see* Dissenting churches.

parachurch: a term for Christian organizations that work independently from and across denominations and denominational boundaries.

Pentecostalism: a form of Christianity that places a high emphasis on the direct presence of God through the Holy Spirit and the expression of that presence through spiritual gifts such as speaking in tongues, prophecy and divine healing. Pentecostalism has its roots in nineteenth-century *revivalist movements such as the *Holiness movement. The movement has formed its own denominations as well as received increasing acceptance since the mid-twentieth century within traditional Protestant denominations and the Roman Catholic Church. It is arguably the fastest growing form of Christianity in the Global South and East.

Pietism: a renewal movement within German Protestantism that has its roots in the seventeenth century, Pietism emphasized a return to personal and practical piety. Much weight was placed on personal holiness and inward feeling, as Pietism was reacting against what it perceived as the intellectualism and formalism of the *state churches. Pietists such as Philipp Jakob Spener and Johann Arndt called Christians to study Scripture, practice confession and repentance, do works of charity and meet in small groups. The eighteenth-century evangelical revivals had strong roots in and connections to Pietism.

pluralism: when adherents of a diversity of religious beliefs are members of the same society or political entity, for example, Jews, Catholics, Anglicans and Dissenters all living in London. Religious pluralism is often used to connote the ideology that all religions are equally valid and none are exclusive in their claim to truth.

providence: the Christian doctrine that holds that God ordains the events of history and outcomes of those events. At times, the concept of providence is personified ("Providence") to represent this sovereign action of God. Some theologians distinguish between general providence, wherein God upholds and sustains the world and all in it, and special providence, wherein God directly intervenes in lives and events.

rationalism: the view that truth can only be attained through reason, and thus all claims must be amenable to rationality. Rationalism was an offspring of the Enlightenment, and during the eighteenth and nineteenth centuries, rationalists increasingly subjected Christian doctrine and Scripture to their reason. For instance, rationalists often disavowed the Athanasian conception of the Trinity or the miraculous accounts in Scripture.

revivalism: the view that individuals or churches need to be restored from nominal or formal Christianity to a vital relationship with God. Revivalism centers on evangelistic proclamation and calls for individual, immediate response; some forms also emphasize holiness, such as the *Holiness movement, or social transformation. While revivalism has roots in the theologically rich tradition of Jonathan Edwards and John Wesley, some later forms tended toward highly emotional and pragmatic approaches.

state churches: those churches given official sanction and status, or operated by a state. State churches function in much the same way as *established churches, but differ in that, in the former, the state exercises authority over the church.

traditionalization: the process of making traditional; used by some to describe the *indigenization of Christianity into traditional African forms.

vernacular translation: a translation of Scripture into the native language or dialect of a particular population.

voluntary: something done of one's own free will. Used to describe a new kind of social and religious involvement that grew up in the late seventeenth and eighteenth centuries where individuals chose to be part of a movement or organization rather than were dictated to by a religious or political authority; also known as voluntarism. The term can refer to a view common in *Dissenting churches that individual believers must choose, voluntarily, to be part of a church—this was seen as mitigating against nominal faith. Historically, evangelicalism has often (but not always) reflected this voluntarist view of religious participation, as well as gaining much by creating voluntarist organizations and societies that provided significant activism and energy behind evangelical mission.

LIST OF CONTRIBUTORS

Ogbu Kalu was Henry Winters Luce Professor of World Christianity and Mission at McCormick Theological Seminary in Chicago.

Donald M. Lewis is professor of church history at Regent College, University of British Columbia, in Vancouver, Canada.

Peter Lineham is professor and head of the School of History, Philosophy and Classics at Massey University in Auckland, New Zealand.

Mark A. Noll is the Francis A. McAnaney Professor of History at the University of Notre Dame in South Bend, Indiana.

C. René Padilla is a New Testament scholar and a founding member of the Latin American Theological Fellowship.

Richard V. Pierard served as professor of history at Indiana State University and was twice a Fulbright professor in Germany. Later he occupied the Stephen Phillips Chair of History at Gordon College in Massachusetts.

Stuart Piggin is associate professor of history at Macquarrie University in Sydney, Australia, and the director of the Centre for the History of Christian Thought and Experience at Macquarrie.

Wilbert R. Shenk is senior professor of mission history and contemporary culture at Fuller Theological Seminary in Pasadena, California.

Scott W. Sunquist is professor of world Christianity and dean of the School of Intercultural Studies at Fuller Theological Seminary in Pasadena, California.

David M. Thompson is professor of divinity and a life fellow of Fitzwilliams College, Cambridge University, in England.

Sarah C. Williams is associate professor of church history at Regent College, University of British Columbia, in Vancouver, Canada.

John Wolffe is professor of religious history at the Open University in Milton Keynes, England.

SUBJECT AND PERSONS INDEX